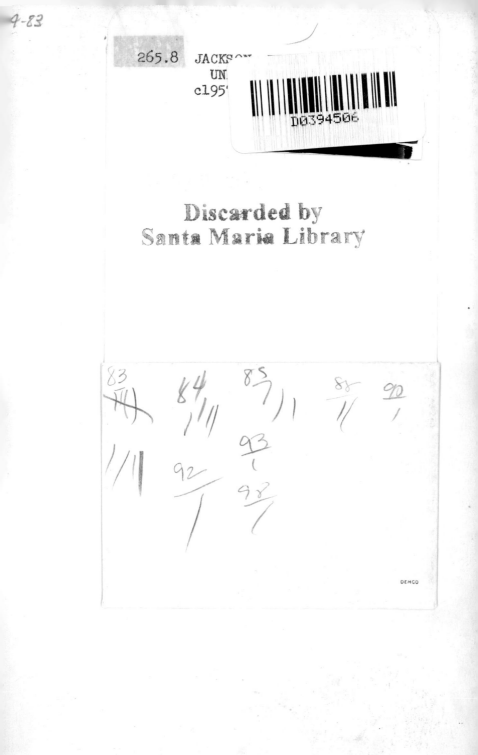

83   84   85   88   90

92   93
      98

DEMCO

Understanding Grief

UNDERSTANDING GRIEF

Its Roots, Dynamics, and Treatment

EDGAR N. JACKSON

ABINGDON   NASHVILLE

UNDERSTANDING GRIEF

Tenth Printing 1978

ISBN-0-687-42854-8

Library of Congress Catalog Card Number: 57-9786

MANUFACTURED BY THE PARTHENON PRESS AT
NASHVILLE, TENNESSEE, UNITED STATES OF AMERICA

to

 EDGAR DUVALL JACKSON

who in fourteen short months taught
much about life and death

PREFACE

Help from many sources has gone into this study, and proper recognition to all would be impossible. While I am trained in the field of formal religious thought, I have had a close working relation with the staff of a psychiatric clinic and owe a debt to them in the development of many ideas.

From the early outline stages, Wellman J. Warner, head of the department of sociology in the Graduate School of Arts and Sciences at New York University and a chairman of the International Congress for Group Psychotherapy, has given encouragement, helpful criticism, and clear insight. Leonard S. Cottrell, Jr., social psychologist for the Russell Sage Foundation, in addition to critical reading of the manuscript, has made available the results of his researches into the dependability of emotional responses, and has permitted the quotation of material not yet published.

Gerhart D. Wiebe, clinical psychologist, assistant to the president of Columbia Broadcasting Company, and president of the American Association for Public Opinion Research, has given time and thought to the plan of the book and careful reading to the manuscript. Soll Goodman, a practicing psychoanalyst and the psychiatric director of the Guidance Center of New Rochelle, has given helpful insights and made available resources that were important for the technical content of the book. Mrs. Sylvia Davis, a psychiatric social worker, has given useful suggestions concerning case material. Mrs. Lewis H. Donaldson, a journalist, has given valuable editorial assistance. Several clergymen have read the manuscript and added their insights.

The staffs at the library of Bellevue Hospital in New York, at the New York Academy of Medicine Library, and at the Baker Library in Hanover, New Hampshire, have been most helpful in obtaining material from a variety of sources for use in this study.

The faculty of the Postgraduate Center for Psychotherapy in New York extended to me every courtesy when, as the only clergyman enrolled in the school, I attended classes for two years and shared the discussions of many of the psychological problems that are referred to in the following pages.

While I am obliged to accept sole responsibility for any of the shortcomings of this study, I certainly must share credit with many persons for whatever adequacy and comprehensiveness it may show.

EDGAR N. JACKSON

CONTENTS

ONE   **The Definition of Grief**
1. The Prevalence of Grief Reactions 15
2. Difficulties in Defining Grief 16
3. Toward a Working Definition of Grief......... 17
4. The Relation of the Clinical and the Creative 21
5. The Plan of This Study 22

TWO   **The Dynamics of the Grief Situation**
1. The Dynamic Quality of Grief 25
2. Four Specific Factors of Dynamic Importance ... 27
3. Expression of Grief Feelings 30
4. Dynamic Comprehension of Death's Significance . 32
5. Basis for an Ego Concept 35
6. Discipline and Deprivation in Relation to Reality 40
7. Age Factors That Modify Ego Response 41
8. Summary 43

THREE   **The Roots and Development of Grief in Man and Society**
1. The Conditioning of Grief Response by Group
   Influence 45
2. Levels of Grief Communication and Expression .. 46
3. Primitive Methods of Dealing with Self-Consciousness and Grief 49
4. Modern Counterparts of the Primitive Methods .. 52
5. Beyond Magical Thinking to a Clear Reality Sense 54
6. The Symptoms of Destructive Repression....... 56
7. Building More Healthful Attitudes Toward Grief 58

FOUR   **Grief and Identification**

1. The Injured Psyche and the Incorporated Object .   60
2. Normal Identification and Techniques of Identity   63
3. Special Significance of Identification Among Women   66
4. Identification and the Personality Structure   67
5. Temporary Identification and Prolonged Manifestations   71
6. Sensitivity to Emotional Response   73

FIVE   **Grief and Substitution**

1. The Injured Psyche and Substitution   75
2. Two Directions Substitution May Take   77
3. Mixed Motives in Substitution   79
4. Three Cases of Substitution   80
5. Substitution and a Weakened Reality Sense   83
6. Unwise Emotional Transfers   86

SIX   **Grief and Guilt**

1. Universal Guilt and Ambivalence   88
2. Techniques for Working Through Guilt   89
3. Guilt Responses Illustrated   91
4. Techniques for Compensating Guilt Feelings ...   95
5. Religious Insight into Guilt Feelings   100

SEVEN   **How a Structure of Values Conditions the Grief Response**

1. A Structure of Values as a Creative Organization of Experience   102
2. A Value Structure Sustains the Logical Mind ...   104
3. Inadequate Ideas Undermine the Value Structure   105
4. Rational Clues to the Meaning of Life and Death   108
5. The Possibilities and Limitations of a Structure of Values   110
6. Religious Values Influence Attitudes Toward Life and Death   112
7. A God Concept as the Basis for Relationship ...   113

8. Seven Minimum Concepts for a Working Faith . 114
9. Faith to Be or Not to Be 118

EIGHT How Religious Practices Sustain the Grief-stricken
1. The Sustaining Power of Symbolic Structures 122
2. New Significance for Old Methods 124
3. Drama and Personification 125
4. Religious Rites and Emotional Responses 127

NINE Types of Grief Manifestation
1. Normal Grief Reaction 130
2. Abnormal Grief Reaction 136
3. When Grief Brings Breakdown 139
4. An Evaluation of Roles in Dealing with the
   Grief-stricken 142

TEN Resolving Normal Grief Situations
1. The Minister's Attitude Toward Grief 145
2. Symptoms of Normal Grief 146
3. What Grief Work Accomplishes 147
4. The Pastor's Role in Normal Grief Situations ... 148
5. Illustrations of Normal Grief 149
6. The Importance of Ritualized Expressions 153
7. Three Recommendations to Pastors 153
8. The Place for Weeping 154
9. What Not to Do 155
10. Nine Areas of Concern 157
11. The Pastor's Personal Role 158
12. The Pastor's Institutional Role 159
13. An Evaluation of the Pastoral Function 160

ELEVEN Resolving Abnormal Grief Situations
1. The Nature of Abnormal Grief 162
2. How Abnormal Grief Is Manifest 163
3. Illustrations of Abnormal Grief 166
4. The Clinical Picture of Abnormal Grief 168
5. Dynamic Factors in Abnormal Grief 168
6. Methods of Treatment 173
7. The Pastor's Role in Abnormal Grief 175

8. The Minister's Abnormal Reactions 178
9. Diagnosis: Professional and Practical 179

TWELVE   When Grief Precipitates Deep Disturbance
1. Definition of Deep Disturbance 186
2. Illustrations of Deep Disturbance 187
3. Prevalence of Deep Disturbance 188
4. The Pastor's Role with the Deeply Disturbed ... 189
5. Cases of Pastoral Success and Failure: A Manic
   State; Depression; The Poorly Oriented and
   Self-destructive; Aggression 191
6. The Pastor and Referrals 199

THIRTEEN   Preparing People for Grief Situations
1. Childhood Conditioning 202
2. Education in the Church 204
3. Preparation Through Pastoral Counseling....... 206
4. Pastoral Self-Examination 209
5. Informal Group Support 210
6. Bibliotherapy: Assets and Liabilities 210
7. A Pulpit Ministry to the Bereaved 212

FOURTEEN   Special Opportunities in Grief Situations
1. Relations with Official Persons in the Community 215
2. Procedures in Dealing with Strangers 217
3. The Problem of Religious Opposition 218
4. Using the Universals in Grief 219
5. The Funeral Sermon 220
6. The Funeral and the Bereaved 220
7. Nine Criteria for Evaluating a Funeral 223

FIFTEEN   Resources for Facing New Horizons
1. Courageous Meaning or Courageous Meaninglessness 226
2. The Counselor's Role in Restoring Persons to Useful Living 228
3. The Importance of Being Related 229

CONTENTS

4. Cultivating a Capacity to Communicate Creatively 232
5. The Place of Active Participation in Personality
    Reorientation 234
6. A Sustaining Faith to Meet Life or Death 235

Notes 238

Selected Bibliography 243

Index 249

ONE

The Definition of
Grief

Although our society seeks to shield us from the stark reality of death, it is prevalent all about us in nature and in human life. When anything is so common, we assume that the reaction to it will be normal, and in most instances it is. Yet increasingly we are aware of the fact that unwise handling of the grief situation is causing personality injury in ways that had not been suspected.

1. The Prevalence of Grief Reactions

Rollo May, in his study of anxiety,[1] gives a careful examination of fourteen cases of acute anxiety. In eleven of these there was death, or its emotional equivalent, in the child-parent relation in the early years of the person examined.

In a study of ulcerative colitis, Erich Lindemann found that thirty-three of forty-one patients had developed the disease "in close time-relationship with the loss of an important person"[2] in their lives.

In a research project at a British hospital for the treatment of mental and emotional illness, it was discovered that nine per cent of the total admissions were listed as "morbid grief reactions."[3]

E. Weaver Johnson, in *Everyman's Search*, indicates that there is a close correlation between diabetes and unresolved grief.

Lawrence LeShan, who has conducted research at Trafalgar Hospital in New York on the treatment of cancer by psychotherapy, finds a relation between the onset of malignancy and acute grief.

These studies point toward the need for a more careful understanding of grief and its aftereffects.

The president of a prominent New England college has said that most of the students now entering college know nothing about death at first hand. A generation or two ago death was not uncommon in a large family, for hospital facilities were limited, and death, like birth, was a part of home life. Now, life is insulated against the physical reality of death, with most dying done in a hospital and in the presence of professional persons. This tends to create a false attitude toward death that is anxiety-creating and reflects itself in a variety of ways which at first seem to be unrelated to acute loss.

A philosophy of life is but half a philosophy until it contemplates death. Thanatology and orthothanasia are relatively new words in our vocabulary, yet a knowledge of death and a proper attitude toward dying are important for a well-balanced way of living.

Our society has entrusted to physicians and clergymen the care of the dying and the bereaved. In recent years the medical profession has made significant contributions to the understanding of grief. It is important that this understanding be made available to the clergy in a way that they can use in their important ministry to the bereaved.

It is hoped that these pages will serve a purpose for all those who would understand what takes place in the process of mourning. Further it is hoped that insight may be gained concerning what can be done to help the mourner through his trying experience without interfering with the important psychological work that is being done as the "libido invested in the lost love-object is gradually withdrawn and redirected toward living people and problems." [4]

2. Difficulties in Defining Grief

Although grief comes close to being a universal emotion and few escape it, it has not received the attention it deserves on the part of careful researchers. Like the common cold, it has been taken for granted by most people. But like the common cold it may be the source of other and more acute reactions that cannot be overlooked. The prevalent experience often evades sharp definition. This may be one of the reasons that grief has been avoided as the subject of research. No one is quite sure what is involved or how it can be defined.

Three physicians were asked to identify the symptoms of acute grief. The first indicated that they are essentially those of emotional shock. The second said they are similar to the symptoms of an anxiety state. The third equated grief with temporary depression as far as visible symptoms are concerned. This shows that in general practice the emotion of grief has not been too sharply defined. While it may well bear a resemblance to shock, anxiety, and depression, such inadequate definition makes it difficult to deal with the specific problem of acute loss.

The writers of the Old Testament knew grief and dealt with it eloquently. The Greek dramatists made the emotion come to life upon the stage. The churchmen of history tried to devise ways of working through the burdens of deep sorrow which their people felt. The problems of the grief-stricken found classic expression in the words of Shakespeare. Yet none of these expressions is definitive. That they are descriptive, and accurately so, there is no doubt. But we must turn elsewhere for the specific analysis and clear definition.

Much of the effort to give a definitive expression to the nature and movement of grief has come through the medical psychologists of the twentieth century. First, Freud, with his paper on "Mourning and Melancholia," [5] and then Karl Abraham, with his studies of depressed states,[6] gave a more explicit understanding of what takes place during bereavement.

Many studies developed during World War II relating to the response of men under stress situations and in the loss of their friends. Differing environmental backgrounds were found to affect significantly the way men met death. The personality structure was shown to have a clear relationship to the way they worked through severe personal loss.

3. Toward a Working Definition of Grief

Much of modern thought, theologically and philosophically, is centered about the problem of being. We seem to have reached a point where the thanatologies of the theoretical psychologists and the theological structures of the more specifically religious thinkers could helpfully cross-fertilize. This would become an important

17

first step in adequate definition. Here the assumption would be that grief is more than a symptom of an ailment. Rather it is an active involvement of the structure of values of the individual in a major situational fact of experience.

We are not dealing with mild sorrow or mere personal disappointment, though the word "grief" is sometimes attached to such states. We are thinking of grief as a more specific and intense form of sorrow that is related to the loss by death of one who is dearly loved. It is more than the instinctual loss that might produce important behavioral conditioning in an animal, or even in a young child. It is essentially the emotional and related reactions that occur at the time of and following the loss by death of an important person in the emotional life of an individual who has reached the state of development where he has the capacity for object love. Grief is the emotion that is involved in the work of mourning, whereby a person seeks to disengage himself from the demanding relationship that has existed and to reinvest his emotional capital in new and productive directions for the health and welfare of his future life in society.

Perhaps it would be helpful to further limit the area of our consideration by making clear the differences that exist between grief and the emotional states that most nearly approximate it. We will omit consideration of the condition sometimes referred to as "shock," because it tends to be a response, involuntary in nature, to severe physical or psychic injury and is in itself not definitive. Also there is a tendency now to use the word primarily to indicate a form of therapy rather than a morbid condition of the emotions or the physical organism.

Anxiety has been more clearly defined and is perhaps better understood by most persons, so its comparison to grief would serve a more useful purpose. Rollo May defines anxiety as "the apprehension cued off by a threat to some value which the individual holds essential to his existence as a personality." [7] Freud points out that the threat involved is related to an object of considerable libidinal investment.[8] Grinker and Spiegel, in their studies of anxiety among airmen, support the view that it must be an object that is "loved, highly prized, and held very dear." [9]

In most instances it is defined as a fear, a dread, an apprehension, that the structure of values which sustain life will be destroyed. It does not need to be an actual threat but may be an emotional response motivated by unconscious forces at work in the personality. Some thinkers relate this unconscious factor with the process of weaning, wherein the trauma of loss creates a deep apprehension and causes an unbalanced relationship in the security structure of the individual. The existence of free anxiety usually means an inability to focus the constructive strength of the personality on a given situation so that it may be realistically handled. Rather, the anxiety generates confusion because the personality strength cannot be focused, and the diffused quality of anxiety tends to generate the conditions that produce even more anxiety.

In contrast, the feeling of grief may hold much of the same quality of threat, apprehension, and dread that is present in anxiety, but it is usually related to a specific fact of experience and therefore does not violate the reality sense but helps to fulfill it. In normal grief the reaction may show comparable symptoms such as confusion, disorganization, apprehension, and poorly focused fear; but the reaction tends to be temporary and is worked through as the personality faces reality and deals with it, even though the process of doing so is painful.

In abnormal grief the loss may serve as a precipitating factor that releases unconscious fears related to unresolved early experience. Then the apprehension and dread refuses to be focused on the actual experience that precipitates it. The personality has difficulty in bringing its ego strength to bear on the reality factor, and the energy of the personality finds a diffused and disorganized expression. Normal grief and anxiety are clearly different as they relate to the reality factor. Abnormal grief and anxiety are more nearly comparable, but the grief becomes the agent for releasing the acute dread which tends to become the chronic emotional state rather than serving as the actual cause of it.

The relation of grief to a state of depression is comparable to the relationship between grief and anxiety. Depression is usually observed as a feeling of inadequacy and hopelessness, with a lowering of psychophysical activity and a tendency to become

19

disorganized in function. The difference in the nature of the reaction is determined by the roots of it. For as anxiety proceeds from a sense of danger to the value structure of the individual, so the state of depression grows from a feeling of injury or dislocation to the narcissistic or self-regarding element of the personality. Depression involves a loss of self-esteem, with aggressive feelings toward the incorporated object. This explains the self-injuring attitude, for the person seeks to injure something beyond himself through himself. The feelings of self-accusation and self-injury are viewed as the turning of aggression against the self when psychologically the injured self becomes also the punishing self through the device of incorporation.

The grief feeling has many of the elements of depression but on a temporary basis usually. The main difference is that in grief there is no less of self-esteem, though there may be a normal amount of self-accusation and feelings of guilt. The feeling of inadequacy and hopelessness coupled with a general sluggishness of thought and action may be evident but it is not necessarily rooted in an injury to self-esteem. Normal grief involves symptoms comparable to depression, but on a short-term basis that is worked through with no residue of self-accusation or self-destructive feelings.

Abnormal grief may involve a situation where the severe loss caused by the death of a loved object may precipitate personality change or adjustment that could bring on a state of depression. This may be true when a person has so overinvested his emotional capital in another that he is destroyed as a person in the loss of this other. This might also be true when the feelings of ambivalence toward the lost love object are so strong that the personality could not do the work of mourning without being involved in a large amount of self-accusation. It might also be true when the reactions to the loss cause a regression to an early emotional state in which the demands of an externally supplied self-esteem are not satisfied by the dependent relation to which the personality retreats. Subsequent chapters will illustrate, through the use of case histories, some of these reactions.

The differences and likenesses shown in the comparison of grief and depression are applicable in the comparison of grief and

20

melancholia, for melancholia is a marked form of depression with more specific motor phenomena involved. As Freud has pointed out,[10] the symptoms are parallel at several points, but differ sharply at the point of the loss of self-esteem and the capacity of the personality to right itself by the use of its own resources. While grief is normally resolved by the "work of mourning," the same economic response from the personality does not follow with melancholia, and the process of treatment is obliged to take into account a different set of dynamic factors as well as a different attitude toward reality.

4. The Relation of the Clinical and the Creative

Thus we see that grief can be defined both by what it is and by what it is not. This approach to definition has depended on the clinical observations of professional psychotherapists whose orientation is essentially secular. Those whose orientation is religious would want to add another dimension to their consideration of grief. It is important at this point to consider the relationship which will be employed between clinical observation and religious application. In this wedding of the insights of two disciplines there may appear to be strong elements of incompatability. These I shall try to resolve at the outset.

As most of the research on grief has been done by persons with psychiatric and psychoanalytic backgrounds, it is inevitable that much of that material would find its way into such a study as this. It is welcomed insight and useful indeed. It is important to indicate that there is a possibility or even a necessity for separating the clinical observations from the philosophical presuppositions of the observer.

My approach to the material has been eclectic. I have used clinical observations with as much objectivity as possible. I have included the insights of various psychotherapeutic schools. No effort has been made to evaluate the philosophical presuppositions of the schools of thought or of the individuals involved. While it is evident that the philosophical premises of anyone dealing with the soul of man are likely to be more significant than those of the practitioner whose chief concern is setting broken bones or employing drugs to defeat a virus, it would seem an impossible task to deal with every clinical insight on the basis of its philosophical premise. What I have tried to do is to accept the clinical findings as valid insight into the workings of the personality. Then I have felt free to define the philosophical framework within which these insights are to be employed. In this way I hope to protect the clinical authority of the material that is used and at the same time make clear my feeling concerning its philosophical adequacy.

A large amount of actual case material has been used in order to give authenticity to the study and also to make explicit the movement of psychological dynamics. However, in order to protect matters of pastoral confidence, the material has been modified insofar as minor details are concerned to make it unidentifiable, while at the same time the essential emotional situation has been preserved. In the use of the material, only that which serves to illustrate the specific matter under study has been included. While this does not permit the illumination of the total personality and environmental picture, it does serve the purpose for which it is primarily employed.

5. The Plan of This Study

The general plan of the book is designed to take advantage of the insights into the secular studies concerning the nature of man and his personality. But it is not limited by such secular observations. There is a specific effort to employ the increased sensitivity that is manifest by both the physical scientist and the scientist of personality as it relates to a plus factor clearly observable in human nature, but less clearly defined or isolated. This plus factor, which is an essential interest of religious thought, can become a decisive factor in determining both the movement and the direction of human experience.

The study of personality indicates four levels of active research and contemplation. First is the dynamic quality of growth itself. Second is the influence of heredity. Third is the reaction of the

22

situational factor on both the dynamic and the hereditary. Fourth is an added factor identified with man's creative nature, which cannot be ignored or denied, but which is in addition to the other aspects of life that can be more easily isolated and studied under controlled conditions.

The dynamic quality of growth and its influence on life experience is the main consideration of the chapter entitled "The Dynamics of the Grief Situation." The valuable insights in the relationship of childhood experience to adult adjustment are considered, as well as the adult adjustment to grief. The efforts of men to deal with this dynamic factor in life, both by acceptance and denial, are considered.

The hereditary influence is considered in the chapter "The Roots and Development of Grief in Man and Society." The efforts of man to deal with the problems of the self, from primitive times to the present, are examined for such insight as they may give to the current problem of understanding grief.

The importance of the situational response to grief, as it is reflected in immediate and postponed responses of defense or adjustment, is considered in three chapters dealing with substitution, incorporation, and guilt. This increased emphasis on the situational response seems warranted because we are actually concerned with the way persons under stress deal with their problems of adjustment.

In the fourth category we deal with man's creative nature, and move into the philosophical, theological, and religious concerns. Some transcendent factors are at work in life to change the quality of response to experience. What is tragedy for one becomes a growth experience for another. What is defeating to one is a stimulus to another. The fact that the matters under consideration here cannot be so sharply delineated is no warrant for ignoring them. These responses are no less real for life merely because they are not subject to laboratory controlled observation. "How a Structure of Values Conditions the Grief Response" and "How Religious Practices Sustain the Grief-stricken" are chapters designed to bring into a useful relationship with the clinical observations the more daring presuppositions concerning life that are the accomplishment of the religious mind.

The last part of the book is concerned with the practical application of the insights of the more theoretical study to the work of those whose function it is to minister to the grief-stricken.

TWO

The Dynamics of the
Grief Situation

We have always known that life is a process and that we are continually in the act of becoming. But we have never been as truly aware of the extent of this dynamic quality of life as we have been in this century. New levels of mental activity have been explored that show depths of being the past had not surmised. While every age has been aware of some mysterious force that seemed to control our behavior, we have never known so well what this force was until we understood something of the layers of consciousness that make up a personality.

1. The Dynamic Quality of Grief

One may examine the growth rings in a tree and feel that the record of the years is a reasonable evidence of the growth of the tree. No one claims that the later rings of growth are more important than the earlier, for they are all essential to the life of the tree. So also it is with personality. Personality is an integral unit. The experiences of the earliest years are written into the rings of growth, and nothing can deny their existence. Later growth may modify the direction in which the personality moves, but every year of life has made its contribution to growth, and all are related to one another. This is especially so when we are dealing with the levels of consciousness; for the earlier years of growth, before the period of verbalization, are recorded only in the preconscious and unconscious levels of the mind's life.

Incidents in later life often serve to precipitate reactions that can be explained only on the basis of the preconscious or unconscious factors that are a part of the mental life of the person. Theodor Reik has indicated that the structure of the personality

25

may be compared to that of an iceberg. One-sixth of it is visible above the water line, yet the five-sixths that is invisible may well determine which sixth is visible. Often the effect of the salt water causes melting, and the weight shifts enough so that the iceberg rolls over and an entirely different part of the berg becomes visible. So it is with the structure of human personality, wherein hidden factors may be so conditioned that they will cause a change in the behavior response of the individual, and a quite different aspect of the personality will be revealed under the stress of circumstance.

There is no place where this may be more readily observed than in the response of a person to the severe loss that comes with the death of a loved one. Deep emotional forces are set at work. Old insecurities may be made manifest. Old patterns of solving problems, long since outgrown, may reveal themselves again. Deep aggressions that have been carefully hidden may burst to the surface of behavior. One does not begin to understand the nature and quality of the human suffering that goes on during acute grief without taking into account these deeper factors of personality that may become operative.

Like all emotional states, grief tends to produce symptoms that are readily observed although perhaps less readily understood. As T. A. Ross has observed: "Disgust may cause retching, or even vomiting: shame may cause that dilation of the capillaries called blushing: anxiety may produce dryness of the mouth and suppression of gastric secretion with inhibition of movement." [1] Similar indications of the grief experience can be described. Feelings of acute discomfort may be manifest in every part of the being. Involuntary contraction of muscles, feelings of weakness, a feeling of emptiness in the abdomen, intense subjective distress variously described as mental pain, tension, or loneliness—such feelings may possess the person so completely that he is temporarily unable to function. This seems to be the nature of the reaction of the person to acute grief. It is a specific emotional state and it tends to have specific emotional and physical reactions.

2. Four Specific Factors of Dynamic Importance

But the quality and the intensity of the emotional reactions of a person to grief are conditioned by a variety of factors. These factors are so real that the type of response can often be predicted with a fair degree of accuracy. Erich Lindemann says:

Our observations indicate that to a certain extent the type and severity of the grief reaction can be predicted. Patients with obsessive personality make-up and with a history of former depressions are likely to develop an agitated depression. Severe reactions seem to occur in mothers who have lost young children. The intensity of interaction with the deceased before his death seems to be significant.[2]

The mature, competent person will feel quite a different emotional response to acute loss as compared to the immature, dependent personality. The immature, dependent person, in his effort to overcompensate for feelings of personal inadequacy, overinvests his emotions in supportive relationships with others, and is thus more vulnerable emotionally to the loss of his love object. More of his projected self is involved in the loss. The emotionally mature person, with his more adequate self-acceptance, is shielded against this type of emotional overinvestment.

The dynamics of the grief reaction may be conditioned in at least four ways: first, by the personality structure of the individual; second, by the social factors that are at work about the individual; third, by the importance of the deceased in the life system of the individual; and fourth, by the value structure of the individual. Let us illustrate these four conditioning factors.

1. Eleanore's mother was rigid, compulsive, and demanding. She had driven Eleanore mercilessly toward accomplishment in every line of endeavor. Eleanore complied because the alternative was the threat of the loss of her mother's love, her mother being the most important person in her life. Eleanore complied regularly and obediently, but there was a part of her being that increasingly rebelled, though the rebellion was never made explicit because the feeling of guilt would have been too great. Eleanore led her class in school, was president of the student body, was

preparing for a senior concert, and in every way seemed to be a superior child as far as accomplishment was concerned.

When her mother was stricken with a virulent cancer and died rather suddenly, Eleanore was lost. She had been so dependent that she was now unable to function. Her backlog of real resentment of her mother's management of her life now expressed itself in feelings of guilt. Though she finished her senior year in high school with difficulty, she refused to play the piano, shunned her friends, went off to college under protest, and was obliged to drop out before the year was over because she could not seem to apply herself. After intensive psychotherapy she is beginning to disengage her own personality from the personality of her mother and to re-emerge as a person with talent and ability. Her bereavement was especially difficult to accept because her personality was so actively involved with that of her mother, both in dependency and in suppressed revolt. The period of disintegration of behavior was indicative of the serious destruction that took place in her personal, social, and emotional patterns of living. Her personality structure had been involved at a critical time when her ego strength was weak and her desire for independence was suppressed. This critical situation within her personality was responsible for the quality and the intensity of her grief reaction.

2. Social factors are also an important part of the dynamic structure of living. They set the framework within which the personality can meet the stress upon it, supported by the actions and attitudes of others. This may be illustrated by the differing ways of approaching death in different communities. Perhaps that of the military community is most graphic. Death there is not uncommon, and the attitude toward it is conditioned by a tradition and a sense of duty. However, human feelings are not so easily fitted into patterns, especially in an army composed largely of civilians. Captain C., the pilot of a B-17, was admired by the men of his crew. He was a bit older, always fair, demanding respect and getting it because he was capable, concerned about everyone in the crew, and their best guarantee of safety. When a

piece of flak killed him almost instantly, the wounded copilot was able to bring the ship back, but the effect upon the crew was marked by anxiety and disorganization. Perhaps this was a trigger situation that released a number of individual fears. The colonel in charge of the unit called the crew together and said that although he felt as bad as anyone else about the loss of one of his best men, he was not going to tolerate any childish actions on the part of his crews. War was played for keeps, and no one in his right mind thought he could get through it without someone's paying the costs. "Sure we feel bad, and it will hurt inside for a long time, but we are not here to nurse our feelings. We have an important mission to perform, and we are going to do it. You'll be prepared for another mission tonight." The pressure of the military situation pulled the crew out of its period of disorganized behavior, and they began to function again with a more mature attitude than they had had before. The colonel, as another father figure, stepped into the vacuum left by the death of the pilot and spoke with an authority that moved the men beyond their fears to their sense of duty. The social factors at work about them had become a strong conditioning factor in the working out of their grief.

3. When Abraham Lincoln was assassinated there was a mass expression of grief. For thousands he was a figure who had represented national security, a way of life, and a promise of peace and victory. The hopes and fears of a war-weary people were bound up in his person. When his tragic death came it released the pent-up emotions through a legitimate expression of grief for a universal symbol. His importance in the life system of many individuals was emotional as well as political. The grief reaction at his death was an illustration of the mass mourning that can develop when a person becomes a symbol for the investment of the hopes and fears of many persons. It also indicated the effect on the mourner when the lost person has held a significant place in the life system of the mourners both as individuals and as a group.

4. The value structure of the individual is also a factor involved in the dynamics of the grief situation. Dr. G. and his

wife had been a campus symbol of marital devotion. They had collaborated on many projects, had traveled together, and had shared many interests. Their lives were about as closely bound together as one could imagine. When Dr. G. suffered a coronary occlusion, he was aware of his limited life expectancy. While he survived the acute attack, he was aware that another might come at any time. Dr. G. was an astute man and sensed the importance of using the remaining time of his life to disengage his wife as much as possible from the dependency relationship she had had with him. In a matter-of-fact way and with no sense of morbidity, he explained his condition and then set about to insure her independence as much as was humanly possible. They talked together of the implications of his death. They concluded certain projects in which they were interested, and closed out their holdings in other ventures that would have involved her in serious disadvantage. He showed no feeling of self-pity, but did express continually his regard for her ability to do what needed to be done. By throwing her on her own more and more and encouraging her independence of action, he was able to help prepare her for his death which came in a few months. Having a mature and perceptive sense of values, he used the time allotted to him to tie together the threads of his life and to disengage himself as much as possible from the burdensome duties that might otherwise have fallen to the hands of his wife. Also, he gave to his wife a feeling of adequacy for facing the future that stood her in good stead for the years that remained for her. He made death not an appalling tragedy, but rather an incident set in a long chain of other incidents. Certainly such an attitude can go a long way toward conditioning the grief reaction of those who are bereaved.

3. Expression of Grief Feelings

Not only is the grief reaction conditioned by personal and social factors, deep inner responses are often involved in its expression. Lindemann, in his study, has indicated that there is not so much a reaction of fright and horror in a sudden death situation as there is an inner conflict and a sense of guilt. This shows again that the grief experience may trigger a variety of suppressed emotional responses and feelings rooted in preconscious or unconscious levels of the mental life. Sometimes these are baffling to the person who feels them. Usually they root in a preverbal period and then the behavior may become what is called irrational or beyond the control of reason. "When a passion can expend itself in words it is less apt to result in deeds," and vice versa.[3] The emotion that is inarticulate tends to eventuate in actions that do not serve the best interests of the person involved. Much great literature illustrates this psychological fact.

Shakespeare was able so to dramatize the problems of deep emotional conflict and irrational action that they came to life and walked about on the stage. Hamlet gives classic expression to that inner conflict that grows from feelings too strong to be made articulate and too powerful to be controlled.

Hamlet's mind is tortured by the actions that grow from his inner conflict, and he is never quite sure what force it is that drives him on to avenge his father, protect his mother, and punish his uncle. It has been referred to as a "diseased imagination" that motivated his action. The unresolved jealousy of childhood may continue to fester in the deep layers of consciousness, so that death of the object of the jealousy brings a mixture of satisfaction and guilt. The child thinks of death not as a final disposition of matters but as a riddance of its source of irritation. The attitude toward death that leads to an adult action based on the child's concept is sure to prove unfortunate. When this jealousy is coupled with an abnormal affection for one's own mother, it produces an inner conflict between the unresolved needs of the child and the adult needs that must remain unsatisfied because of false associations. Hamlet, with an emotion oriented about the needs of his childhood, was unable to be content as long as there was any thought of infidelity on the part of his mother. Even though he destroyed himself in the process, he felt obliged to protect this image of fidelity. There may be some reason to believe that his inner problem was so disruptive of his equilibrium that he would have welcomed a chance to die in guaranteeing such fidelity. However we may interpret the inner conflict of this unhappy adult, we are justified in believing that it had its start long before his mind was concerned with reasoned action.

Extensive studies of the past half century, inspired by Freud, have taught us that a psychoneurosis means a state of mind where the person is unduly, and often painfully, driven or thwarted by the "unconcsious" part of his mind, that buried part that was once the infant's mind and still lives side by side with the adult mentality that has developed out of it and should have taken its place. It signifies internal mental conflict. We have here the reason why it is impossible to discuss intelligently the state of mind of anyone suffering from a psychoneurosis, whether the description is of a living person or an imagined one without correlating the manifestations with what must have operated in his infancy and is still operating.[4]

One can see how the early attitude toward a love object, feelings of ambivalence in childhood, insecurities in child-parent relations, and fears related to insecurity might seriously affect the problems in working through acute grief. Similarly, any difficulty in establishing a clear reality relationship complicates the problem of honestly and effectively working through the emotional aspect of bereavement.

4. Dynamic Comprehension of Death's Significance

As Shakespeare has indicated in the case of Hamlet, more than one of these factors may be operative in any given situation. No personality situation is simple and uncomplicated. The accumulated experiences and attitudes of life come to bear on every new situation. The complexity of each human relationship is so great that the ramifications cannot be detailed in any simple description. Any effort to illustrate the movement of human emotions will be aware of the elimination of much related material in the effort to make the main factors of the emotional picture more clearly visible.

Religious systems have always indicated the importance for life of the attitude toward death. Psychiatrists have more recently tried to find the basis for the importance of such attitudes. Interestingly, they have turned to the myths and the works of creative artists who have been able to express more fully the totality of human emotional need. The creative artist is not as precisely scientific in his approach and for that reason is able to take into account aspects of life that are not subject to exact measurement. Scientific disciplines tend to limit the interpretations of human experience because the scientific method must eliminate much that is not verifiable under laboratory controlled conditions. The creative artist, like the religious thinker, being less restricted in his method, may include larger areas of feeling in his consideration. While his interpretation may be in error, he is at least able to acknowledge those areas of human experience that he observes. The great mythologies as well as the great religions have taken into account the totality of human experience and have tried to find for it meaningful explanations. While the explanations may fall short because of inadequate interpretative equipment, the human experiences revealed stand because they are the authentic record of the feelings of sensitive beings.

So Eissler, in his study,[5] turned to the Parcae of ancient Greek mythology to find a balanced picture of the dynamic forces at work in life to determine the response of the individual to life. The Parcae are the three sisters who represent the fates. They preside over the destinies of life itself. There is no life without the influence of the three, and everything in life is conditioned by all three. Modern thought has often tried to ignore or deprecate the function of the third sister, but only to the detriment of the total life picture. True religion never makes that mistake. Clotho, who presides at the spinning wheel, is busy creating the thread of life. She represents the "fateful tendencies each one of us brings into the world." Lachesis is the disposer of fates who determines the experience of life or the length of the thread. Under her control is the variety of incident and event that makes up the warp and woof of life itself. Atropos, the familiar figure with the shears, is the symbol of death, or the cutting of the thread. In our effort to think of the dynamics of living we are likely to ignore the last figure. But the preconscious forces at work in our being are more aware of this third sister than we frequently realize; and the apprehension, the concern, and the desire for her company are built into the basic structure of being.[6]

Less specific as a concept, but no less real in its meaning, is the symbol of the potter's vessel that is prevalent in Hebrew literature. In the drama of Job's experience he indicates this trilogy at work. "Did not one fashion us in the womb?" (31:15.) "The spirit of God hath made me, and the breath of the Almighty hath given me life. . . . I also am formed out of the clay." (33:4-6.) Speaking of the experience of life, the Old Testament writer says: "Then I went down to the potter's house, and, behold, he wrought a work on the wheels. And the vessel that he made of clay was marred. . . . As the clay is in the potter's hand, so are ye in mine hand" (Jer. 18:3-6). Speaking of fate, he says, "He hath made me an empty vessel" (Jer. 51:34).

And of death he speaks in this fashion, "I am forgotten as a dead man out of mind: I am like a broken vessel" (Ps. 31:12). The figure of the vessel holds true—from the early days of life when the vessel is newly formed and beautiful, and "the evil days come not, nor the years draw nigh, when thou shalt say, I have no pleasure in them," through the times when the vessel of life is poured full to overflowing with the experience of being, until the days come when "the silver cord is loosed, or the golden bowl is broken, or the pitcher is broken at the fountain, or the wheel broken at the cistern" (Eccl. 12:1, 6). So also it is fulfilled: "Then shall the dust return to the earth as it was, and the spirit shall return unto God who gave it" (Eccl. 12:7). Wherever life has been examined with freedom from the self-imposed limitations of any discipline, the full implications of death for a philosophy of life have been evident.

Modern man, in his preoccupation with the structure of personality, cannot do justice in his thinking unless he deals with each of the three sisters, or with the potter's vessel from the time it is formed, through the period when it is filled full of experience, until the time comes when it proves no longer able to hold experience and is thrown out as useless upon the potter's field.

34

5. Basis for an Ego Concept

In our effort, then, to deal with the dynamics of the grief experience, we will not only consider the importance of early object relationships but will also interpret the attitude of the person toward the end of life. Our current preoccupation with the early years of life in the formation of character makes it more difficult for us to interpret the deep emotions that are involved in the feeling that "dead are we all and dying." No grief situation can be considered without taking into account the attitude of the bereaved person toward his own eventual death. This significant dynamic factor in the total picture of the handling of grief has been largely ignored. But Shakespeare, the Greek mythologists, and the writers of the Old Testament encourage us to create a philosophy of life that looks realistically at death.

Having made this observation we can proceed to the examination of early life experience as it relates to deprivation. Whether it is fortunate or not, it is undoubtedly true that the answers to most of the basic questions of life are given before the child gains verbal competence. The answers are given in a sum total response to life itself. The answers are assimilated from the actions and attitudes of adults in the family constellation. They are written into the fabric of human relationships and become bound up with the structure of personality in so basic a way that they become the unconscious bases for action rather than the material for logical thought processes. Such ideas are involved in every experience of grief, for they are related to the competence of the individual. They are bound up with the idea that life is good or bad. If life is not an acceptable experience emotionally, then death will also have an unacceptable quality. If life is essentially good, it is easier to accept the experience of death, for then all experience is undergirded by a quality of acceptance.

Just how would this operate in more specific terms? The mother or mother substitute plays an important part in the development of an adequate attitude toward life and death. Much of what she does is built into the unconscious or preconscious levels of the mind's life. The very nature of her biological relation to the child is a binding tie that cannot be equaled in emotional content. Security in this relationship is basic to the development of emotional security, and emotional security is important for effectively doing the work of mourning.

As religious activities are concerned with building a basic security into life, so theology is concerned with the answer to questions relating to that security. Yet often we do not realize that the important answers to all the major theological questions are given before the verbal period of life. Therefore, the conditioning factors of a philosophy of life are related to these important answers stored away in the preconscious and the unconscious. As the grief reaction is essentially a sum total response of the organism to deprivation in its most acute form, we must look to the early conditioning of the personality to see how it develops a tolerance or an intolerance to deprivation. At that point the early answers to the important theological assumptions about life are important. These are the questions in their simplest form: Who am I? Who are you? What am I? Why am I?

Who am I? One does not watch the explorations of a baby without seeing the wonderment of the child's discoveries. There is the hand before the eyes, and the wiggling fingers, and sometimes for hours the two hands go through all sorts of manipulations in an effort to comprehend how it all works, and how these wiggling fingers are a part of one's self. Then comes the discovery of the feet and the equally interesting explorations of that part of the anatomy. Day after day the child is involved in discovering himself. Who am I? During these early days the loving mother gives the answer, not in words that as yet have no meaning, but in acts. In her loving care she says over and over again: "You are a person, a precious person. Every part of your little being is precious and valuable. I kiss your hands, I kiss your feet, I hug and fondle you, and in every way I can I try to let you know that you are precious to me. I listen for your cry, I anticipate your needs, and I am an expression of the love you deserve when you are introduced to yourself, so that you will learn to value yourself as I value you." When anything else is said it is a tragedy for life and the scars are deep. The child, without an aptitude for language or reasoning, feels an emotional response of love. He begins to know something of life and what he knows is pleasant. He begins life with the feeling that he is a being of worth. Into the fiber of his being is built a response to the quality of his acceptance that becomes the basis for his self-esteem.

The ability to accept the self without uncertainty, fear, or low self-esteem is important for grief reactions. The person with uncertainty, fear, and easily stimulated feelings of guilt is excessively vulnerable to the strong emotions released by a major deprivation experience. His overdependence or underacceptance makes him susceptible to those abnormalities of response that can deny legitimate self-expression and stimulate destructive escapes and a distorted reality sense. The person who from early years has felt emotionally secure is able to meet the most disconcerting experiences with a measure of inner adequacy that serves him well.

Who are you? What are you doing here? What is my relation to you? Naturally, the child's first response to others in his world is to a nebulous force that is beyond himself, yet related to himself in the satisfying of hunger, in warmth, and in relief from irritation. Gradually these responses begin to organize themselves into a pattern, with a voice that sounds the same and means soothing comfort, strong hands that lift without fear of falling, a warm body and nourishing food, and the combination of sights, smells, and tastes that take form in another being, the mother. This discovery of another person in the world is as important for the baby as the discovery made by Robinson Crusoe when he came upon the footprint of Friday. It marks the beginning of the social life of the individual. How important it is for the context of later social life that this first experience of another being be sound and secure! When a baby can express the inarticulate equivalent of, "There is another with whom I can have a satisfying sense of relationship; there is one who needs me as I also need her; there is another person in whom my yearning nature can find a fulfillment," then the child has formed the basis for a healthy interpersonal relation that is solid enough to build on in the rest of living.

The ability to deal with another with this sense of relationship that fulfills the self but does not deny the self is important for withstanding the acute deprivation of bereavement. When a child's first human relations are rejecting and unsatisfactory, the life of that child is likely to be off balance in other human relations. He becomes anxious and apprehensive, self-conscious and steeped in inferiority feelings. He wants to placate others and unreasonably seeks to gain their approval. When acute grief is experienced he is likely to feel uncertain in his response. He may feel guilty and punish himself. He may feel insecure and become disorganized. He may even in adulthood be unable to meet the death of another without feeling that somehow remotely it is a judgment upon himself. However, with secure human relations from the beginning, he can establish a healthy reality sense and can feel the pain of loss without unreasonable judgments concerning himself and others.

What am I? Self-consciousness soons leads to value judgments. Self-knowledge leads to comparison. Early in life there is consciousness of sex differences, dress, and status. The early years bring to life comparisons of good and bad, smart and stupid, slow and quick. The answers to such questions are significant for self-respect and for the capacity for initiative and a feeling of personal adequacy. Some persons are never able to achieve emotional maturity because the answers they have received about themselves in this early stage have injured self-confidence to the place where they are unable to feel equal to other people or able to get along with them on an even basis.

What am I? This question is basic to any ethical structure, for it poses the primary questions that deal with values. When these questions do not find a reasonable and constructive answer in early years, there is an uncertainty at the core of life. The child grows up to be more concerned with unreasonable competition than he is with fulfilling the basic needs of his own personality. When his value structure is built on an uncertain basis, he may be continually about the task of self-justification and compulsive action to sustain a place of significance in his own eyes. When serious loss is sustained, the measure of self-regard may be so weak that the being is not able to organize its resources for the more constructive work of mourning, but rather takes upon itself the added tasks of self-punishment, self-justification, or the building of magical explanations for the facts of life that could be more satisfactorily dealt with by a strengthened reality sense. Lack of a reality sense may lead to the destructive self-pity which assumes that life deals mercilessly with one and not with another, and that some cruel force is at work to punish or to destroy the object of self-pity. Quickly this attitude of mind weakens the ability to deal wisely and well with the problems of living. Fortunate indeed is the person for whom the early questions concerning value and quality were answered with a respect for individuality and a concern that the young child be made secure in his acceptance of self and others.

Why am I? Here one comes to grips with the whole matter of the purpose and meaning of life itself. The answers given here, even by indirection, can become basic to life and its value to the individual. To indicate that one is an accident is to make the qualities of human personality a cosmic joke. To exist in order to satisfy small selfish purposes is to limit the scope of life. To exist only for others is to deny major concerns for the self. The element of purpose in life tends to become a major determinant of the drive and direction of life. The positive answer that the life of each individual is related to a purpose larger than the self, within which larger fulfillments are realized, changes the level of living. A feeling of cosmic purpose changes the level of living. The achievement of values that do not begin and end in the self gives to life a capacity for relationship that would not otherwise exist. The purpose and meaning of life cannot easily be separated from the purpose and meaning of death.

If life is a cosmic joke, then death itself becomes the bitterest defeat administered by a cosmic jokester. If death is the end of selfhood, the nature of the concept of self is involved. Selfishness and selflessness find a limited meaning in a life with a limited meaning. If the question "Why am I?" can be answered in actions

39

and attitudes that lend to life true personal, social, and cosmic significance, the individual life is surely enhanced. The venture of faith that religion makes is concerned primarily with granting to life a meaning and purpose large enough to explain its highest aspirations and to give direction to its most daring assumptions. These aspirations and assumptions about life tend to become the measure of the quality of life itself. Beyond the meanings produced by fears and illusions, there is the meaning that is a spiritual achievement. This meaning is created early in life and becomes the basis for the evaluating of life experience. This meaning becomes important for establishing the adequacy with which a person meets the acute loss that comes with the death of significant persons in his personal and social framework of existence.

The child who has had the early experience of life surrounded by affirmation, acceptance, and affection has had built into the structure of his being certain attitudes that condition his approach to life experience. Such attitudes also provide the raw material out of which the problem of death can be competently handled. Because most of the material of these early years is stored away at preconscious levels of mental life, it becomes the basis for the sum total emotional responses to life experience. While the child who has been grounded in an adequate emotional security will face tragic circumstances with confidence, the insecure child will be disturbed by deep anxiety. So the early attitude toward the mother, ambivalence in childhood, fear and insecurity in early years, as well as a clear sense of self-acceptance and acceptance of others, become the dynamic force at work in shaping a thanatology.[7]

6. Discipline and Deprivation in Relation to Reality

The capacity to respond healthfully to stress is not unrelated to an environment of realistic discipline administered with a loving concern that is so interpreted by the child disciplined. Here is it not so important what the parent thinks about the method of discipline as it is what the child feels about it. The child seems to feel more secure in a framework of firm but loving discipline. When American military personnel went into Okinawa after a period of terrific bombardment, they found few evidences of anxiety states. The children submitted to preventive medical activities with no fearful apprehension. They did not seem to feel hurt by the injections. The reason seemed to be that the children had been made to feel so secure in parental love that they could not easily think of an adult willfully hurting them.

For fifty years the Santi family, at an orphanage in Portici, Italy, has been meeting the needs of children, with expressions of loving concern and a rather strict form of discipline. The children feel a sense of security within the framework of the discipline but never seem to feel that it is punitive. During World War II, when Naples was under the pressure of military attack, the children were evacuated to caves, and the physical bases of acute anxiety were abundantly present. However, the children were calm and disciplined and seemed to feel secure in the provision that was made for them. Furthermore, in their own individual beings, they seemed able to withstand the stress of tragic circumstance with a good degree of equanimity.

When children are allowed to grow with a proper balance of freedom and responsibility, when the "dos" and "don'ts" are in the right proportion, the personality grows with a healthy acceptance of external circumstance. When such circumstances are tragic, the personality withstands the stress because the pattern of response to deprivation has been established. Because the results of grief on the psychic structure depend on this pattern of interpersonal responses, it is important to understand the significance of the early years of life as the important dynamic element in the consideration of grief responses for all the rest of life.

7. Age Factors That Modify Ego Response

The dynamic factors that become apparent in the acute experience of grief are not different from the dynamic factors at work in all the rest of the person's life. They may be revealed in a different way, but if we have learned anything about the personality of man it is that it is all one. There are characteristic responses at different periods of life. But these again are responses to the dynamic elements of life modified by age factors. The grief expressions of children are not likely to be shown in the same manner as those of mature years. The child's grief is more likely to be shown in physical symptoms and behavior difficulties than in the symptoms described in Chapter X. Often what is referred to as juvenile delinquency can be traced to a grief experience. The years between adolescence and senescence, when a strong capacity for object love marks life, are the years in which both the normal and abnormal grief reactions are more clearly defined. The discussion of these reactions is the main purpose of Chapters X, XI, and XII.

The dynamic factors at work among aged persons are again quite different from those of the adult in the prime of life.[8] Among the aged (referred to as over sixty-five but in most instances considerably older), careful study of a number of cases indicates a paucity of conscious guilt feelings. As guilt is a major factor in most bereavements among younger persons, this is significant. However, there seems to be a replacement of guilt feelings by somatic equivalents, with the development of specific infirmities, characterized by those eye weaknesses that may express a desire not to see, and hearing weaknesses that may indicate a desire to withdraw from communication. Also rheumatism may comparably indicate a desire to withdraw from activity and responsibility. Interest in life wanes and the impulse toward creative action decreases with it. There is a common distortion of the image of the deceased with an unreal glorification and a tendency toward self-isolation coupled with a growing hostility toward family and friends. In children there is an absence of the normally associated grief symptoms because in children the ego strength is yet too weak to respond. In the aged, the ego strength seems to be correspondingly weakened and the symptoms of the grief reaction are modified accordingly. Quite in contrast to the studies of Lindemann, which dealt with the acute grief reactions to violent death among adults, Stern's study defines different types of reaction among the aged. This is probably due to the fact that there has been a long period of time for the development of identification characteristics, and these show their influence rather than the guilt that ambivalence normally generates. Ambivalence is probably present with the aged but it is expressed through a different set of mechanisms.

8. Summary

When we are able to understand the dynamic factors at work in the personality to develop the reaction to severe loss, we are in a better position to deal with them creatively and to direct the personality toward productive mourning work. Klein points out that suffering can be productive in the release of new talents under the stress of frustration.[9] Paradise Lost can also have its Paradise Regained. The important thing is to relate the precipitative emotional experience to the resources of the total personality for meeting stress. Emotional maturity is the best assurance for meeting stress with competence. Environmental factors may be brought to bear to help resolve the stress. Artificial forces such as counseling aid may also be used to relate the person constructively to his experience and to the future that is still his.

But of great importance is the health of personality that the person brings to the precipitating emotional experience. It is seldom that a healthy personality is disorganized for long by the experience of grief. The dynamic factors in healthy growth become the important determinants of the grief reaction. Therefore, we take into account all of life in dealing with the grief-stricken, and we employ all the opportunities of life to prepare the personality for the inevitable experience of bereavement.

THREE

The Roots and Development
of Grief in Man
and Society

Now that we have examined in relation to grief the dynamic factors in the growth of the individual personality, we are prepared to look at the contribution of the group to individual personality.

Grief is not only deeply rooted in the personality structure of the individual; it is also firmly implanted in the nature of man as a being with a long history of development as a social creature. One cannot easily understand the individual man without understanding the human group. Social and anthropological studies help us to interpret the development of the nature of man, and to illuminate the devices that man has traditionally used to protect himself from the forces he could not understand or control.

While we can study the individual man vertically, so to speak, we must also study him horizontally, for he is the sum total of the group experience. In a physical way this is rather dramatically shown in the growth of the fetus. The whole process of evolution— from the one-celled creature, through the lower forms of life, through the early mammalians, up to the full potential of the human—is recapitulated during the nine months of gestation.

In a less dramatic but no less significant manner, the growth stages of full self-consciousness are restated in the life of each individual. As preverbal man had limited equipment for communication, so he had but a limited concept of himself as a being. The early stages of language, according to Emil Froeschels, developed with the grunts of satisfaction in a shared meal. The early communication related feelings with specific symbols in a way that gave a direction to social relations. As man developed skills in communication he also was able to develop a self-awareness that brought something new into life. Language became the equipment of abstraction and secondary symbolization. He could talk about things he could not see but could feel. This was not unrelated to the growth of those strong feelings that became a basis for socialization and self-consciousness. This self-consciousness, in turn, became the basis for the growth of a capacity to feel grief. It is not probable that there was a feeling of relatedness in preverbal man strong enough to become the basis for the strong emotional response to deprivation that we call grief. While there might have been a sense of loss, insecurity, or deprivation, it would have been oriented about limited needs and a limited concept of self.

1. The Conditioning of Grief Response by Group Influence

The development of more adequate modes of communication, along with the effect that such communication had upon social organization, stimulated those qualities in man that sought expression in mutual dependence. The tribal hunter, off alone for long periods of time, had less of the interdependence that makes grief acute than had the agrarian man. The man who lived in small towns probably had more capacity for it than the agrarian man, for the fabric of interrelations in his life was greater. Only when man loses his sense of need for others, as in the life of a great, impersonal city, does this social factor in grief become diminished.

Those developmental factors that appear in man's movement toward socialization, and toward the capacity to communicate deep feelings adequately, are restated in the life of each individual as he matures. The preoccupation with self is usually followed by strong social impulses that ripen into family and community life. During the early months of life the complete self-centeredness is without active self-consciousness, and the organism is totally occupied with the satisfaction of basic physical and emotional needs. This is followed by a stage of consciousness of others, but only as the concept of "other" is a more adequate organization of relationships bent on the satisfying of the infant's needs. Then

45

there comes a time of response when an effective and meaningful communication begins to be established with another being. The content of the communication has a different quality for the adult than it has for the infant, but it is an evidence of the growing capacity for relationship. The emotional quality of the relationship is still oriented about the primary needs of the small child. All these stages would have been achieved before the period of verbal communication is established. During none of these stages would there have been a capacity for grief as we have defined it. There could be a sense of loss, insecurity, anxiety, or deprivation, but it would be oriented about the satisfaction of the infant's primary needs. The infant has no concept of self or death, so it cannot have any concept that would hold the meanings that the adult normally puts into grief.

During the early verbal stages, from two to five or six, the child is still primarily concerned with the satisfaction of its own emotional and physical needs. Even during the latency period from about seven to eleven, when the child is learning the essentials of the culture and the fabric of human and social relations, the capacity for a concept of death is only partial, and related more to an idea of separation and temporary "going away" than the final and unalterable concept that brings grief for the adult.

2. Levels of Grief Communication and Expression

It seems that the ability to form a concept of true grief depends on what Harry Stack Sullivan means by a tertiary level of abstraction and symbolization. The primary level of symbolization would be the word itself as it stands for something. The word "cow" gives a primary relationship to some picture of a cow in the mind of the person who hears the word. A secondary symbolization might be indicated by such a statement as, "Two and two are four." The two is a secondary symbolization, for it does not necessarily stand for a particular two, such as two cows or two oranges. The tertiary level of symbolization and abstraction comes when we use such as phrase as, "Love is eternal." Here the essential words are not reducible to any simple category of measurement. The reality of their meaning is related to an accumulation of experience

46

that gives body and substance to the abstraction. The child does not seem to be able to gain a true concept of grief until he is able to handle abstractions at the tertiary level.

In the individual or the group the capacity for strong feelings of interrelationship is essential to grief as we define it. With preverbal man, with young children, or even with the aged whose sense of relationship is diminished, the feelings of loss fall short of the concept we are dealing with when we speak of the grief of a normal adult.

As we know it, grief seems to be inseparably bound with the capacity for self-consciousness. One must come to the place individually and within the group where his nature as a person has commanding status in his thought life before he can begin to develop the feeling of concern for the loss of it. This is essential to that feeling of acute pain which is the core of the grief feeling.

Animals seem unable to know grief as we have defined it. They have no capacity for symbolization above the primary level. A dog may know his name, and show remarkable intelligence in certain limited areas, but he cannot feel a contemplative concern about his own death or the death of another. His reactions are instinctual and limited. Humans like to read into their pets their own feelings and find satisfaction in doing so, but it does not change the nature and quality of the animal's feeling. The almost human response of a dog to the loss of his master is cited often as an evidence of a grief reaction at the animal level. The animal's concern however seems to be primarily that of maintaining the elements of the security framework of his life as he has known it. Studies of animal psychology have been unable to establish any other basis for the behavior of animals than that related to primary instinctual satisfactions. It might also be observed that some human beings seem to be singularly devoid of any higher capacity for response, and the callous response of the person shows up poorly in contrast to the instinctive devotion of a faithful animal.

Studies of apes, man's closest relative in the animal realm, indicate that the instinctual drives are primary as a basis for interpreting behavior.[1] When an old ape begins to lose his powers, the younger males fight for the desirable mates. Their fighting may be so vicious as to destroy the very mate for whom they fight. But the ensuing death seems to produce no feelings of grief. Driven by instinctual forces they may be led to copulate with the dead female, but not to express other feeling than frustration at the loss of a desired partner in fulfilling basic instinctual drives. It seems logical to conclude that there is nothing at the animal level that is comparable to the feeling of acute grief of the adult human.

It also seems reasonable to assume that the human child is not able to formulate a concept of death such as is essential to the adult form of grief before the period when tertiary abstractions are handled. This does not mean that a child cannot have a severe sense of loss or trauma related to deprivation. But it does mean that it must be dealt with in a different manner, as the studies of Redl, Wineman, and Bettelheim have so clearly established.[2]

Self-consciousness is thus both a privilege and a burden for life. The fact that man was early aware of this burden is shown by the efforts that primitive tribes made to deal with the elements of the unknown which he was aware of but could not understand. This was especially obvious as it related to matters of death and grief. Without developing a philosophy to interpret his feelings, he moved directly to work out a system of rituals and social relationships that could give expression to his emotional needs. While we may judge his efforts to be unsatisfactory for us we cannot escape the fact that our own methods tend to incorporate many of his techniques in modified fashion. Primitive man tried to work out meanings as well as his limited resources permitted. His scientific resources were limited but his imagination was not. Many of the things he did were logical interpretations of his observation as it was limited by lack of organized scientific knowledge. His interpretations took the form of logical projections, animism, fetishism, and magic. Let us look more closely at these modes of expression, for they can give clues to some of the comparable grief expressions of modern man.

3. Primitive Methods of Dealing with Self-Consciousness and Grief

Sir James George Frazer gives a whole chapter in his study to the rituals developed surrounding death to try to cheat death of its finality.[3] Many primitive tribes have rituals of death and resurrection, and the initiation rites of the youth of the tribe are related to a theory of life and death. By means of a ritual in which the person could become actively involved, the individual was able to feel that he had gained some mastery over the force that was beyond his understanding or control. All magical thinking seems to have this element about it, whether it is the ritual of the primitive man or the magical rituals of modern man as he institutes them in relation to the important incidents of his life.

The philosophical counterpart of these expressions is the myth—the effort to give verbal expression to the fellings stimulated by those basic relationships that involve creation, life, and death. Though they start with basic facts of experience they move on toward interpretation, with the feeling that understanding can give a measure of control. In his study *Myth in Primitive Psychology*,[4] Malinowski writes: "Every myth possesses as its kernel or ultimate reality some natural phenomenon or other, elaborately woven into a tale to an extent which sometimes almost masks and obliterates it." The myth may deal with the moon, the sun, the stars, life, death, or sex. But for the people who have made the myth a part of their philosophical equipment for understanding life, it becomes more than a myth. It becomes a force to control the world of external things through understanding. The frightening is not so frightening after we understand it. It may be as deadly, but understanding makes it lose some of its dread. In the same way the myths of childhood are a part of the prelogical equipment by which understanding tends to bring a measure of control over those things that are too large to handle in any other way. Admittedly it is an emotional control and not physical, but it serves its purpose. Stories such as "Jack the Giant Killer" give the child a way of expressing with safety his aggression against the adults who as giants exert control over his world. The ability to express the aggression makes it possible to tolerate it more adequately. So the primitive, through his mythological structures, gained a capacity to tolerate those things he could never really control physically. In effect, he is working to gain for himself a measure of psychological control. This is clearly evident in relation to death myths and the physical reality that stimuates their development.

Through the processes of animism, primitive man tried to deal with the problem of his own self-consciousness by investing with self-consciousness the other parts of his environment making a quite natural assumption that he would then be in a better position to understand and control. The idea of the soul, which is impossible without self-consciousness, is so difficult to define that early man tried to escape the burden of definition by denying the very uniqueness that was peculiar to his self-consciousness. By sharing with other objects, both animate and inanimate, the qualities of a self-conscious soul, he escaped some of the burdens of his uniqueness and removed the major problem of definition. This was partly necessary because he was seeking to establish communication with his environment, but primarily because of his lack of equipment for dealing with the uniqueness that was the core of his selfhood. What Homer did at a much later time was to deal with those same anthropomorphic projections in a more artistic way by selectively relating the needs of man to the family of gods rather than to indiscriminate animals and things. All polytheisms are essentially refined animisms and are projections of the self-conscious nature of man into an environment that he would seek to understand and control. To invest the dead with another life could well be another method used by primitive man to deal with a problem he could not understand. Also by reinvesting his emotional capital in devotion to the soul of the deceased, he would protect himself from the burdens of guilt that normal ambivalence usually produces in mourning.

Fetishism seeks to invest inanimate things with spiritual powers. Sometimes these are things that are made by the hands of men and granted special powers. Golden calves, images, and amulets would come under this heading. At other times they are things that, in one sense, are not living, yet in another sense they seem to have a life of their own. Waterfalls and rivers come under this heading. Sometimes this special quality can be resident in an office that a man may hold. Even more advanced cultures have kept a certain amount of fetishism: for instance, the crown and scepter, or even more primitive items such as the stone of Scone. The basic conflict of powers is still operative in the efforts to bring political cultures under ecclesiastical control, or to prevent such rapprochement through the separation of church and state. In its more active relation to this matter of life and death, we see the effort to remove from the state the power to exact capital punishment, as if to say that men trespass on the realm of the gods when they assume the power of life and death. Ultimately, it seems that the revolt against the ruthlessness of totalitarianisms is rooted in this disinclination of man to allow secular power to long hold final control over what he considers to be the destiny of his soul.

The structure of magical practices is but a further and more explicit effort to bring the unknown under control. Sometimes the magic is resident in a person, and sometimes in a process such as a sacred ritual. These formulas are adopted to insulate man against stern realities that he is not prepared to face. The medicine man is embued with magical powers. Some of the little-known powers of the mind are evidently related to magical practices. Psychological powers are also involved, and in relation to long-established taboos this power is so great that persons are actually brought to death. Not only was it evident in primitive tribes, but also in scriptural times such incidents are recorded, as in the case of Uzzah, who touched the sacred ark and died (II Sam. 6:9), and Ananias, who violated the sacred truth and died. (Acts 5:5) In such instances it seems that the explanation may be physiological, with an emotional excitement that builds up an intolerable adrenalin content in the blood with no adequate means for working it out of the system. Such magical factors are not unrelated to the more modern practices of bringing a restoration of divine substance to the physical elements of a ceremonial meal. In some instances the magic seems an effort to wall off and control the unpleasant aspects of experience, and at other times to break down the walls and restore that which is desirable. Such simple practices as closing the

51

eyes of the dead may be rooted in a fear that the soul of the departed may see what is going on after his death and return to seek retaliation. Here again the inadequate and primitive understanding of the dream is undoubtedly a factor also, as well as the sense of guilt that is related to the normal ambivalence in most close human relations. (Chapter VI contains a more detailed discussion of this phenomenon.)

4. Modern Counterparts of the Primitive Methods

Jung finds a modern counterpart in the interest in magic manifested by those who have adopted the mind-over-matter cults and other phases of Oriental religious practice:

We have not yet clearly grasped the fact that Western Theosophy is an amateurish imitation of the East. We are just taking up astrology again, and that to the Oriental is his daily bread. Our studies of sexual life, originating in Vienna and in England, are matched or surpassed by Hindu teachings on this subject. Oriental texts ten centuries old introduce us to philosophical relativism, while the idea of indetermination, newly broached in the West, furnishes the very basis of Chinese science. Richard Wilhelm has even shown me that certain complicated processes discovered by analytical psychology are recognizably described in ancient Chinese texts. Psychoanalysis itself and the lines of thought to which it gives rise—surely a distinctive Western development—are only a beginner's attempt compared to what is an immemorial art in the East. It should be mentioned that the parallels between psychoanalysis and yoga have already been traced by Oskar A. H. Schmitz. . . . Need I point to the Asiatic origin of Christianity? [5]

Pursuing further the magical factor that modern man seems willing to grant to such Oriental thought, he writes:

The Theosophists have an amusing idea that certain Mahatmas, seated somewhere in the Himalayas or Tibet, inspire or direct every mind in the world. So strong, in fact, can be the influence of the Eastern belief in magic upon Europeans of a sound mind, that some of them have assured me that I am unwittingly inspired by the Mahatmas with every good thing I say, my own inspiration being of no account whatever. This myth of the Mahatmas, widely circulated and firmly believed in the West, far from being nonsense, is—like every myth—an important psychological truth. It seems to be quite true that the East is at the bottom of the spiritual change we are passing through today. Only this East is not a Tibetan monastery full of Mahatmas, but in a sense lies within us.[6]

The western world that has long had a secular orientation, from the time of the Greek interest in the glorification of the body and the early Christian concern with political preferment, is now sharing the quest of primitive man in a search for the important meaning of being. While we have more adequate tools to work with in our quest, we are also hampered by mental predilections that condition the use we make of the tools. In some respects we have come up with about the same answers as our primitive ancestors, with the exception that we have clothed them in the styles that are more fitting in our day. We do not begin to grasp the basic insights of an adequate philosophy of life and death or a personality satisfying set of rituals and symbols for dealing with it, until we understand where we are and where we would want to be. Perhaps our present state of scientific devotion to the development of tools of mass destruction and total extinction cannot be disassociated from our essentially secular and nonspiritual view of the nature of man. Until we sense the importance of the soul's vitality we will not adequately deal with either life or death.

But this soul's vitality is a sterile and dangerous thing if it is thought of as pure individualism. The acceptances of life are never fulfilled without the sense of relationship that is an essential part of the soul's growth. Personality is formed through interpersonal relations. There would be no soul as we now know it apart from this meaningful growth of human relationships. As Bergson has pointed out so well, this is the source of a privilege and of a burden:

Man outwits nature when he extends social solidarity into the brotherhood of man; but he is deceiving her nevertheless, for those societies whose design was prefigured in the original structure of the human soul . . . required that the group be closely united, but that between group and group there should be virtual hostility. . . . Man, fresh from

the hands of nature, was a being both intelligent and social, his sociala-
bility being devised to find its scope in small communities, his intelligence being designed to further individual and group life. But intelligence, expanded through his own efforts, has developed unexpectedly.
It has freed men from restrictions to which they were condemned by
the limitations of their nature. This being so, it was not impossible
that some of them, specially gifted, should reeopen that which was
closed and do, at least for themselves, what nature could not possibly
have done for mankind.[7]

5. Beyond Magical Thinking to a Clear Reality Sense

These special gifts, and the burden of responsibility that accompanies them, oblige man to move beyond the level of magical
thinking to the establishing of adequate cause-effect relations. The
ability to move beyond mere consciousness to creative self-consciousness involves the ability for object love, but it also involves
the threat of object hate. One cannot apply reason to the affairs
that have to do with object love, and expect to apply magic where
object hate is involved. The aborigine could do that. He had no
consciousness of the workings of his nervous system. He could
think, "Finger move," and his finger moved. It was not illogical
with his limited knowledge to feel that he was also able to think
rain and have it rain, or think death and cause it. Because of his
ignorance of his nervous system and its mechanism, he had a feeling akin to omnipotence. The only limit was the power of his
thinking, his ability to make "strong medicine." But as social
beings, we fall far short of our responsibility if we let our knowledge of the functioning of our nervous system become our excuse
for not dealing creatively with our emotional states. The aborigine
was neither a mechanist nor a determinist. He was sure that there
was something about himself that was a creative, determining force.
He acted on the basis of that belief and set up his system of social
controls accordingly. Modern man because of subtle and increasingly dominant mechanistic and deterministic factors at work in his
thinking, has surrendered the right to create his philosophy and his
social controls with a concern about his own deep emotional needs.
This is especially shown in relation to his group thinking about

death. This is illustrated in the phenomenon of the Nazi state, with its pathological reversion to primitive thought modes and action patterns. The antiscientific designation of the Nordic race as the superfamily of a frightened people gave group cohesiveness, but the price it exacted was a reversion to intertribal hostility that destroyed effectively the structure of values that civilized man had laboriously developed concerning life and death. Its essentially nihilistic thought patterns were tinged with enough magical thinking on the part of its leaders to satisfy the superficial emotional needs of those who were uncertain of their place as mechanistic automata of the state. The attitude toward an act of group devotion willingly accepted was maintained in group action; but when the group broke up into frightened individuals again, the courage turned to cowardice and unbridled sadism. For those who were able to enter into the primitive modes of magical thought and action, the problems of physical health were improved. Problems such as those created by the aged were dealt with directly and the nonreligious philosophy justified the action. The concerns of life were sharply defined and a philosophy fitted to meet the definition. The main effort of that philosophy was directed toward destroying the sense of responsibility for applying reason and truth to public affairs; at the same time hate was being aroused as an essential human motivation.

In American life a comparable but modified process has been taking place. We have accepted the practical values of a competitive society, and it has made its imprint upon our concept of life and death. It is reflected in our international dealings that are essentially power-centered, with money for our friends and threats of nuclear bombs for our enemies. This has so conditioned our thinking that we have found it difficult to express the deeper feelings we have about life and death. We must not think death is so bad if we are willing to deal in it in wholesale terms. Yet individually we are frightened by the thought of death, so that we build a curtain of defenses against the philosophical reality of death. With the pressure of such an unresolved emotional situation, the only thing we seem able to do is to make physical death common and to ignore the other implications. This we do with pictures, movies, television, and literature steeped in the physical aspect of death. But still something in man is not satisfied with this answer. He feels he has destroyed something valuable within himself. In destroying the souls of others by proxy he has done something devastating to his own soul.

6. The Symptoms of Destructive Repression

In his effort to defeat his feelings by making physical death so common that he can ignore it as a too-familiar part of his experience, he does not take into account the reactions of his total being. What is suppressed for long finds other channels for expression. While he may rationalize his thinking to conform to his materialistic philosophy, he cannot prevent his sublimated feelings from taking other forms of expression. So we see a sick society producing its symptoms in psychosomatic illness. A number of organic disturbances of psychogenic nature are almost categorically accurate in defining their emotional origin. For instance the aggressiveness of a competitive society, with its suppressed chronic anger, is not unrelated to the prevalence of stomach ulcers. The thinly veiled atmosphere of fear under which we live finds expression in the prevalence of heart disease. The suppression of the irritation we feel but dare not express is able to find an outlet in the skin diseases that have made dermatology one of the prominent areas of medical specialization. The overburdened and those overwhelmed with the problem of their humanity are easily immobilized by arthritis. Of what value is it to get a million dollars if one has to spend it at the Mayo Clinic. How strangely familiar is this modern echo of a statement made centuries ago: "Whoever would save his life will lose it; and whoever loses his life for my sake and the gospel's will save it" (Mark 8:35 R.S.V.). The values involved in life must be adequate to sustain that life. If they fall short, tragedy ensues. Modern man is paying the price for his distorted values concerning life and death.

A neurotic flight into work merely prevents the type of contemplation that can give the ultimate and satisfactory answer. The neurotic pattern in the individual and in the group reflects a failure of values. In the Middle Ages when a plague came the people killed their dogs. This increased the danger of the plague, for they should have dealt with the rats rather than the dogs who helped to destroy the rats. The neurotic approach to the problem is that of dealing with the dogs rather than the rats. The inability of modern man to develop a realistic attitude toward death is largely due to the fact that he seems unwilling to approach the problem directly. When the individual faces his grief directly, he is in a better position to resolve it. When a society faces the implications of its lack of a philosophy of life and death, it is in a better position to evolve one. The inability to evolve a realistic view of life and death merely increases the potential for destructive behavior. In the individual it often takes the form of self-destruction. In society it may produce a generation that glorifies its capacity for self-destructive action at the same time that it ignores the meaning of this self-destructive potential. So we see the development of men with a diseased soul living a marginal existence resistant to truth about himself and his motives. He resists the responsibilities for true socialization, and in return becomes increasingly lonely and more deeply neurotic as he destroys the social roots of his emotional health.[8] Unfortunately it appears that too often the intellectuals in society have been the leaders of the movement toward nihilism and away from the expression of the natural healthful feelings toward self and others. In place of the expression of creative emotion they place their intellectualization. In the place of rituals that give meaning to life (see Chapter VIII), they institute the rituals that deny it. In the place of values that enrich the life of the soul they practice the values that deny its worth.

Franz Alexander has defined the thought movements of "our Age of Unreason." We have failed to see the meaning of this for our acute and somatic expressions of grief. Because we cannot face our grief in terms of normal expression, we must work out the more costly details of a neurotic grief. Primitive man faced his grief directly and worked out a system of personal and social rituals and symbols that made it possible for him to deal with it directly. Modern man does not seem to know how to proceed in the expression of this fundamental emotion. He has no generally accepted social patterns for dealing with death. His rituals are partial and unsatisfying. His funerals are apt to be meaningless and empty. Either he is so afraid of normal emotion that his funerals are sterile, or they are so steeped in superficialities that they remain meaningless, and the more normal emotions remain unengaged.

7. Building More Healthful Attitudes Toward Grief

So modern man, aware of the function of his nervous system, but unaware of the sum-total nature of his being, unconsciously builds substitute rituals and stumbles on the symbols of those deeper meanings that fulfill his soul's desire. During one week recently the listing of best-selling books in a New York book-review section showed seven books dealing with the sea. The sea is readily accepted as a symbol of the eternal, but it is also a symbol of that all-engulfing source and end of life that originally produced us and eventually will claim us. In the sense that Freud used the symbol, it is the all-encompassing, all-sustaining, all-satisfying state of well-being that existed before birth and continues to exist as the basis of unconscious symbolization of being and nonbeing at one and the same time. So while we do not have the articulate philosophy of life and death to give us values and to determine our individual and group behavior, our unconscious needs drive us to find the symbolic satisfactions that our reasoned approach to life would tend to deny. So we continue to speak, with the sanction of this unconscious symbolism, of being engulfed in grief and being in a flood of tears.

The capacity for grief is an achievement of a being capable of true object love and involving both self-consciousness and other-consciousness. It is a product of advanced interpersonal relations. Primitive man, in his response to life, realized this in his actions even if he did not realize it in his articulate philosophy. By so doing he developed for himself what might be called security measures to protect his integrity as a spiritual being. His soul was not denied.

Modern man, with his emphasis on mechanical manipulation and hedonistic satisfactions, has ignored a major part of himself. Modern psychiatric interest has tried to restore it to a place of significance in life, but in many instances the deterministic preoccupation of modern psychotherapy has at the beginning denied that important part of human nature which was the end result of the therapy. Until modern man can find the equivalent for the attitude toward life and death that was existent among primitive men, he cannot begin to gain for himself a mastery over the individual and group sources of unreason that destroy his happiness individually and may destroy his collective life socially.

Grief is essentially an individual response to a social fact. It is the acute response to deprivation at the highest level. It grew with man's self-consciousness and the capacity for true object love. It is resolved in those attitudes and actions that can restore a proper balance between the integrity of the bereaved self and the emotional demands of the lost love object. But unless the capacity for resolving the balance exists in the individual and in society, untold suffering will persist. But as the suffering self is a product of the social inheritance, it is important for the society of which he is a part to deal with the basic problem of the meaning of life. This our society seems unwilling and unable to do.

FOUR

Grief and Identification

In addition to the important personality-determining forces of growth and heredity there is an active ingredient that is operative in human life created by the actual precipitating incident. Where the factors of growth and inheritance meet at a given focal point in life, something new is in the act of being made. When the focal point is a circumstance charged with deep emotion, much that is significant can happen to change the course of life or refine its progress. Grief is such a circumstance and the personality develops responses in the form of identification, substitution, and guilt. The next three chapters deal with these situational responses.

1. The Injured Psyche and the Incorporated Object

The psyche injured by acute grief seeks to make the experience tolerable by a situational response called "identification," or sometimes "incorporation." The terms may be used interchangeably. The bereaved person seeks to overcome the pain of grief by becoming one with the lost love object. It is not uncommon in every day speech to hear a person say something like this, "I love you so much I could eat you right up." The inverse of this same emotion is involved in severe loss, when a person might say in effect, "In your death something in me also dies."

Wilhelm Stekel defines the process in these terms:

With the aid of identification a lover can transfer his passion upon any object that stands in some sort of relation to his beloved. It is in this way that fetishism sometimes results. . . . Thus there runs through the soul of man an endless chain of identifications ranging from the normal to the pathological.[1]

Dealing with the same device in more technical terms, Edoardo Weiss writes:

As duplications of the mental data of other persons, living a proxy existence within the ego, they follow the mental vicissitudes of the object to which they are related and from which they are never disconnected. When the ego has a bodily and mental object representation of the other person, and also duplicates within itself the mental and emotional experiences attributed to the person, the result is a psychic presence whose reactions have an effect upon the ego equivalent to those of the actual person represented.[2]

Under normal circumstances this is not an unusual occurrence. Any child will take on characteristics and mannerisms of its parents. Adolescent girls will adopt the hair styles and clothing fashions of the moving-picture stars whom they emulate. Boys will affect the simple rituals of big-league stars in their actions on the baseball diamond. Such examples are so common that they are not generally credited with psychological significance.

The behavior of Mr. L. is more significant. People commented on how Mr. L. had changed since his wife died. Mrs. L. was an active, energetic little woman, very much involved in church and community affairs. She was even elected to the school board in town and was quite a figure in the community because of her vigorous stand on public issues. On the other hand, Mr. L. was retiring. While he never interferred with her affairs, he seldom participated. He was always ready and willing to help, but always as the chauffeur, the financier, and the behind-the-scenes collaborator. He was seldom seen at public meetings and never attended church though his wife seldom missed a Sunday. He preferred to work around the house and in the garden, which was his pride and joy.

The Sunday after Mrs. L. died, her husband came to church and sat in the place that she usually occupied. It was assumed that this was an act of devotion toward her memory, but no one expected to see him there again for some time. However, in the two years that have elapsed since her death, he has missed the regular service of worship only during vacation time and when he was away on business. Not only that, he indicated that he would like to serve his wife's unexpired term on the school board. Some persons smilingly remarked that at last he was able to possess his own soul and speak his own mind; but something deeper seemed to be taking place. He continued to move into other community activities. He took a place on the budget committee of the Community Chest. Although nominally a church member for years, he was not active in organizational work. Some of the church members thought that the death of his wife brought a new religious awareness to Mr. L., and they felt that her death did more for his spiritual life than the combined efforts of neighbors over the years. At the same time the garden and the property showed signs of neglect. He did not devote the time or interest there as he had formerly done. In many respects he was a different person. Though he had not shown any marked signs of grief at his wife's death, there was evidence that his life had been profoundly changed by that emotional experience.

Turning again to the interpretation of Weiss, we may get a clue to what was taking place in the structure of Mr. L.'s personality.

A similar transformation can be observed in a person who has lost someone he loves. At first helpless to control his id-cathected longing for the lost one, he engages in the "mourning work" in a process of bodily identification with the deceased, at the end of which he loves, instead of the actual person, the egotized, autoplastic restoration of that person within himself. Only to the extent to which the deceased person can actually be substituted by such an internalization does the ego feel emotionally free from the lost love object. This phenomenon accounts for the acquisition, by the mourner, of many characteristics of the deceased, just as the child comes to have characteristics of the parents from whom he has freed himself by a similar process of bodily identification. As Freud points out, the process leads to self-hate and self-reproach when the person incorporated is the object of ambivalent feelings of mixed hate and love.[3]

Mr. L., in his complete devotion to his wife and her interests, seems to have identified with her personality through an act of incorporation. In a response to deep emotional need, his own personality has been sublimated to the point where her personality and her interests have become primary. His inability to enter upon the normal work of mourning indicates that he has been unable to separate himself from the dominance of her influence. While he may function adequately in the eyes of the community, it is undoubtedly true that his identification has been made at considerable cost to his own personality. At his age, in the middle fifties, there may be no evidence of acute breakdown as far as his ability to function is concerned; but it might occur, especially if some precipitating factor should release an amount of guilt or self-recrimination. This might occur, for instance, if at the next election he seeks to win the support of the electorate and is defeated. It would not be his defeat, but rather the defeat of the incorporated love object, and at this point the unresolved emotional problem might present itself.

2. Normal Identification and Techniques of Identity

A certain amount of identification is essential and desirable. When someone asks us a question we automatically identify with that person in order to interpret what the question means as he asks it. When we go to a play we identify ourselves with the characters who appear before us. The more completely we identify the more likely we are to enjoy the play. In the process of establishing empathy or expressing sympathy we become, as it were, emotionally sensitive to the needs and feelings of another. Others come to know us as the sum total of the acts and attitudes that make up the structure of our personality. The natural and normal fabric of identification can be disrupted, however, when the personality is so deeply injured that it feels it must become more essentially another in order to tolerate the intensity of emotional pain. This marks the difference between normal short-term identification and the abnormal and long-term type.

Often the emotional needs of the persons are so important that the structure of reality is modified to meet that need, at least in the mind of the person involved. We call such a condition irrational, and the evidences of it irrational behavior. But from the point of view of the injured person it is all quite logical. It involves a rearrangement of the syllogism to the place where the personality finds what satisfies it. The syllogism, "Man is immortal; I am a man; therefore I am immortal," may be fallacious but the logical structure is clear. But when a sorely disturbed person tries to find satisfaction through a logical transposition of subject and predicate, the irrational appears. For instance, "Napoleon was a man; I am a man; therefore I am Napoleon." The emotionally disturbed make that illogical deduction in response to their needs. Between the normal identification and the clearly disturbed there is a large area of logical practice that is determined by emotional need and not by cool logic. The grief-disturbed personality readily employs such methods. This is seen in the displays incident to public mourning, wherein a person attaches an emotional significance to even the garments he wears. It is revealed in attitudes of mind and personal activity. In such instances it shields the bereaved person from the full implications of his grief. If it becomes a device through which the implications of the grief can be increasingly accepted, it is well and good, for it is temporary. But if it becomes an irrational escape from which the personality cannot extricate itself, then it is clearly damaging and injurious to the self and to others.

When a mother whose young son was killed in military action enlisted in the WAAC, she was saying in effect, "I can stand my grief if I share your death." As the military service was the cause of death, her sharing of that service seemed logical to her suffering personality. As time went by and she participated more actively in the military service with its acceptance of death, she resolved her grief. When she completed her period of service she had shared his death so completely that she was now ready to live her own life again. Her grief had been constructively worked through.

Quite the opposite was true of a little Italian lady in a small New England industrial town who lost a child in the early school years. She made a sacred vow that she would visit his grave every day. Each day she trudged up the hill to the village cemetery, rain or shine, summer or winter. The years have come and gone. Her other children have grown and she has many grandchildren. She will never go to visit them if it involves being away so long that she cannot make her daily pilgrimage up the hill to the cemetery. She has so completely identified herself with that grave that she is willing to kill much of the other experience of her life. She is completely enslaved by an unbreakable emotional tie. In her simple way she explains a bargain that she must keep, for it is a sacred pledge. But the vow made under the pressure of acute grief has about itself the element of enslavement that appears when an identification is carried on so long that the normal life of the bereaved person is seriously handicapped. What her neighbors take for unusual devotion and faithfulness is more nearly described as the irrational behavior that is the product of an unfortunate state of unresolved emotional disturbance.

Unfortunately, such behavior is often misinterpreted as worthy and truly religious. Instead, it is a form of regression and psychological incorporation that should be discounted and discouraged. Regression is not cured by accepting it. It must be actively opposed, for it becomes worse if it is encouraged. It then loses its original purpose and becomes an expression of the disabled portion of the being. A person should be encouraged to live in terms of the future rather than in terms of the past. Even if an illogical vow is made under the burden of grief, it should not be made so binding that it cripples life when the circumstance that originated it has been left well behind. Too many cemeteries become the burial place of the living as well as the dead. In that sense we have not improved on certain primitive and barbaric practices.

The employment of mourning clothes is a clearly visible form of identification, for the dead body was traditionally wrapped in clothing comparable to sackcloth and burned. Even now we use some of the terminology when we speak of "ashes to ashes." The mourner in black garments has but slightly changed the use of his clothing in an effort to identify with the deceased through an approximation of the sackcloth and ashes. Various traditions in the use of such clothing indicate the methods of withdrawing from the work of mourning as one gradually uses less and less of the symbolic clothing until the period of mourning is over and the grief is worked through. In that sense it may well be a useful ritual for symbolizing the process that takes place as the person suffers the pain of personal loss and gradually emerges from it to deal with the rest of life free from the burden of unresolved grief, just as he is symbolically free of the burden of visible grief by the divesting of his garments.

While most persons meet the mourning situation with a desire to weep, those who remain dry-eyed and seemingly unrelated are likely to be the ones who identify their own lives with the lost person and institute processes of incorporation whereby they do not lose the dead person but rather become integrally related. The person who weeps is resorting to a technique developed in childhood for ridding one's self of annoyance. If a foreign object is lodged in the eye, tears will work on it quite directly. If the pain is located somewhere else in the body, a form of emotional release seems to be involved in the flow of tears. Bereavement is an amputation of a part of the emotional structure of life, and the use of tears may help to wash away the pain of separation. Those who cannot easily employ a flow of tears at bereavement may well be showing the early stages of a process of incorporation.

3. Special Significance of Identification Among Women

Women, whose techniques of emotional release are usually less inhibited, may cry easily about the milder forms of emotional discomfort, but be less inclined to do so when emotional loss is great. The structure of our society makes it important for the woman to be identified with her husband. She is dependent upon him for many of the essentials of life, socially and economically. She may deny and compensate as vigorously as possible, yet the psychological fact remains and is indicated by numerous conditions that are visible in everyday life and verified by psychoanalytic studies.

The quality of pride in the woman's make-up becomes an important factor in the device of identification. Theodor Reik writes:

We should conclude thence that pride is more developed in the life of women than of men. . . . It appears as nothing but a reaction to injured self-love. . . . It is not extant from the very beginning, but originates as a reaction-formation to an injury . . . and serves the purpose of defense against future damage. . . . Pride is best compared to a tumor which by building new tissue produces a pathological increase of volume.[4]

In some societies, when a woman became a widow her competence to carry on a useful existence was called into question. In some extreme practices she was buried with her mate. Such extreme measures but accentuate an attitude that is prevalent in milder and more subtle practices in every society. In most countries special legislation has been required to guarantee for the widow a measure of the social and economic security she possesses. Faced with that kind of an injurious judgment, the woman is forced to protect herself against emotional injury. This, in part, explains the emphasis women place on both bodily charm and modesty, for both are devices employed to enhance self-esteem. Such a severe blow can be struck at this essential self-esteem by the loss of a husband through death, that the process of incorporation or identification becomes the logical protective device in many instances. This only emphasizes the fact that the feeling of self-esteem is inseparably related to some form of useful or accepted function in the social structure. The widow, stripped of that easily observed function by death, seeks to preserve self-esteem by becoming so obviously identified with her husband that her pride is not dealt a fatal blow. So the woman, in our society, becomes a breadwinner, takes over the management of her husband's business, runs for the public office he held, or continues to maintain the home as if she were fulfilling a dual role. In such an instance the device of identification is socially imposed and may have quite a different meaning for the individual than the identification that is unconsciously assumed by the individual in response to emotional need.

4. Identification and the Personality Structure

The unconsciously assumed response is observed in a strong inclination toward oral incorporation, wherein a regressive behavior shows itself in eating habits. Mrs. K., a slight young woman who weighed about one hundred pounds, was widowed suddenly when her husband developed a brain tumor. She had given some evidence of emotional instability in her past history. Almost immediately after his death she developed a ravenous appetite, and it has been characteristic of her since that time. Her weight has doubled, and she has taken on a rather grotesque appearance. Instead of taking skilled employment for which she was qualified, she took work as a housekeeper in order to work with food. Though she showed few signs of active emotional involvement at the time of her loss or since, she has shown marked evidence of the change of physical and emotional aspects of life that can be brought on by the act of psychological incorporation.

One of the aspects of the work of mourning is the effort of the normal mature person to resist the type of incorporation that could enslave or destroy the personality. This is often observed at the time of the death of a loved object when the bereaved loses all desire to eat and when forced to eat indicates that the food does not taste like food and has become unpalatable. One of the earliest forms of relationship to an object of need is through the mouth in breast feeding. When an acute loss is suffered the inclination toward regression is very strong. The possibility of retreating to an early emotional level where the object is possessed through the mouth is usually resisted. It is interesting to observe how persons will say again and again that they have no interest in food until the funeral is over and the remains of the deceased are properly interred. Then the bereaved persons will return home and gorge themselves in a variety of the foods that the neighbors have brought in, with the symbolic idea, "We have successfully passed through this stage of our mourning work and we have freed ourselves of the danger of enslavement by incorporation, so now we can relax and eat to our heart's content." It is similarly worth noting that those who seem unable to resist the tendency toward oral incorporation feel guilty and express their feelings in some such remarks as these: "I don't know what is the matter with me. I am ashamed of myself. I can't seem to control my appetite. I have been eating six or seven times a day. I never eat like this at other times." Much the same emotional process may be at work with those who deal with their grief by excessive drinking.

In acute deprivation when an important object is withdrawn or taken away permanently, the personality makes an effort by the use of psychological devices to restore the significance of the lost object. The identification that often results may take different forms, and the classification of the forms may be helpful in understanding what is taking place. Calvin Hall mentions four different types of identification.[5] First is the narcissistic identification characterized by a love of one's self in other people. The person who prefers those who share his opinions and his interests may be susceptible to this form. Many group activities make use of this tendency by which people do together the things they enjoy doing but could not do alone. So we have golf clubs, yacht clubs, and comparable group activities built on this type of identification. Second, goal-oriented identification grows out of a desire to emulate or become like someone else. Children often do this in relation to adults. When a goal-oriented person is bereaved, he feels that a part of himself has also died and the result may be severe. Third, object-loss identification is more often encountered in the grief experience. When death is not involved a lost object may be restored by a change in behavior, and the effort at reform is often a basis for a renewed human relationship, as in marital reconciliation. When death is a factor that separates, then one cannot restore the dead person by any change in behavior; but an effort to do the equivalent is often observed when a person tries to placate the gods, and many of the sacrificial rites of religious groups may be related to this effort to restore the lost love object. Fourth is the form of identification wherein the bereaved person would identify with the prohibitions of an authoritative person. He might relate himself to an aggressor in order to defeat the aggressor. In life he might marry the boss's daughter. In death he might seek the emotional equivalent of death in order to defeat death. In the case of William W. which follows, we see this form of identification.

William W. was forty-seven and had never had any serious complaints as far as his health was concerned. He worked regularly on his milk route and had a good record of service. Immediately after his death of his father, a condition developed that was causing him difficulty on his milk route. His collections dropped off seriously. He was called in for an explanation and at first gave an evasive and unsatisfactory answer. Because of his long record of good service he was given another chance. At the end of the second month the condition had worsened, and he was told he would have to correct it or seek other employment. He then reported that he couldn't understand why it was, but he couldn't leave any bills since his father had died. Those people who asked him how much they owed were allowed to pay for their milk, but no regular monthly bills had been left with the customers. The milk company quickly remedied the situation by taking him off his route and making him an extra to cover the off days. This solved their problem but not his. It seemed that he had become afraid to ask for anything, even what was rightly his. Family and friends were puzzled as well as William W. himself. After some time the matter was brought to the attention of the pastor. The father had been a dominant man who always demanded strict behavior from his children. While he was fair, he was stern. He laid down simple laws of conduct such as, "What is worth having is worth asking for," but, paradoxically, he also made the rule that no child of his should ever be caught asking anybody for anything. It was part of his plan of life to be independent of everyone and to pay for everything you get. Without being aware of what had happened, William W. had unconsciously incorporated a part of his father's admonition so completely that it became irrational out of its context. His grief has led to identity, and as soon as he was aware of the problem he corrected it.

In hypnosis the psychologist deals directly with the subconscious mind of the subject and is able to produce results posthypnotically that are determined by the hypnotic suggestion at work rather than by the conscious thought pattern. Under some circumstances a person may create the suggestion for himself or may have it done by some dominant person in his life. William W. evidently had some subconscious force at work in his being to determine his behavior. His father, being the dominant sort of person he was, had evidently so exerted his control over the lives of his sons that they felt a compulsion to do as he would want rather than as their own judgment dictated. A strong superego manifestation can reveal itself in the relation between father and son, and the grief reaction might bring to the surface a behavior pattern that had been previously suppressed.

5. Temporary Identification and Prolonged Manifestations

As Karl Abraham has pointed out, there is temporary introjection in normal grief. This form of activity brings consolation in the feeling that the loved object is not gone, "For now I carry it within myself and can never lose it." The danger of this sort of emotional reaction is acute when the word "never" is taken seriously. Normally the identification wears off just as the mourning clothes are gradually laid aside. But sometimes the emotional involvement in the process becomes so demanding that the personality is seriously crippled. The following illustration indicates something of how this crippling process can work in the life of a child.

May L. had long been involved in the family conflicts that existed between her father and her mother. For reasons that seemed sufficient to her, she had sympathized with her father and had taken his part. When he died as the result of an accident, she was eleven years old. She met the grief situation by identifying with him emotionally. She tried to act as he had acted. She stood for the things he had stood for. In family matters she was the proponent of his ideas. As she grew older she began to have a series of unfortunate love relationships in which she fell deeply in love with men she could not possibly have, either because they were uninterested in her or were happily married to another. The problem became so serious that it was interfering with her work and her health. She began to develop a serious eye weakness and had stronger and stronger glasses made, though they did not seem to improve her condition. Finally through the insistence of her family, she began psychotherapy. At first she was resistive and non-co-operative. She spoke of her father with reticence. After a considerable period she gave evidence of seeing for the first time what the relationship with her father had meant and its influence upon the rest of her living. With a burst of insight she said, "Now I see it all." Immediately there was a marked improvement in her

71

vision, and she is on the way toward an adjustment of the emotional relationships of her life.

Often when an important person in the life of a child such as May L. dies, there may be little expression of emotion, for the child is not capable of sensing all the ramifications of death. But a chain of attitudes and feelings may be set to work that can disturb the child for a long time. When this is the case, it may take special therapy to bring about a solution to the problem. Sometimes this is the sort of relationship that develops indirectly because of the effects of the mourning of an adult, and then it may be more difficult to understand or interpret.

Karl Abraham tells of a case that came to his attention which involved a child who was disturbed by the parent's reaction to the death of an older child, and who showed acute emotional disturbance for a number of years.

The parents of the boy were in deep mourning over the loss of an older sister. Love and attention were withdrawn from the remaining child, and the mother retreated to her room, ignoring his needs and feelings. Because the mother could not stand the associations with her home, she prevailed upon her husband to take up residence in a hotel. Here the young boy was more completely lost because he could not relate himself either to places or people who were familiar or concerned. Because he had lost all ties with his mother, and because his needs for her were so great, he introjected the mother image. Emotionally he solved his problem by incorporation. As the years went by he acted more and more as if he were a female emotionally. When he became a youth he was homosexual. His incorporation had become so complete that in effect he was a woman and wanted the attention of men. The simple dynamics of his case were that he needed his mother so much that he became his mother emotionally through introjection, and the symptoms of his disturbed emotions were but the externalizing of his emotional state. Abraham comments that "in the normal person the process of introjection is set in motion by real loss to preserve a relation with the loved object to compensate for the loss but is never unaware of the loss." [6] When the process is unconscious and not understood,

72

then the results within the personality are likely to be abnormal and show up in specific problems in behavior.

6. Sensitivity to Emotional Response

The pastor who notes a complete lack of apparent emotional involvement at the time of bereavement may suspect that this is due to an active identification with the dead person. The pastor should be careful not to encourage identification by the things he says, for as Otto Fenichel has pointed out:

The illusion that the lost person still lives and the identification with him are closely related. Every mourner tends to simplify his task by building up a kind of substitute object within himself after the real object has departed. For this he uses the same mechanism all disappointed persons, including the depressed ones, employ—namely, regression from love to incorporation, from object relationship to identification. It can often be observed that a mourning person in one or other respects begins to resemble the lost object, that, for example, as Abraham reported, his hair becomes gray like the hair of the person he mourns; he develops cardiac symptoms if the object died of heart disease; he assumes one of the peculiarities of speech or gestures of the lost person. . . . All this gives evidence of an identification with the dead person, subjectively perceived as an oral incorporation occurring on the same level as in psychotic depression but of lesser intensity.[7]

This shows that the dangers may be not only physical and emotional but basically disruptive of the total personality.

Although the pastor may be aware of the dangers of the extreme forms of identification, he may well bear in mind that such mechanisms are essentially normal when used in relation to a healthy reality sense. Freud said, "It may well be that identification is the general condition under which the id will relinquish its object." [8] Fenichel further observes:

Apparently, for a normal person it is easier to loosen the ties with an introject than with an external object. The establishment of an introjection is a means of facilitating the final loosening. Mourning consists of two acts, the first being the establishment of an introjection, the second the loosening of the binding to the introjected object.[9]

Those who mourn or who work with the bereaved may well understand what is going on in the emotions of the grief-stricken. The mechanisms that are operative need to be understood so that the boundaries between normal manifestations and those that need special attention may be more easily determined. The process of identification and incorporation is probably the most often employed and most easily resolved. The continued manifestations of its use tend to be easily observed and treated, unless complications such as strong ambivalent feelings are involved. There the sadistic possibility is specific and skilled psychotherapy is advisable.

FIVE

Grief and Substitution

We come now to the second of the situational responses of the personality to acute grief. As the first involved the effort to destroy the pain of grief by a maneuver that internalized, incorporated, and identified with the lost love object, so the second seeks to destroy the pain of grief by an active effort to exteriorize, project, and substitute an image or an object for that which has been lost. The grieving person seeks to invest his emotional capital in something or somebody else. Where identification tends to be personal and internal, substitution tends to be external and more impersonal. For that reason it is possible more easily to convert such a mechanism to physically constructive purposes through memorials such as scholarships or hospitals, while at the same time it may be more difficult to resolve the feelings involved when they are abnormal for they are separated from the grieving person's emotions by a false but powerful effort.

1. The Injured Psyche and Substitution

Just as identification involves an incorporation of the object the better to control the feelings toward it, so substitution involves a projection of the loved object the better to be separated from the distressing feelings related to it. It seems to involve an effort at intellectual denial of what the emotions cannot deny. The matter can be seen at a rather simple level in the case of the student who does not like to study but, rather than admit it, says it is of no use to study for the professor is unfair and asks questions on the examination that are not in the book. Or the woman with feelings of low self-esteem criticizes her neighbors for not coming to call on her because they do not like her. Or the defeated Germans after Versailles could not accept their defeat so they projected it into the lives of a minority group and made of them a scapegoat. Such devices are continually at work in everyday life and we recognize them as such. But when the involved emotion of acute grief exists, it may be more difficult to follow all of the devices that may be employed to alleviate the stress on the personality. Substitution may be employed as a temporary measure to withstand the stress of grief. As a temporary measure it is not so likely to be dangerous to the personality. As Sandor Rado points out, it is "the failure of emergency adjustment [that] lies at the bottom of all disordered behavior." [1] And the habitual devices employed by the person are easily adapted to major crises. The person who is always blaming others for his misfortune is the one who will probably employ projection in major crises. And these devices are not developed in adulthood usually but are a part of a long-range emotional development well rooted in childhood responses.

The devices of substitution find expression in fetishism, and the number of practices whereby we invest objects with a quality and quantity of emotion that is extrinsic rather than intrinsic. It is also easily demonstrated to be a way of transferring thought from the painful to the less painful, for the person is more comfortable when he is dealing with something that is within the range of his emotional competence.

Karl Menninger illustrates such a device in the case of a small boy who was treated by a friend of his:

The boy had suffered from a slight inflammatory tightness of the foreskin and, at two and a half years of age, was taken to a surgeon who relieved the condition by means of stretching. The little fellow had behaved very well indeed and was praised by the surgeon who gave him a piece of candy. After the child was dressed and was saying good-by, the surgeon, still quite jovial, laughingly said to the little fellow that he had been a pretty good boy this time but next time he would "cut the whole thing off for you with these," showing him a large pair of surgical scissors. The surgeon laughed in a friendly way but the child ran to his father with a cry of terror and "trembling with agitation sobbed in my arms." The parents endeavored in every way to assure the child that the surgeon had been joking and gradually he seemed to forget the episode. A year later the child had a slight inflammation of the penis which responded easily to local bathing; in connection with it he began of his own accord to speak of his experience of the previous year with the surgeon. He recounted cheerfully and with remarkable accuracy all the *unimportant* details of what had happened in the surgeon's office, mentioning many items which the parents had forgotten. But concerning the final episode, the joke about the scissors, he did not say one word. Thinking that he might help to remove the painful impression of the experience, his father asked him if he did not remember anything else—something the doctor said. No answer. "Don't you remember the joke he made?" No answer. "Didn't he have a pair of scissors?" The child laughed. "Oh, yes, a pair of scissors. He made a joke about the scissors."

But in spite of prompting from his father he could not remember what the joke had been. Finally his father asked him if the surgeon had not talked of cutting off something. Immediately the child cried out merrily, "Oh, yes, I remember, he said he would cut my hair off.[2]

This incident illustrates how a person, when faced with a distressing situation, may unconsciously repress the unpleasant and so alter the recollections that they are within the range of competent handling by the individual. The boy was not threatened by the cutting of his hair, the device of substitution having served its psychological purpose. Other more complicated injuries to the personality are often treated by comparable devices.

2. Two Directions Substitution May Take

The process of substitution works in two different directions. One method of employing substitution involves the act of changing the meaning to something that is more readily acceptable by substituting a completely different but related meaning for that which is too painful to accept. The case of the small boy shows how this method works. The second method relates the emotional meaning to an external object, person, or idea as a substitute for the internal feeling one would escape. Sometimes this may be desirable, creative, and useful, or it may be disruptive to the emotional life of the person involved and merely serve to postpone the useful and normal work of mourning.

A certain amount of substitution is probably involved in every normal grief situation, for the bereaved person in carrying on the work of mourning tries to separate himself from the ties that bind him to some other person. If these ties can be related to an external object he is able to release the inner bonds that might enslave him. Substitution is a form of exteriorization that serves to rid the personality of its overinvolvement emotionally.

A strange process seems to take place when people are able to exteriorize even that which is close and personal for them. This is made clear when persons deal with their own bodily secretions. That which has been an intimate part of themselves becomes a rejected part merely by exteriorization. Persons would swallow their saliva all day and think nothing of it, for it is within, but to try to drink a glass of their own saliva would probably cause them to gag, as Gordon Allport has pointed out. What would be true of secretions of the body is also true of parts of the body itself. A person shown the appendix that had been removed from his abdomen shuddered and wanted it taken from his sight. The reaction at the sight of blood which some persons have is probably related to this feeling toward what is exteriorized.

That this same feeling is involved in the work of mourning is clearly indicated by the activities of persons in clearing up the affairs of a bereaved relative. In fighting against the tendency toward fetishism, they try to dispose of the personal effects of the deceased as quickly as possible. The more personal they are the more urgent is the desire to remove them from the daily routine of life. Personal effects are given away. The more impersonal possessions are preserved, for they do not present quite the same threat to the progress of the mourning work.

Those who want to expand educational facilities are alert to the opportunity to encourage a family to endow a chair in memory of the deceased or to finance a new building that will bear his name. Here is a legitimate and useful way of exteriorizing some of the grief feelings by investing an external structure with some of the qualities of the personality that has died. A fine building that can serve the educational needs of youth is a valuable form of substitution, for it gives creative expression to the interest and quality of the deceased person. Sometimes it serves an added

78

purpose in helping to idealize the memory of the person so that a measure of guilt is resolved. So a person who never attended church may have a church dedicated to his memory. A questionable character who won a reputation for sharp dealings may have a university named after him because his heirs want to create a memory different from that which was created in life. It would be somewhat different if an equal investment were made in an effort to release the soul of a supposedly tormented person from a man-made nether region which exists only in the folklore of an institution. This would be a less acceptable form of exteriorization. It may be an effective technique for allowing persons to deal with the felling of ambivalence that exist in any love relationship, but it does not necessarily serve as the best or most justifiable technique.

3. Mixed Motives in Substitution

Many institutional representatives have difficulty with the donors of memorials who make the effort of exteriorization through their memorial gifts and then find that they have not made the process of separation complete. They then try to possess again what they have given in a consuming emotional interest that may impede or block the effective use of what they have given.

Sometimes the substituted object becomes not only a form of emotional investment but it may become also a tool for the expression of aggressive attitudes. After her husband died, Mrs. L. arranged with the pastor for a new set of altar candelabra to be bought in his memory. She made the stipulation that no one should ever touch the candelabra except the pastor himself. It seemed like an unreasonable attitude for Mrs. L. to assume, but the pastor did not challenge it because it did not seem to be the appropriate time to set up that kind of discussion of trivial details. However, as time went on the trivial detail became the source of disruptive action and the expression of Mrs. L.'s aggression. She came early to church to make sure that the pastor was fulfilling his obligation. When any special group was at the church for a service she was also there to make sure that no one approached the altar. When a state convention of the women's guild met at the church, she created such a scene in the presence of guests that it was difficult for even her friends to interpret such behavior. Because the pastor was out of town she refused the use of the altar furnishings at the state convention. The problem became so much a matter of parish concern that the pastor and the officials many times wished that they had not accepted the gift in the first place. The aggression that is a normal part of the grief reaction had been localized and given an extended life by relating it to a specific memorial object. For her the obligation to the object became the justification for her hatefulness. No candelabra were ever bought for so great a price as that exacted from the pastor and the church which agreed to receive that memorial gift. An object may so easily become the substitute for a being that it serves as the channel for expressing emotions toward that being. Then the gift may stand the recipient in double jeopardy.

An object may serve a therapeutic purpose in drawing off strong emotions that might otherwise do severe injury to the personality. So the reduction of tension within a person can be achieved by a shift of the emotional investment from the lost object to one that is readily available. Normally the personality develops by a series of energy displacements or object substitutions. This is the process of extended growth relationships. Yet under abnormal stress the process may take on abnormal characteristics. The emotional investment in the object may become so great that the normal functioning of the personality is crippled.

4. Three Cases of Substitution

The devices of substitution or replacement as they are worked out in grief may be illustrated. First we will indicate how the replacement of the person by an idea or an image can be acceptable to an elderly person whose intensity of emotional feeling seems to have been replaced by a state of semiawareness comparable to that of a child.

Two elderly ladies had lived together all their lives, neither having married. They had considerable wealth and administered important business holdings inherited by them in the New England industrial town where the family home was located. One assumed a male role, driving a car of foreign make, supervising business matters, and manipulating local politics with a mildly Machiavellian hand. The other assumed the female role, supervising the servants, doing the marketing, making floral arrangements, and caring for other details of the household.

The masculine sister died rather suddenly of a masculine type of heart attack. The pastor assisted with funeral arrangements. He was interested to note that the sister who had suffered the loss seemed to show no outward indications of her mourning. He drew her out in conversation and received this reply: "I know my sister is not really dead. She is here with me now just the same as she always was. She couldn't really die, not my sister." She went through the activities of the funeral and the next few days with a smile and a cheerful word for everyone. Again and again the pastor heard her say to friends: "Ruth isn't really dead. My faith wouldn't let her die. I believe she is still here with me even though I can't see her. Why should I be sad? We will always be together."

As time went along the pattern of her life became clear. She was keeping up the play upon her sister's presence with complete sincerity and candor. Two places were always set at the table, and though no food was served the dead sister, she explained, "In the spirit body we don't need food. We just don't want to be ignored." Flowers were kept in her sister's bedroom. Her clothes were left hanging in the closet untouched except for an occasional cleaning. As much as it could be acted out, the presence of the sister as a spiritual being was accepted. When guests came, she would say, "I know Ruth would want me to thank you for coming." When Christmas gifts or cards were mailed, they were signed, "Minnie and Ruth."

Because of the loss of such a close relative, companion, and dependency figure was more than the personality could tolerate. Minnie refused to accept fully the fact of death and with her own particular technique substituted the spiritual presence of her dead sister in her structure of personal and social living. She closed her mind against the realities and refused to accept the facts beyond those that were forced upon her. At her age and in her circumstances it does not present too serious a problem, for her life has set its pattern and has almost run its course. But the same device used at an earlier age and under different circumstances could easily be destructive to normal, healthy living.

Sometimes the process of substitution appears to be present in the response of younger persons. Then it is expressed in different dynamic factors but the emotional needs are served in a comparable way. Such was the case of LeRoy F., a sixteen-year-old boy at a time of the bereavement that was so important in conditioning his behavior. The emotional life of the adolescent is turbulent and uncertain, and this affects the grief response.

LeRoy F. was the only son of a rather compulsive father. For years there had been considerable conflict between the boy, who was strong-willed, and the father, who was determined to exert a rigid parental control. The mother, a rather timid person, was unable to function effectively in her role as a mediator between the two masculine members of her family. She was vacillating and defeated by the situation. When the father died suddenly of a heart attack, the mother was filled with fears and became quite thoroughly disorganized. LeRoy reacted with no obvious emotional expressions, but shortly afterward he started on a round of adolescent pranks that brought him into trouble with the authorities again and again. His mother was even more deeply disturbed by these happenings and could not cope with her son. Finally she gave up and said, "I can't do anything with you. You will just have to make your own way from now on."

Those words seemed like a declaration of independence to LeRoy and almost immediately his role shifted. He became more protective and solicitous of his mother. He applied himself at school. He made a good report for himself both in school and in part-time employment. His mother could not understand the change that had taken place. It seems that LeRoy had taken a substitute role in the family as the protective male when he had at last assured himself of the fact that he had broken the strangle hold he felt was laid on his personality by the effort at rigid parental control. He demanded more of himself in the new role than his father had demanded of him, but he was satisfied for he was taking the initiative himself. His grief was fulfilled when he was able to give expression to his feelings in behavior through a substitute role.

Sometimes an adult will become involved in an emotional response to acute grief that indicates that he has substituted another person for the deceased in his emotional framework, with little or no awareness of the realities of the new relationships.

When Mrs. T. died, Mr. T., who had been very dependent upon her, seemed to be lost and disorganized. Mrs. W., a widowed friend of his wife, moved into the emotional vacuum and soon he had transferred much of his dependency feeling toward her. In a few weeks he was sure that he was in love with her. Although there were marked differences in background, religious training, and temperament, he was willing to make any adjustment to fulfill his emotional needs. It seemed that everyone but Mr. T. himself understood the mechanism at work in his emotional transfer. Friends tried politely to caution Mr. T. against an unwise step, but he was not open to suggestion. He had invested another and quite different personality with the ideas and feelings he had toward his deceased wife, and he married his wife's friend, only to find that his idea and the reality were quite different. The person toward whom he had adopted a dependency attitude soon became a dictator, and his life was bound by an unbreakable tie to one who had capitalized on his emotional need at a time when he seemed helpless to interpret his own feelings.

5. Substitution and a Weakened Reality Sense

Among primitives the acts of substitution are visible in fetishism and comparable devices. A similar primitive type of thinking works in the individual to distort reality to a more acceptable form through regression. As Fenichel puts it, "It no longer fulfills, it is true, the function of preparing for future actions but becomes, rather, a substitute for unpleasant reality." It is often observed that the regression to a dependent attitude may involve the pastor. It is necessary to understand the meaning and purpose of the regression and to accept it on a temporary basis as an important service to the bereaved who is in the process of learning to handle his human relations again on satisfactory terms. The pastor may use the temporary dependency attitude toward him to make unnecessary the type of unfortunate alliance that a dependency need created for Mr. T.

Many grieving persons ask for advice in such a way that they could be easily taken advantage of by the unscrupulous. For that reason it is probably wise to encourage people to think over for a while any decisions that might seriously involve their future.

Edoardo Weiss indicates that there is often a reversion to the feeling structure that existed in the distant past, especially as it related to parents. When this is so, the possibility of action on the basis of the immature feelings may take the place of the more mature judgment that should be operative.

In a moment of great or immediate danger a person often experiences a rapid and extraordinarily vivid review of his lifetime, which is not merely recalled but is relived with the previously experienced effects. An analogous phenomenon also occurs in grief reaction. After the loss of father or mother, or any figure of similar importance in one's early development, there is frequently a re-cathexis of an early ego state. The memory of the lost love object as he appeared, often many years previously, frequently seems to replace entirely the actual person as he was at the time of death, and the mourner's early emotions, feelings and affects are intensely re-experienced in the mourning work.[3]

When such an early ego state assumes control of behavior, it tends to function without regard to present realities but with a regard for earlier emotional states. Though the condition would usually not last long, a person should be protected from making long-range decisions under such stress.

Sometimes persons make of a substitution process a form of slavery. Through what appears to be a form of self-punishment, they bind themselves to an object or a behavior pattern and then let it exert an unreasoned influence over their living. Such is the case with Dr. L. and his wife.

Dr. L., a dentist, and his wife were bereaved by the death of their beautiful and talented only child, Betty, through complications at the birth of Betty's first child. They found it impossible to reconcile the fact of her death to the intensity of their feeling. Though their life seemed to be quite normal in other respects, they built up a ritual that made it possible for them to condition the reality to meet the intensity of their emotions. Each Sunday afternoon they made a pilgrimage to the mausoleum some miles from their home where the casket with Betty's remains had been placed. There they would sit in the little alcove before the vault and visit with each other and talk over all the things they thought their daughter might be interested in. Then at the end of the two-hour visit they would go over and pat the slab of marble at the end of the vault and say, "Good-bye for now, Betty. We'll be back next Sunday." By establishing a time and place in the world of external things for focusing their grief, they seemed to be able to find the needed factor about which they might organize their emotions, so that while they accepted a part of reality they were also free to reject another part of it. In this partial state of acceptance they have continued to harbor their grief; and rather than achieve a freedom from the object of their love, they have built a practice that symbolizes their desire not to be free.

In the consideration of the substitution of an idea for a person, we might consider what takes place in the use of wry humor. Humor is a form of language that conceals rather than reveals its deeper meaning. Much as is the case with dreams, a special understanding is needed to break through the disguise and deal with the real meanings of the humor. Humor may be a device used to exteriorize a sense of loss, in that it creates something which may be laughed at instead of contemplating something that should be cried about. Often at the gatherings of the bereaved in funeral homes and cemeteries, there is a use of humor that at first seems inappropriate. Martha Wolfenstein, in her study of humor,[4] indicates that humor is used to disguise a painful reality, transform an unpleasant thought or feeling, bring down to a size that can be handled a large and painful experience, and make it possible to deal with something that is beyond easy understanding.[5]

We are familiar with the types of humor that are related to undertakers, cemeteries, skeletons, and death. They are similar in purpose to the types of humor that relate to sex and the relation of the sexes. Areas of emotional involvement which are

85

fraught with concern and anxiety that make them too large to handle normally are brought down to a more comfortable size by changing the emotional mood in which they are considered. An understanding of the types and modes of laughter can be a clue to the emotional activity going on in the laughing person. Laughing, like crying, serves a purpose of expelling irritants, and in that sense is a substitute activity.

6. Unwise Emotional Transfers

Sometimes a professional person related to the bereaved during the active stage of the mourning work becomes the subject of substituted emotions. An obstetrician who delivered a woman of a stillborn child soon became aware of the fact that the woman had assumed an attitude of unreasonable attachment toward him. He was wise enough to understand something of what was going on in the emotional life of the bereaved woman and with skill used his relationship as a professional person to interpret to her the meaning of her feelings and help her to work through them without loss of self-regard.

A somewhat similar condition sometimes develops with the clergyman who seeks to give spiritual help during bereavement. What is at first an acceptable dependency relationship that should be resolved in a short time becomes an abnormal attachment that interferes with the normal working through of the grief experience. Pastors need to be aware of the development of such conditions. At first they may feel that they are important for the stabilizing of the emotions of the individual. However, this period of normal and helpful dependency may lead to a condition that serves no useful purpose and actively retards the desired work of mourning.

As incorporation may produce conditions that are either acceptable or damaging according to the nature of the emotional intensity and personality conditioning effect of the incorporation, so also substitution may work for good or ill. The person who deals with the bereaved must be alert to the limited and useful forms of substitution and encourage them, but he must also be equally aware of the dangers that develop when external objects are invested with too great a degree of emotional capital. The relation of strong emotions to objects or other persons may be a factor in preventing the normal working through of the grief experience.

SIX

Grief and Guilt

A third situational response that is almost universally present in grief is a feeling of guilt. Few escape such a reaction and they would be classed as subnormal emotionally. Even those who have lived exemplary lives do not escape such a feeling, for as Kierkegaard has observed, "The greater the genius, the more profoundly he discovers guilt." [1] The more morally sensitive a person is, the more he is likely to have the personality structure that will feel guilt.

Erich Lindemann, in the study previously mentioned, has indicated that the nature of human relationship breeds the possibility for guilt responses and that his observation shows such responses to be universal among normal people. It is a testimony to the ambivalent nature of the love relationship.

1. Universal Guilt and Ambivalence

The love relationship produces a certain amount of inner conflict. Death is so final that the person contemplating it is almost always inclined to regress to an earlier level of emotional reaction. This level is dominated by the superego, the inherited values of life. "Whether we call it conscience or super-ego, the moral sense is almost always involved in any serious conflict. . . . The consequences of violating the super-ego are known in modern parlance as 'guilt feelings.'" [2] The effort to evaluate the reality of a grief situation is complicated by the dominance of the superego, which temporarily challenges the status of the ego.

In these cases where the super-ego disapproves of action taken by the ego under pressure of the id, it manifests its disapproval by a condemnation of the ego which causes the ego to feel a sense of guilt. This is akin to the feeling of loss of love that the infant experiences when he feels his mother or father has withdrawn the love so necessary to his psychological well-being. It is a feeling of unworthiness, of insecurity, of having evoked hostility.[3]

The feeling may have no basis in fact but may be stimulated by some long-past feelings of child-parent relations that have left their mark. Death, with its loss of love, may project these same feelings again into the forefront of life.

There may be real feelings of guilt in grief related to neglect. There may be neurotic feelings of guilt related to other than the situational factor involved. It is important to know the difference. Wise says:

Real guilt is the sense that one has broken a fundamental law or that one has done something that has severely injured himself or other people. The feelings are commensurate with the seriousness of the act and are consciously related to the act. In neurotic guilt the feelings are greatly exaggerated beyond the act which the individual confesses, or the person is unable to relate his feelings to any act or situation.[4]

Both types of guilt are stimulated by acute loss.

Ambivalence is a by-product of love. Wherever love exists there is also a certain amount of reaction against it, for love demands limitation on freedom and responsibility. Though the loss or limitation of freedom is readily accepted and feeling about it is seldom articulate, the personality again and again reacts against it, and the reaction is likely to be stored up as unexpressed aggression. Sometimes it becomes explicit and we have lovers' spats and marriage conflict. Often, however, it remains unexpressed. Then it builds up a backlog of the kind of mixed feelings that can stimulate inner conflict at the time of the death of the beloved.

2. Techniques for Working Through Guilt

Bereavement precipitates feelings of guilt that must be worked through for the health of the personality. This can often be done by talking about it. One of the reasons that the bereaved often spend much time in idealizing the deceased is that this is probably the simplest and best form for resolving the guilt feelings that exist.

It is a way of paying off the emotional debt. Ancient Jewish custom allowed for a week of mourning during which the bereaved and his friends were allowed to talk only about the deceased and his virtues. This was a wise and healthful custom. It is not only dangerous to wall up the means of expressing feelings, it is also purposeless. Though general custom prevents the expression of aggression against the deceased, it readily accepts the efforts to compensate for such feelings through active idealization. The counselor of the bereaved consciously encourages such expression, for it invariably serves a purpose in releasing guilt feelings.

Some of the rites employed by primitive man were designed to meet this psychological need. They gave expression to the ambivalence with rites that would pay respect to the physical remains at the same time that they prepared to destroy them, that would seek to meet the future needs of the deceased at the same time they denied the existence of these needs. Malinowski describes rites of cannibalism where the mourners partake of the flesh of the deceased in pious rituals that are followed by violent vomiting. Probably there is no more specific illustration of the desire to accept and reject, to retain and to expel at one and the same time. The primitive is afraid of death and does not want to accept it, but the facts are self-expressing and he cannot deny it. Since his fears and his feelings of guilt are bound up so closely that he cannot separate them, he develops rites that can do two things at once. While it is illogical, it is also psychologically sound. Modern man also employs in modified form the rituals that accept and reject, the rites that preserve and destroy, and they too fulfill the needs of his psyche to give expression to ambivalent feelings in his love. So we remove the jewelry from the body and then place the remains in expensive caskets. We collect on insurance and deny the reality of death. We give verbal acceptance to the spiritual and actual acceptance to the material. We accept the testimony of the senses and deny the meaning of that testimony. The ambivalence that is evident in love and death becomes the source of feelings of guilt that are either successfully resolved or persistently destructive to the health and happiness of the bereaved.

3. Guilt Responses Illustrated

Perhaps the mechanisms of grief and guilt can be illustrated by the attitudes of children. Bill had a puppy called Spot. Bill loved the puppy and cared for him regularly. He even took Spot to bed with him and there were times when only the puppy's nose could be seen above the covers. His attitude toward the little dog was essentially one of consideration and responsibility. One day he took the puppy with him to visit a friend and crossed a busy highway. The friend's parents did not want the puppy in the house, so Bill sat his puppy on the steps and told him to wait until he came out. The puppy looked as if he understood, and Bill went about his play. After a few minutes the puppy was tired of waiting and started for home, only to be killed by a car. Bill was filled with feelings of guilt mixed with his sorrow. He said, "I was always so careful with Spot. Why did he get killed the one time I was not careful?" He blamed himself. He would not have another puppy because that would be an act of unfaithfulness. After a time he said that Spot had taught him a great deal about life by his death, and that Spot would always be a part of him as far as his education was concerned. He learned the price of carelessness and also something of the obligations of love. His guilt was real and it was resolved only by certain mental processes that made the loss seem justified.

The problem of Vernon L. was quite similar in nature but more difficult to resolve, for any guilt was indirect rather than direct. Happily married and anxious for a child, his wife was informed that her pelvic structure was such that she would probably be able to bear a child only through a Caesarean section. This the couple agreed to do, and all proceeded normally until the time of the operation. Then complications developed and both wife and child died. Vernon L. was thrown into acute grief complicated by severe guilt feelings. He felt that he was responsible for the death of his wife. If he had not allowed her to become pregnant she would still be alive. It was her love for him that made her do it. He was depressed, self-condemnatory, and critical of those who tried to help him resolve his guilt. Finally, through the help of

91

his pastor, he was able to talk the matter through, coming to a realization that he could not accept responsibility for all unforeseen factors in life, and that in certain circumstances the risks of life are disproportionate. When he remarried a few years later he was quite apprehensive about childbirth. His wife, a mature and well-balanced individual, aided him in the matter and gave him emotional support. It was only after the child was born that he seemed to be completely free of the feelings of guilt and apprehension that were related to childbirth.

Some guilt is related to feelings of responsibility for death. Some is felt concerning aggressive feelings expressed in the past that might have made life more difficult. At other times guilt is related to unresolved feelings growing from aggressive feelings that have been felt but never expressed. Then there is guilt that is related to previous feelings for which the death stands as a form of punishment.

Two cases that follow illustrate the feelings of guilt that have normal and obvious roots. Both are related to parents and involve the conflict between ego and superego forces within the personality. That of the army captain will probably be worked through because of his age, his generally healthy attitude toward life, and his willingness to exteriorize his feelings. That of the elderly spinster may well become worse as she grows older because she is unconscious of its cause, and because the pattern of her life now tends to make it important for her to express her emotions in some such self-punishing manner.

Capt. C. was a regular army man, thirty-four years old, well disciplined and self-contained. He had served fourteen years and looked forward to retirement. He had joined the army when economic conditions at home were difficult and he was not on good terms with his family. He seldom wrote home and had been home for brief visits only two times in ten years, and not at all for the last four years, excusing himself on the basis of military necessity. Actually, he was letting his leave time accumulate for terminal leave so that he might retire sooner. The army had become his family and his home.

Capt. C. was stationed in Athens with military intelligence

during the Greek civil conflict. It was while there that he received word that his mother had died. He immediately sought out the chaplain, for though he was not particularly religious he was on good terms with the chaplain. "I just got a telegram that my mother died. I haven't been home in years. What do you do in a case like this?" He had been in the army so long that he thought there was an item of issue for every emotional as well as physical need.

The chaplain suggested, "Let's take a walk. How about climbing to the top of Lycabettus?" The mountain loomed over the city from a height considerably above the Acropolis and was topped by the chapel of St. George. As they walked across the city toward Lycabettos, Capt. C. smoked cigarette after cigarette and said little. Neither said much until they reached the top of the mountain an hour and a half later. Then after looking out over the ancient city and the sea, those symbols of eternal things, the captain began to talk about his childhood and his mother. He recounted incidents; he recalled humorous activities; he engaged his emotions and wiped his eyes occasionally.

After some preparatory talking around the subject, he finally told why he had left home. He pointed out that it was not his mother's fault, but he had never been able to get along at home. His parents were of a European background, too strict, and unwilling to grant him the privileges that other American youth had. After a few years of this he felt so stifled that he blew up one day; after a round of unpleasant words he left home for good, with the exception of a few brief visits. While he had felt justified in what he had done, he also felt guilty about it; and now that his mother had irrevocably been removed from his life, the sense of guilt became more specific. He talked about it rather freely, and at some length, and again and again he would sum up his dilemma in words such as these, "How do you deal with a situation like this?" He had dealt with it in the only way he knew but still he was not satisfied. Now he was re-examining what he had said and done. Now, years later, unmarried, unattached except to the army, he looked back over his life and felt that something important was missing. He was still working through some of the unfinished business of his childhood and suddenly realized that the business was irrelevant. After several hours of sharing their thoughts, the chaplain and the captain parted at dinner time. Though the captain had talked himself out with freedom, the chaplain left the door wide open for any further discussions that might be desired.

Several weeks went by and then one day the captain sought out the chaplain and said, "I think I will adopt one of these war orphans." With considerable length he outlined his plan. He had seen a partcularly bright youngster whose parents had been killed. He had become friendly, and although his conversation was meager due to language difficulties, he felt a sudden burst of warmth toward the youngster, a preadolescent girl. It was obvious that he was serious about the proposal and had already made inquiry of authorities as to arrangements for such an adoption.

The chaplain questioned him at several points as to the child's welfare, the basic motivation involved, and about provisions that could be made for home life for a youngster of a regular army man stranded in a new and strange land. None of these lines of questioning seemed to dampen his ardor for the project, and he was continuing with his plans when higher headquarters ordered his transfer to a base thousands of miles away, where it became difficult to work out the details of adoption and it was not consummated.

It seems that the motivation for his sudden desire was not unrelated to his recent experience of bereavement, though he was probably not aware of it. His feelings of grief were strong as they related to his mother, and his behavior over recent years had caused strong feelings of guilt also. Because of the circumstances that made it difficult for him to work through realistically his feelings of guilt, he sought some form of expression that could serve as an approximate method for relating cause and effect. To do something important for a female for whom he could assume a filial or paternal role seemed to be an adequate expression for his pent-up feelings. That the needs of the child had so little specific attention indicates that the plan was designed primarily to satisfy his own emotional needs.

4. Techniques for Compensating Guilt Feelings

One cannot ignore feelings of guilt. They may be denied or compensated. The captain unconsciously tried to work out a plan that satisfied his emotional needs. The chaplain lost contact with the captain after the transfer, but even the contemplation of such a plan as the adoption probably served a useful purpose.

Quite the opposite is likely to be the case with Marie M., whose age and status will tend to make her condition progressively worse. At sixty-six, she had kept house for her aged father during most of her life. Her mother had died when she was nineteen, and as the oldest of seven children, she had assumed the burden of household responsibilities and had never been able to get beyond them. For her it was a grievous burden. As the years went by and she saw the chances for marriage and home life fading away, she became resentful and adopted the role of a martyr. When her father lived to be ninety-two, it seemed that her role was carried to its illogical conclusion. Through the years she had carried out an external practice of religious devotion and often said she did not know how she would bear her burden without the help of her religion.

During the last years of her father's life he was an invalid, and the burden of caring for him had been accentuated. She never missed a chance to point out to the younger children what a price she had paid for their happiness. During the years of her father's helplessness she was sharp-tongued, critical, and mildly abusive. While she assumed more responsibility than was required of her, she complained about it, as well as about her father's habits and his attitudes. For years he did little but read and sleep, and for some unknown reason got up every morning at 4:15 to make a cup of coffee and read a magazine. After he was bedridden he continued to awaken at the same time and always managed to awaken his daughter also.

After his death, many persons expressed appreciation for the faithfulness of Marie through the years and said she must feel real satisfaction in having been such a wonderful daughter. She felt a mixture of relief and loneliness at his death, and shortly thereafter a reaction set in. At first without realizing why she was doing it, she got up every morning at 4:15. Even when she was visiting other members of the family, she seemed compelled to arise at this unreasonable hour. At home she wandered about as if lost, and when away from home she was so restless that others were distressed by her. Her father had had a peculiar hacking sort of cough, and now she developed one quite like it. In contrast to her former state of irritability, she developed a resigned air much like that of her father, who had quietly taken whatever came his way.

The rest of the family noted that she made regular pilgrimages to her father's grave, by the most devious and torturesome route possible. Instead of taking a train and a taxi, which she could easily have afforded to do, she took a series of buses and used up the best part of the day in so doing. Increasingly she spoke of feelings of guilt about the way she had treated her father. She developed ways of punishing herself. She went without things because she wanted to put flowers in the cemetery. She paid for masses to be said at her church over and above what would have been considered necessary. Although her father had never been an active member, she made regular contributions to the Italian American Club in his memory.

In many respects she seemed to have developed an inner conflict between the attitudes, "You shouldn't have lived so long," and "You shouldn't have died so soon." Feelings of guilt generated by the conflict became the basis for a pattern of self-injuring and self-punishing activities that now dominate her living. So guilt feelings may become a major characteristic of grief reaction.

Where the matter of acute grief is related to feelings of guilt and punishment for former sins, real or imagined, the process of resolving it is more difficult. Here the grief is not related so much to the sense of loss as it is to an interiorized feeling of condemnation. The chance to relate the guilt to rational factors of readjustment is limited, and even the loss is interpreted not as a loss primarily but as a form of cosmic retribution. The whole process is taken out of the area of bereavement as a primary cause and is related to the intensely personal problem of guilt and retribution. That cosmic retribution should take such action against another and loved person only makes more acute the sense of personal guilt that involves the lives of others.

In the two cases that follow, the relation of guilt to punishment is shown. The air-force pilot deals with the social implications of the destructiveness of war, and the young Jewish man is dealing with the feelings of guilt that are related to violation of a closely-knit religious and national tradition. In each instance the grief itself is complicated by the other major problems of life, and the bereavement is not resolved until the other major problems are attacked and interpreted in such a way as to make it possible for the grief to be accepted for what it really is.

John B. was intelligent, sensitive, artistically inclined, and skeptical in matters of religion. He came out of a background of strong social consciousness and superficial religion. At twenty he enlisted in the Air Force and was trained as a pilot in a heavy-bomber squadron. He saw long and effective service in the Pacific and flew many bombing missions over Japan. He returned to the United States on leave two or three times during his service in the Pacific. On one leave he married a girl he had known for some time. On his next leave she became pregnant, and when he was returned to a training center for duty as an instructor, he was greeted by a three-month-old son who was named John B., Jr. He seemed to enjoy the role as father and retreated to it with satisfaction.

John B. was glad to be done with the fighting part of the war. He had seen more than his share of service in combat and had dropped hundreds of tons of jellied gasoline and heavy bombs on Japanese cities. He had been trained in early life to think that war was a stupid and useless business, and although he participated conscientiously in his military assignments, part of his mind remained unconvinced. He started going to the chapel regularly and expressed feelings of guilt about the ruthless destruction of aerial warfare. He was called on the carpet for too free an expression of opinion but the war was ending at that time and little attention was paid to such matters. Because of his high point standing he was released from active duty shortly thereafter and returned home to civilian life. A few months after returning to civil status, his son, then sixteen months old, was killed in an accident. Though John B. was not at home at the time, he assumed full responsibility and blame. He made all arrangements for the funeral. He specified cremation though the nearest crematory was at some distance. He remained dry-eyed and coldly efficient throughout the days though his wife seemed devastated by the loss. After the funeral he claimed the ashes of his son and carried them to his home. While his parents and friends watched in dismay, he ran his fingers through the ashes and let them sift from his hand as he talked rather incoherently about the price that he had to pay universally for ruthless destruction. He said, "I did this to a thousand parents. I can never live long enough to undo the damage I have done. I have had to pay so little." His wife was frightened by his attitude. She did not dare talk with him, for he had a far-away look in his eye and a curt and hurtful word on his tongue.

After a few months he began to visit a pastor in a neighboring town whom he chose because of his service as a chaplain in the Air Force. Without ever mentioning his own personal tragedy he spent hours discussing involved philosophical and theological problems dealing with love, hate, forgiveness, and restitution. The pastor heard indirectly of John B.'s personal loss and mentioned it to him, hoping to relate it fruitfully to their other considerations. John B. cut him off abruptly, saying that he did not want to discuss his own personal problems and discontinued his visits with the pastor. Shortly thereafter, however, he notified his wife that he was going to a theological school and that he was going to become a minister. At the theological school he came to the attention of a counselor who arranged for sessions with the school psychiatrist. He had regular sessions during two years of seminary study and, at the end of that period, transferred his credits to another department in the university, where he now teaches social psychology.

The case of John B. represents a variation on the usual theme of guilt as it relates to grief. Usually the person feels a sense of guilt for attitudes and actions expressed toward the deceased. In this case the loss was interpreted as a form of punishment exacted of him because of actions and attitudes expressed by him during military service. It illustrates the rather long and tortuous way that many men with moral sensitivity have had to follow in working through their feelings of guilt.

It also illustrates the fact that religion serves not only as a source of comfort, but often as a source of discomfort for one who relates bereavement to punishment. John B. was fortunate to run into a series of religious counselors who understood the nature of his problem and helped him to work his way through it. His emotional disturbance might have been capitalized on by less perceptive religious agencies to enslave him through his sense of guilt and fear of punishment. As it is, he is living usefully and employing his own experience, and the insight that came through it, to enrich the lives and understanding of others.

David S., in his middle thirties, is an artist of considerable ability. He had not been known to the pastor before the time of his bereavement and did not have any active contact with him until almost a year after the death of his father. Mr. S., Sr., was an orthodox Jew and felt a strong sense of obligation to both the national and religious traditions of the Jewish people. He had long been disturbed by the attitude of his son, who felt that too active an interest in Jewish traditions was detrimental to the life of individuals in America at the present time. He did not share his father's interest in religious or secular Jewish matters. In fact, in what might be considered overt rebellion, he became engaged to a Protestant girl of fine character and ability. It brought on a vigorous argument between father and son; and though the father did not disown the son, he made it clear that he was disappointed in his son's attitude, which had caused the father no end of humiliation in the Jewish community as well as deep personal sorrow.

Things went on for ten years, with a rather difficult adjustment having been achieved by both sides. The father did what, for him, was a difficult thing and made his son's wife and their three children welcome in his home on their occasional visits. The son, while he tried to understand his father's attitude, could not share it and carefully avoided any further discussion of it. This was the state of affairs that existed at the time of the father's death as a result of a heart ailment. The son and his family were not able to participate fully in the traditional funeral rites but did what they could. The strained feelings projected themselves into the circumstances surrounding the death of the father.

The matter was brought to the pastor's attention about a year later when David S. went to see him ostensibly about joining the church. He talked briefly about matters of doctrine and then said that he just had to do something quickly to rid his soul of the feeling of guilt that was becoming unbearable. He told of going to the rabbi, who admonished him severely and indicated that there was no freedom from guilt for him until he had fulfilled the demands of his father and his father's fathers. This he could not do in good conscience, either on his own account or for the welfare of his family. He was precipitated into gloom and inner conflict. He became ill and sought help from a psychotherapist but felt he had not come to grips with the problem that bothered him. He said that understanding his condition did not solve it. After one session he failed to return.

A few months later he became ill with infectious hepatitis and was hospitalized. When the pastor called on him, David looked at him with frightened eyes and his first remark was, "Is this also a punishment for my sins?"

This opened a discussion of religious history and religious values that both reassured him and gave him a new sense of relationship in his tradition. For the first time in his life he began to see his father as a person as well as an authority in his life. The father's attitudes could then be valued for what they were, and his own feelings could be accepted without a sense of guilt. During the eleven or twelve hours of counseling that followed, he was able to accept his father as a person and to differ with his judgments as he would those of any other person. Then he could think of his father's death as a personal loss but not as a threat to his own integrity or adequacy. His other symptoms gradually disappeared, and he is now largely free from the sense of guilt that had so severely disturbed him.

5. Religious Insight into Guilt Feelings

Because religion has long made it an area of primary concern, the person representing the religious tradition is in a position to help resolve the complications of grief that involve persistent feelings of guilt. The danger is that the representative of the religious institution will present a dogmatic statement concerning guilt and restitution that does not apply to the emotional needs of the individual disturbed by the guilt related to grief. It is perhaps safer to encourage an exteriorization of the guilt feelings, with the minimum of interpretation, and no preaching; for the personality usually has the inner resources to find the meanings that meet its own needs if the exteriorization is adequate. It may be the function of the religious counselor to relate the expressed feelings to a pattern of larger reality.

A soldier with guilt feelings reacted to the death of his buddy by making a travesty of his own life as if he were deliberately setting out to destroy all that he valued about himself. When he was referred to the chaplain for counseling he stated his premise quite simply. He said, "The bullet should have got me, not him." Then it was important to relate his feelings to the larger aspect of his emotional life to see why he felt that way, and to determine the basis for his feeling that he should be able to control even speeding bullets in their course. Finally the basis for his inner reproach was found to have no relation to the actual event involved, but rather to be related to a basic attitude toward life that he had adopted since childhood when he felt rejected, thought he was adopted, and believed his parents wanted him out of the way because he was a nuisance. The expressed feelings of guilt and emotional disturbance had been set off by the sense of loss for a buddy with whom he had quickly developed a feeling of rapport. When his buddy was killed he felt deserted and needed to prove again the thesis of his life that he was unwanted and undesired.

When strong expressions of guilt find outlet at the time of bereavement, it is important to allow time for the exteriorizing of the chain of feelings behind them. While it is accepted as an established fact that all grief involves some feeling of guilt and that it should be expressed creatively, it is important to be aware of the situations of acute guilt that are precipitated by loss. It is here that deeper problems may reveal themselves. It is in this area that the alert pastoral counselor can assist in working through the guilt and freeing the personality from the deep and disturbing feelings that might cripple it for an indefinite period.

101

SEVEN

How a Structure of Values Conditions the Grief Response

We come now to a section that is particularly important for the handling of grief: namely, the consideration of the creative response of the total personality to the given situation. The person is a composite of his dynamic nature, his cultural and hereditary conditioning, and his situational response. But he is also something more. He is a contemplative being, capable of creative mental and spiritual activity. This, too, can be cultivated over a period of time as well as stimulated by a given situation. Mankind through the years has developed a variety of rational, intellectual, and emotional expressions of this creative nature. In this chapter and the next we will give our thought to these expressions.

1. A Structure of Values as a Creative Organization of Experience

Every person, in some fashion or other, develops a thought structure wherein he tries to make reasonable for himself the experience of life and also a logical way of handling grief. Some do it in rudimentary form, while others devote their lives to a never-ending quest for form and structure in their experience and in the experience of others. In this chapter we are not so much interested in the details of a traditional and complete thought structure as we are in those postulates that may be accepted by a person who wants to look at his life and his death, and the life and death of others, with enough understanding to give stability and enough insight to give self-mastery.

Sometimes this is done in negative terms. When a psychiatrist[1] was treating a suicidally inclined patient in terminal illness, he capitalized on the lack of religious faith and the nonexistence of belief in the patient to re-enforce the concept of the meaninglessness of life:

The most decisive interview—at least in my opinion—was that in which I tried to convince the patient that life in whatever form or phase is meaningless. . . . This patient had no religious ties and did not believe in the immortality of the soul. . . . Her life—like life in general—had been futile and without meaning even before the onset of her disease. From the beginning philosophers have vainly tried to find the meaning of life. The only difference between the two phases [health and illness] she had in mind was that in one she was able to attribute a meaning to life, whereas in the other she was incapable of doing this. In reality, I told her, both were bare of meaning and sense.

In this instance the psychiatrist used the approach of the meaninglessness of life to indicate the meaninglessness of suicide, and considered that by such an interpretation he was instrumental in preventing self-destruction with its personal and social ramifications. Here we see an example of the use of the value of meaninglessness.

The modern thinker can as easily postulate those positive values that give life its deeper meaning. Henri Bergson writes:

We cannot reiterate too often that philosophic certainty admits of degrees, that it calls for intuition as well as for reason, and that if intuition, backed up by science, is to be extended, such extension can be made only by mystical intuition. . . . Now, who can fail to see that, if philosophy is the work of experience and reasoning, it must . . . question experience as to what it has to teach us of a Being Who transcends tangible reality as He transcends human consciousness, and so appreciate the nature of God on the facts supplied by experience? The nature of God will thus appear in the very reasons we have for believing in His existence. . . . Distinct from God, Who is this energy itself . . . ? Beings have been called into existence who were destined to love and be loved, since creative energy is to be defined as love.[2]

In fact, even the most skeptical seem compelled to contemplate the positive facets of life's values. Bertrand Russell, who long upheld the view of life's meaninglessness and spoke of "unyielding despair" and the courage required to face life at all, has come with the years to say:

103

The root of the matter is a very simple and old-fashioned thing, a thing so simple that I am almost ashamed to mention it, for fear of the derisive smile with which wise cynics will greet my words. The thing I mean—please forgive me for mentioning it—is love, Christian love. If you feel this, you have a motive for existence, a guide to action, a reason for courage, an imperative necessity for intellectual honesty. . . . Although you may not find happiness you will never know the despair of those whose life is aimless and void of purpose.

It is not difficult to see the relation of this type of constructive thought to the personal resources with which a person meets either life or death. While death may be no less an enemy, the nature of "creative energy as love" or "Christian love" adds to life a dimension that is not dominated by physical circumstance. While the death of a beloved one is in one sense a more acute loss, it is in another sense not a loss; for love is a value, and values cannot be destroyed by physical incidents. The orientation of the person grounded in such a concept as "Christian love" is not lacking a motive for life. Nor is the motive so bound with physical things that it is destroyed when its physical counterpart is destroyed. The intuitive value that transcends physical consciousness has a perspective not limited by physical facts. This Christian love postulates a faith in creative values that is neither denied nor defeated by death, but rather operates with the assurance that in the relationship of these creative values there is a quality of being completely removed from death's destructiveness.

2. A Value Structure Sustains the Logical Mind

The approach to the value of life can be useful in aiding the thinking of those who like to live close to established logical principles. The problem is more than one of being versus nonbeing, or of meaning versus nonmeaning. It is the problem of the dynamic nature of life in active relation to the experience of life and death. As we have indicated in an earlier chapter, the ancient Greeks and Hebrews did not ignore this aspect of their thought. The meaning of death was for them an important item in establishing the attitude toward life itself. The meaning of death is still an important element to be considered in establishing the value of life. Those who approach death with a medieval attitude toward hell and eternal punishment are induced to consider their life as a period of preparation that they dare not trifle with. Those who believe in no life after death can make the pleasure of the moment more important than other considerations.

We look at the tragedy of unfulfilled hopes, sacrifice, and struggle and feel that there is something irrational about a life that creates spiritual values merely to have them destroyed. Sir Henry Jones, in the Gifford Lectures of 1921, claims that a logical view of the universe demands immortality of the soul, for it would be illogical for a Creator to create that which could not be sustained by his creation:

> Man's rights spring neither from his discontent nor from his desires. They arise from his intrinsic nature, the final purpose of his life and of his world. . . . No stronger proof of immortality is either possible or necessary than that which shows that it is a necessary condition to an orderly universe.[4]

So it is that a structure of values attaches meaning to life as a purposeful creation, and in so doing limits the meaning of death. It does this in a way that satisfies the demands of the mind for a reasoned answer to life at the same time it is satisfying the needs of the emotions. However, for the systematic thinker, the rational comes first and may limit the bounds of his creative presuppositions.

3. Inadequate Ideas Undermine the Value Structure

As the thinker works to strengthen the creative significance of this inner world of response, so he also works to make more important the influence of the product of that creativity for the world of external relationships. His judgment is more than a subjective response, for it becomes a determinant of the meaning of objective reality. Things then become less important, and ideas about things more important. When we are considering the matter of the meaning of life and death, it is quite obvious how important ideas can become, especially when we illustrate them from life experience.

Philip W. was well along in his seventies when his wife died. He said quite simply, "Well, this is the end of her. I can't believe anything else. I have been a physiologist all my life. I know how the organism works. The mind is a function of the brain and when the brain ceases to function there is no mind. The personality, or soul as you call it, is a product of the total being. When the physical equipment that is responsible for the personality is dead, then the soul is dead too. I would like to believe otherwise, but nothing else seems to make sense, and I cannot deny my reason to satisfy my feelings."

From the point of view of his basic premise, Philip W. was correct and honest. But he was making the mistake of measuring the greater by the lesser. Physiology is an important part of life, but life is more than physiological functioning. The higher aspects of life cannot be interpreted by biology alone, so they cannot be measured by the limitations of biological measurement. Almost at once we are faced by the man-made limitations of measurement, and the measurements are for our convenience, not for limitation. For having developed measurements of space and time does not mean that we have developed a control over space or time. Nor does it mean that by establishing measurement we have placed bounds on the unmeasurable. As no interpretation of life is adequate that limits man to organic function, so no measurement of life is adequate that limits it by the very measurement man has developed as a convenience in trying to understand the life he would measure. He does not gain control by measurement any more than a man gains control over the sun by knowing it is ninety-two million miles away. To say that life is eternal is to say that there is something about it that is beyond the bounds of measurement that man has developed for his own convenience.

The person who speaks of life as being snuffed out like a candle is dealing with the limitations of sensory capacity and practical measurements. Insofar as he speaks in limited terms, he is correct. But one cannot really snuff out the light of a candle. What one does is to interrupt a process of rapid oxidation that generates for our sensory system what for convenience we call light. One does not put out the light. It had already started its course at 186,000 miles per

106

second in whatever direction was open to it. With an instrument sensitive enough to measure it, that light persists in its progressive diffusion; it is not destroyed or put out. It is merely moved beyond the capacity of our sensory equipment to measure it. It would be illogical to say that the limitations of our sensory equipment were also the bounds of objective reality.

To approach the same matter from a somewhat different angle, we might speak of the destruction of matter. If we burn a piece of wood we get so much smoke, so much ash, and so much energy. The form of the wood has been destroyed but not the essential matter. The First Law of Thermodynamics does not say anything about philosophy or immortality, but it does give a clue to the economy of nature in dealing with its own structure. Carnot postulated the principle that matter, in changing its state, produces energy. This is the principle that is almost universally used for motor power in our age. The principle shows that nothing that is material is ever destroyed. It merely changes its state. We look at such a principle and ask, "Is it logical that everything material is preserved from destruction while the only thing in all creation that is singled out for destruction is the soul of man which gives meaning to all the rest?"

For many the group relationship is a sufficient form of creative self-expression, and their lives find their ultimate meaning in the preservation of the social order. This view of life, like the physiological, measures the total by one of its parts. The total life of man cannot be separated from society, but the social consciousness of man is but one part of his being. When the nature of man is made subject to the function of society, we have emerging a life philosophy like that encouraged by the Nazi and Communist states, wherein the state is the end and man is the means. Man's nature lives within society but is never completely fulfilled by it. His soul is never entirely within the compass of social controls. There is in the soul of man something that is more than any social composite of man. While a society can carry on the ideas of a person, and make his contributions last, it is always a fractional view of man to see him as living only for the community or his family. The social sciences are tempted to place the same

107

limitations on man as the physical sciences when they employ a measurement of the parts to limit or determine the whole.

4. Rational Clues to the Meaning of Life and Death

But the social scientist, like the physical scientist, can give clues to the meaning of life. We can adapt the ideas of the social scientists or the scientists of personality to our over-all value structure. The psychologist, for instance, has an axiom that perception is a habit. We perceive what we have been trained to see. Perception is not merely a matter of seeing, but of the training of each of the senses. The conductor of an orchestra can hear an off note when no one else would notice it, for he has cultivated a habit of auditory sensitivity. The bank teller can feel a counterfeit as it passes through his fingers because he has been trained to be sensitive to such feelings. Philosophical perception is also a habit developed by a person who makes a sustained effort to penetrate more deeply into the meaning and purpose of life. Such insight is a product of training, cultivation of attitude, and a spiritually sensitive being. One does not achieve such an awareness of the nature of the soul without effort, but one does not ignore its meaning when it has been achieved. This is what led Plato to be able to speak of his own soul with such assurance:

From all that has been said, consider whether the soul is most like to that which is divine, immortal, intelligible, simple, indissoluble and ever the same and identical with itself, while the body is composite, dissoluble, and never the same with itself . . . but when the soul withdraws itself from bodily influence, it passes to that which is pure, and eternal, immortal and immutable. And as the soul is akin to this, she cleaves ever to it, when she belongs to herself, and is capable of it.[5]

This is the judgment of one who has made a habit of being sensitive to the existence of a soul rather than the denial of it. Neither denial nor affirmation are scientific measurements, but they can become the expression of the person's response to life. As a psychologist, Plato was sensitive to qualities of being that were well beyond the realm of statistical measurement.

One of the major contributions of modern depth psychology

has been a concept of man, not as a body of statistics, but as a dynamic being. The problem of the self is not considered as a problem of mathematics or physics. Those who discredit the writings of Freud as too speculative cannot deny that he has rescued the concept of human personality from the limiting measurement and has released a whole new era of concern about man and the meaning of his consciousness. For even though Freud's psychological presuppositions were mechanistic, they merely proved he was a creature of his time. Within his speculations were the active ingredients that destroyed those same mechanistic concepts. William McDougall goes even further to say:

Here, then, we have yet another line of evidence that each man is not what to so many scientists he has seemed to be, a fortuitous concatenation of physical forces, but is rather a ripple of the mighty ocean of spirit, an individualized ripple, small and feeble, yet sharing in the nature of the whole and not wholly detached from it.[6]

This puts the concern for the meaning of life back in the area of values, for the scientists of personality clearly indicate that their contemplation of man demands that they move beyond the inadequate and the partial to the type of judgments that are worthy of the major concern of the problem of being. In writing of Mosaic religion, Freud, in his last work, says cautiously:

Although I do not wish to retract anything I have said before, I cannot help feeling that it is somehow not altogether satisfactory. The cause does not, so to speak, accord with the result. The fact we are trying to explain seems to be incommensurate with everything we adduce by way of explanation. Is it possible that all our investigations have so far discovered not the whole motivation, but only a superficial layer, and that behind this lies hidden another very significant component? Considering how extraordinarily complicated all causation in life and history is, we should have been prepared for something of that kind.[7]

Such speculation brings the problem of being into sharp conflict with the equipment which the mind usually uses as the basis for its speculations upon the concepts of space, time, and eternity. When this happens we are again moving close to the area of eternal things, for life's eternal meaning is merely that which is beyond the man-made measurements of space and time. Reinhold Niebuhr makes this specific:

The fact is that there is no escape from the "rational absurdity" of the real self because it is at once in time and beyond time. It is spatial and yet non-spatial. And there is no sharp distinction between its spatial and non-spatial dimensions. Yet this double fact, which outrages the sense of rational coherence, is a fact of daily experience. The philosophers since Plato and Aristotle have eliminated the absurdity of the self which is in time and yet beyond time and space by reducing self to mind and identifying mind with form and thus establishing it as congruent to space and time. Modern psychology has no such simple way out of the dilemma. It is committed to the study of the empirical self as the object of its study. If any part of that object seems to elude it, the inquiry becomes embarrassing, for only an object in space and time can be the subject of a scientific study according to its own presuppositions.[8]

5. The Possibilities and Limitations of a Structure of Values

This, then, brings us to the place where we can see both the possibilities of speculation on values for our present study and their clear limitations. This approach can give logical answers to many of the problems that arise concerning life and death. It can help to establish sound bases upon which a thought structure can be built. But as soon as it defines the extent of its speculations by the limits of scientific measurement, it predetermines its speculation to ultimate inadequacy, for the mind of man is never satisfied by functioning within the bounds of its own mind-made tools. As soon as man tries to find another base for his speculation, he moves beyond the capacity for self-measurement and proof. Kant tried to shift the base of contemplation from pure logic to ethics: "The ideas of the reality of human personality, of life after death, and of the being of God, which were discounted on intellectual grounds, are reinstated and accredited as valid ideas on moral grounds.[9]

Morals do have something to do with this idea of life's ultimate meaning. Life is not breath, mere persistence. The nub of the problem is not a quantitative extension in time, but a qualitative extension in value. The concern is not with how much there is of life, but with how well it is lived. Too often we think of immortality in terms of time, of living after death. We need to think of it as the act of living a good life here and now. Its quality alone determines whether or not it deserves the right to survive that incident we call death. Socrates disdained the effort to escape execution, for the mere quantity of life made little appeal to him: "No harm can come to a good man in life or in death." Ethically, the burden of proof falls upon the person who is entrusted with the experience of life. If we think death is an enemy we defeat it by making life good, not in terms of a Methuselah who merely lived a long time, but of a Jesus of Nazareth, who lived life full of confidence in its spiritual quality. He had sublime confidence in the life of quality and assumed that the cosmic structure undergirded his confidence.

It is at this point that we see the creator of values become more the poet and less the scientist. His life is realized not by limitation but by moving beyond limitations. His nature is made manifest not by a detailed examination of the parts of life but rather by a quest for life's essence. So it is that the poet Goethe is both the poet and philosopher when he says:

It would be thoroughly impossible for a thinking being to think of the cessation of thought and life. Everyone carries the proof of immortality within himself and quite involuntarily. But just as soon as a man tries to step outside of himself and become objective, just as soon as a man wants to prove or wants to understand personal survival dogmatically, and in a narrow way make that inner perception clear to himself, then he loses himself in contradictions.[10]

The poet, the moralist, and the psychologist all point to one conclusion, that the ultimate concern for the meaning of life may be amplified by the mind of man, but it is fulfilled only in the soul of man.

The mind may go far in giving meaning and purpose to life through creative speculation. But the mind recognizes the limits of

111

its capacity, for life is more than reason or logic. There are areas of human desire and aspiration that are satisfied only by a daring venture of both mind and spirit. Here the bounds of logic with their restraints must be broken, so that the speculative capacity of man may function with a concern for the total needs of his nature as a spiritual being. This is not an irrational area of speculation, but rather a superrational area of creative mental and spiritual activity.

6. Religious Values Influence Attitudes Toward Life and Death

We have seen how a thought structure, through understanding of the facts and principles of life, can also invest death with a meaning that makes possible a more effective handling of grief. Let us now see how the religious thinker's understanding of the nature of life and God can illuminate man's attitude toward death and also how that understanding will affect the reaction to grief.

Everyone assumes faith as a working premise in life. Those who have no faith soon cease to function normally. Acute mental illness involves a breakdown of faith at one or more of these levels: in things, through a disorientation of reality; in people, through fear and suspicion; and in the cosmic structure, through apprehension and a dread of meaninglessness. For some, faith is a matter of personal revelation. For others, it is a spiritual achievement produced by insight through the growth of mind.[11]

The faith of the grief-stricken person may do much to determine how the incidents of life influence him. Faith is a deliberate projection of mind, emotion, and will into the creative process. Religious faith is a deliberate and clearly defined structure of relationships that give substance to faith itself. The primary object of religious faith is a prime mover for that which moves, a goal toward which movement goes, a mind that is the source of the intelligence that the cosmos reveals, and a will that is the causative agent. The concept of God is always subjective, for the conceiver is limited by his sense capacity, his creative imagination, and his reasoning processes. The concept of God is an economical answer to the multiple problems of the individual and the universal experience of life. While for man the concept of God is always of necessity subjective, this does not mean that there is not a God of objective reality. In fact, it is the function of faith to project the subjective into the objective, just as it is the function of faith to use language with the belief that our communication can be understood. The amount of imagination and daring in the former is infinitely greater than in the latter, but the type of process employed is similar.

7. A God Concept as the Basis for Relationship

The creating of a concept of God is essentially an effort to communicate for the very purpose of giving meaning to life. Religious thought initially moves beyond negations, beyond projections of fear and despair, beyond the pattern of emotional abnormalities, to the creative fabric of relationships that give a firm basis for self-consciousness and self-acceptance, for social consciousness and the acceptance of others, and ultimately God-consciousness and the feeling of at-homeness in the universe.

When a person can comprehend his religious thinking as a rational projection that fulfills the most exacting demands of his mind at the same time that it fulfills the demands of his emotions, he can find the emotional security in adulthood which can give a meaning to life that makes it worth the living, and to death that makes it but another form of fulfillment, as natural as birth and growth.

The bereaved, at the time of acute loss, needs that which can fulfill his deepest emotional needs without destroying the integrity of his intellectual processes, and without confounding his sense of what is real. For that reason it is important for him to have some idea of what he does when he makes the investment of himself in the positive commitment of a faith. Also it is important for him when he makes that commitment to make it large enough to sustain him whatever the stresses of life may be. He must seek the resources to achieve a quality of life that makes death a secondary consideration. His faith, as a mature commitment of mind, emotion, and action, should have at least the following seven components.

113

8. Seven Minimum Concepts for a Working Faith

A Concept of Purpose That Is Adequate to Give to His Life and the Lives of Others a Significant Meaning. The quality of meaning that a person places upon his life determines in large measure what his life will be. The pragmatic argument works here. If life is considered as sacred, it bears sacred fruits. It was Jesus who indicated the importance of the pragmatic measurement, "By their fruits ye shall know them." The fruits of purpose and meaning are an upward spiral of worth. Where there is no purpose or meaning for life the downward spiral is rapid and catastrophic. A purpose for life is a primary element in any theological structure that can sustain a person under stress.

A Concept of Man as a Being with Sustaining Spiritual Value. The theological question "What is man?" has to be answered in such a way that man has status in his own eyes. The Bible places him little lower than the angels, with dominion over the earth and sea. In this recognition of his unique nature as a being who can make choices, use tools, feel shame, know remorse, laugh, cry, sing, exploit the world of nature for his comfort, and organize himself into a society that guarantees his security while it protects his essential freedom, man is aware of his unusual place in the world of creatures. A religious faith that makes a place for his uniqueness and gives responsibility commensurate with its privileges enhances the concept of purpose and makes that purpose explicit. This responsibility leads directly to a working morality that relates to the purpose and calls for a disciplined mind, a purity of heart, and a body dedicated to useful pursuits. It also leads to a responsibility for social relationships predicated on a respect for the rights of others who share a common uniqueness and a concern for the needs of those whose humanity has been threatened.

A Concept of God as Essential Goodness. Man's moral nature cannot exist in a vacuum. It finds its sustaining meaning in the concept of God's goodness. This postulate is a product of the observation of dependability in nature and the moral concern in man. The dependability of nature emphasizes the reign of law and order in the universe. This law and order is not always friendly to the interests of man's will, but if he learns to subject his will

114

to the law and order about him he can find a security that would not be otherwise possible. Ignorance and willfulness are operative to destroy man in nature, and man can never know enough to adapt perfectly to the moods of nature, but he can try. Man never breaks the laws of nature. He can break himself against these laws. Gravity can be destructive unless man learns to co-operate with its great force. This sounds like the ruthlessness of an unconcerned power that cares not whether it destroys or preserves. How can such force be called good? It is good in that man has a capacity for intelligence which can learn to obey and co-operate. His effort to co-operate is his security. The structure of ethical principle is built upon an effort to know and follow these laws. The laws have been projected into human conduct as well as into the mechanical operation of the universe. The effort of man to co-operate creatively with the structure of law and order about him produces his moral nature. The effort to make this law and order good is another evidence of the positive affirmation of religious thought. To make the universe evil and destructive would plague man's life with futility and conflict. To affirm a quality of goodness as the purpose behind the law and order gives man a feeling of "at homeness" in a friendly universe. Then he is not only able to co-operate more effectively with the law and order, but also he is able to find the fulfillment of his deep emotional needs. Then he sees the tragic events of life not as the basic mood of the universe but as the evidence of his sinfulness, willfulness, or limited knowledge. He then puts understanding in the place of blame, and acceptance in the place of bitterness and frustration. So death becomes not the final triumph of evil but is another evidence of the working of the inexorable law within which man finds his security.

The Concept That Death Is Relative. The values of life and death are often held in a balance and persons are obliged to choose. There are situations in which persons quite readily say that the circumstances are such that they choose death to life. Evans Carlson, commander of the Marine Raiders, risked his life again and again to save men under his command and simply interpreted his action by saying, "Those who cringe from death deserve to die, for

they lack the faith and the breadth of vision to be useful in life."
He loved life but he valued responsibility more. When men have
been faced with a choice between death and slavery, they have
been willing to risk death or accept it rather than to lose their
freedom. In the structure of values of the God-conscious individual, there are times when persons must be prepared to face
ultimate choices. Sometimes this involves sacrifice. Always it implies that there are values ultimately greater than the mere extension of physical existence. Such a concept gives to life a relative
value and tends to make death not an end but a means to an end,
and therefore incidental rather than final. When war demands the
sacrifice of life for group goals, the minds of the grief-stricken find
a perspective they would not otherwise have when they grasp the
possibility for the creative use of death itself.

The Concept of Jesus Who Communicates God's Redeeming
Love. Theological abstractions, in and of themselves, are seldom
comforting. They need to be made real and personal in life. For
many who choose to make a further venture of faith, Jesus becomes
a mediator of the divine nature and brings into human form that
which man can accept as the mark of the divine. In his life and in
his death he teaches more about the nature of God than man has
learned in any other way. When one tries to explain the life of
Jesus, he comes up against the inexplicable. How does one explain
the life of a tradesman in a third-rate, subjected nation who was
without formal education, never held a position of influence, never
wrote a book, never traveled farther than a long walk from his
birthplace, never led a popular movement, but in the space of a
few years was able to impress mankind so deeply that he has the
loyalty and devotion of more persons than anyone who ever lived?
This sort of thing does not happen without the union of important personal, social, and historical qualities in the life of one who,
with unexplained psychic power, sees farther than other men have
seen, and in so doing reveals that which other men feel they need.
The contemplation of such a life adds meaning and stature to all
human effort. The symbol of the Cross, which could have spelled
death but for him meant new life, speaks a promise to the grieving.

Trial, tragedy, grief, and death take on a new dimension, and man is more fit to face them after having known the life and teachings of the Nazarene Carpenter. In this sustaining relationship is a personal quality, a friendship, that does more than ideas alone. It brings comfort and hope on a person-to-person basis. It makes a God of redeeming love a personal reality.

A Concept of Historical Continuity. Life is sustained by a feeling of relationship with those who have met the problems of life in the past. The Christian tradition furnishes the Church as a living symbol of fellowship across the ages, and the Bible as a storehouse of the wisdom and insight that have sustained men in crises.

The Church has maintained worship as a central act wherein men can be alone together. Without breaching the privacy of their innermost thoughts and feelings, they can share a supportive relationship with those who have a common tradition and a common loyalty. To be able to sing together gives identity and aspiration. To be able to pray together gives strength and unity of spirit. To participate in ancient rites gives the support of a sustaining tradition.

The Bible makes available the wisdom of the past for the needs of the present. In language that has survived the test of time because it has said effectively what needed to be said to suffering and searching humanity, it continues to speak to our age. Perhaps no other words have spoken so directly to so many bereaved people as the words, "Though I walk through the valley of the shadow of death, I will fear no evil: for thou art with me." Both in availability and in its direct and economical language, the Bible relates the emotions of the present with the emotions of the past and brings strength to life.

Here a sense of oneness with struggling, suffering humanity through the ages, not in futility and defeat, but rather in faith and the achievement of meaning and value, sustains life. The security of being part of something bigger and more permanent than the self is a foundation upon which shattered feelings can be rebuilt.

A Concept of an Undying Quality in His Own Soul. One evening a woman came unannounced to a pastor's counseling room. He had not seen her before, nor has he seen her since. Like a wraith out

117

of the night she posed her eternal question in new form. With the anxiety of those with threatened values who stand naked before the threat, she said she was a Communist and that the man she loved had died. Was that the end of life? Nothing in her Communist textbooks could satisfy her, but from her non-Communist past came a remnant of a belief that death was not the end. Almost furtively she sought an answer. There must be something more to life than death. It was not possible to develop for this troubled woman a concept of the soul that would fit her philosophical conditioning, and she went out again into the night, still troubled but with some ideas that might give new direction to her thinking.

The problem raised by this troubled woman is not unlike the problem raised increasingly in our world. How can I believe in the undying quality of the soul and make that belief compatible with the truth I have learned about man and his nature through science?

That question can be more easily answered now than it could have been fifty years ago when the minds of scientists were well insulated against other areas of human need by complacency and seemingly adequate theories. Now, instead of being members of a group who hold the searchlight of truth on the world and man, they are a number of individuals, each with his own little flashlight, sending feeble rays out into the unlimited night of man's unknowing. One cannot begin to answer the questions about man's spiritual nature unless and until one has made the venture of faith that accepts that spiritual nature. The denial of that nature precludes the meaning of the nature denied. Acceptance opens the door of a structure of new possibilities through faith. This faith takes a great courage, for the leap of faith must be made in the face of the practical and logical difficulties, but when it is made the results are self-sustaining.

9. Faith to Be or Not to Be

Paul Tillich has defined the problem well:

The popular belief in immortality which in the Western world has largely replaced the Christian symbol of resurrection is a mixture of

118

courage and escape. It tries to maintain one's self-affirmation even in the face of one's having to die. But it does this by continuing one's finitude, that is one's having to die, infinitely, so that the actual death never will occur. This, however, is an illusion and, logically speaking, a contradiction in terms. It makes endless what, by definition, must come to an end. The "immortality of the soul" is a poor symbol for the courage to be in the face of one's having to die.

The courage of Socrates (in Plato's picture) was based not on the doctrine of the immortality of the soul but on the affirmation of himself in his essential, indestructible being. He knows that he belongs to two orders of reality and that the one order is transtemporal. It was the courage of Socrates which more than any philosophical reflection revealed to the ancient world that everyone belongs to two orders. . . . For encountering God means encountering transcendent security and transcendent eternity. He who participates in God participates in eternity. But in order to participate in him you must be accepted by him and you must have accepted his acceptance of you.[12]

This sharing of eternal values is then not so much a logical process in time and space as it is a religious process involved in the values beyond time and space, but which is determined by the amount of courage that marks the faith of the individual believer.

The leap of faith can be more acceptable for scientists whose whole scientific structure is now based on the abstract speculations of a violin-playing mystic who looked out into the universe with awe and formed his mathematical formulas that change the course of history long before they can be proved.[13] The proving does not make the truth. The truth has a speculative daring about it that can neither be defined nor denied. The more the proof-chained mind of the would-be scientist retreats into his world of established facts, the more he denies the very courage that makes science a magnificent venture of faith. Surely there is need for the pedantic soul who reduces daring concepts to proven formulas, but we do damage to the grandeur of human imagination and intellect if we somehow think the formulas that are proven take precedence over the as-yet-unproven flights of creative imagination that lend to the human soul its ascendent place in the world of nature and ideas.

The religious thinker, of course, needs to keep his flights of fancy within the bounds of reason, sensitive to logical fallacy and aware of scientific discovery, but he does not need to wait upon proof in order to embrace ideas that give life stature and significance. The proofs may well come with time. Even now, the careful studies of parapsychologists are defining and explaining many of the phenomena that have given wings to men's flights of fancy. They are proving that what seemed beyond reason is quite within the bounds of newly established frames of reference. The psychologist, with his study of the unconscious, is finding out new things about the idea of death itself. It seems almost impossible for man to imagine his own death. He may be aware of his dying, but his ability as a being to conceive of his own nonbeing seems to be an impossibility.

Perhaps it is the demand of his unconscious mind that projects a logical structure that fulfills the demands of his emotional need to extend his pleasure of living. To contemplate these and similar theories merely extends the area of conjecture about the subjective realities of death and immortality. The objective reality remains untouched.

Here again the courage of a faith is needed, to move beyond the finite to the infinite, from the mortal to the immortal. Faith gives value to life. Faith makes explicable the inexplicable. Faith makes it possible for man to move beyond the boundaries of man-made measurements of space and time that chain the brain. Faith is the "open sesame" to a structure of creative meaning. The ventures of the disciplined mind into the realm of faith are the grandest achievements of mankind.

The value-conscious individual will not be denied his insight merely because it is not bound to a body of established and laboratory-tested fact. He would rather assume the function of one whose imagination and insight become the invitation to the search for more knowledge. When his insight serves the deepest needs of the spiritual nature of man as shown in its ministry to the bereaved, he does not stop to quarrel about details. He continues his search confident that even in his unknowing he is approaching a transcendent meaning that combines the *summum bonum* of philosophy with the body of established truth of science and the revelation of the nature of God in theology.

EIGHT

How Religious Practices Sustain the Grief-stricken

Philosophy and theology are creative resources for the meeting of acute bereavement, but there is also a third voice at work, more nebulous, more difficult to define, but no less real in its effectiveness. There is a symbolic structure at work in society, and especially in its religious institutions, that sustains persons in stress. The symbolic structure is the product of a long period of historic accumulation. It was not planned nor is it the product of conscious design. It seems to be the unconscious accumulation of the meanings that meet the need of the preconscious mind. The life of every society is rich in its symbolization as an unspoken language, and though the origins are obscure the purpose is clear to students of human personality.

1. The Sustaining Power of Symbolic Structures

It is to these symbolic rituals and dramatic acts, rather than to the more self-conscious religious practices such as prayer, that we turn our attention now. These more personal and individual worship procedures will be mentioned in Chapters XIII, XIV, and XV.

Nearly every religion starts with the premise that there is something about the nature of the self that is too valuable to allow its extinction. There seems to be a basic need for maintaining the idea of creative self-consciousness. The ways in which this need has been met have varied greatly from culture to culture and from period to period in human history.

For instance, Ruth Benedict points out[1] that the Plains Indians met life's crises with terror while the Pueblo Indians accepted them calmly. The difference in the group attitude undoubtedly had an effect upon the way the individual within the group responded. But whether the crises of life, such as birth, puberty, marriage, death, and sorcery, were met with terror or accepted as natural phenomena, the individual had a sense of group support. When the phenomenon was death, the group support involved a belief in the survival of the personality of the deceased. In the society where terror dominated, the survival was surrounded with threats that had to be dealt with by ritualized precautions. In the society where calm acceptance was the pattern, survival was not a matter of a battle won but rather of a basic faith in a universe without good or evil, without sin or struggle. As all is essentially good, there is no denial of goodness in death. There was "no resignation, no subordination of desire to a stronger force, but the sense of man's oneness with the universe." There is no conflict between life and death, the here and the hereafter. All are essentially one. Man's faith gives him a sense of oneness with the universe and therefore leads him to a calm acceptance of death.

Of even greater significance, however, is the fact that though the form of expression may differ from one culture to another, the psychological necessity that exists behind the expression remains the same. The human mind, with its capacity for self-consciousness, seems impelled to deal with the mystery of its survival. To this end man develops a variety of logical, social, and magical formulas that tend to satisfy his need. Over the centuries man has built a spiral of thought and theory that has become both consciously and unconsciously an almost insurmountable barrier to the clear and objective weighing of the factors that relate to his survival as a human soul.

Perhaps it is for this reason that many with a purely scientific interest avoid the subject, or dismiss it with a glib reference to "wishful thinking" or "whistling in the dark." One can read dozens of psychiatric treatises and never find a reference to this aspect of the study of the soul. Perhaps it is clearly recognized as an aspect of life beyond the scope of verifiable investigation. Yet even here, recognition has been made in recent years of influences at work in the life of the mind not adequately explained by previously accepted psychological thought.[2] Gradually it is being recognized that that concern of modern man for avoiding the reality of death cannot be corrected unless he can bring together his concept of personality and his awareness of the basic needs of that personality. These deeper needs seem to be met only by a symbolic structure that speaks directly to the more primitive aspects of being. Here Christian symbolism has a validity for each level of man's response.

The great truths of mythology, which met the needs of the total concept of being with its unconscious and preconscious mental activity, have come to new status psychologically. Studies of communication have developed a new sense of their relevancy, for this communication is a source of healing life. The rituals and rites that men have developed to sustain their souls have come to hold a respected place in psychological thought. Their justification is not dependent upon how much sense they make to the conscious mind, for they may serve a more important purpose in communicating with the lower levels of consciousness.

2. New Significance for Old Methods

This new importance for supplemental modes of communication gives support to methods traditionally employed in Christian practice. Symbolization, as the art of making real that which is too real to be adequately expressed in ordinary speech, has achieved new dignity, for we now know that the symbol is not the reality but rather the clue to the reality. In similar fashion the lowly myth has come to be a dignified participant in intellectual activity; it is a vehicle to carry a combination of thoughts and feelings too great to be handled otherwise. And the drama that symbolizes the myth and makes it possible to accept it and also to participate actively in acting it out, then becomes a crowning achievement of the total mental and spiritual life. The symbolization and acting out of the Christian drama of Lent, Holy Week, and Easter then become, not an archaic inheritance to which we pay a grudging tribute, but rather the crowning achievement of the struggle to make explicit what is both the individual need and the inherited achievement of the group. It is the crowning effort by which man seeks to equate his burden of self-consciousness and God-consciousness with the opportunity for meaningful self-expression and group expression. Here the drama becomes more than dramatics. Here the rituals become more than rites and forms. Here the heroic effort for self-realization in man finds its cosmic counterpart and is fulfilled.

Perhaps it has never been possible for man, bound to the more traditional interpretation of this cosmic drama, to sense its full significance. Perhaps now for the first time we have the equipment of psychological understanding, social research, and scientific insight to bring this drama to its level of highest meaning.

The drama of Holy Week seeks to make explicit the revelation that could never be made in the abstract. It must be in the person of a being who fulfills the obligations, bears the burdens, and achieves the possibilities of true selfhood. It is a relation that accepts all the limitations of biological origin and, in spite of that, achieves all the possibilities of spiritual fulfillment. It is a drama that makes explicit the relation of God to man as the expression of that eternal struggle between the self and the larger than self. Here the concept of God as love becomes meaningful, for love is that capacity of the individual to relate himself creatively to that beyond himself.

3. Drama and Personification

The factors in the struggle are also explicit and can be made to live and walk upon the stage of human history. There are persons who illustrate the forms of man's denial of the possibilities of his spiritual nature. Judas represents the denial in which man, with careful calculation and dependence on his own reasoning capacity, decides how he shall proceed with the revelation of God.

Peter, the blustering disciple, is well cast in the role of the fearful being who reflects his fear in every aspect of his nature.

There is the denial through weakness. The disciples were heavy with sleep, and when the struggle between the nature of man and the nature of God was at its height, they went to sleep.

The denials of design, fear, and weakness, however, have their counterparts in acceptances that the drama reveals. The mother, who had misunderstood her son and tried to dissuade him from

125

his ministry, is found among the grieving at the time of his death. The importance of relationship even at the biological level is recognized here. This basic relationship may become the basis for the true revelation of love, as a sense of self-consciousness that is fulfilled in a form of creative otherness.

Mary Magdalene represents the acceptance that grew out of a deep sense of need. Her life had been crippled by a slavish devotion to physical desires. In relationship with Jesus she found a new dimension for life and began to realize those possibilities that are often dormant when the struggle of the limited self is related primarily to the fulfilling of instinctual desire. It meant the awakening within herself of a new horizon of living. Her love then became more than a satisfaction of drives and developed into a sensitivity to undeveloped resources as well as a creativity of human relationships based on recognized spiritual needs. In traditional terms, she found an abundant life in the place of a self-destroying slavery to the impulses that limited her capacity to know that such an abundant life existed. It was the subdrama of sin and salvation.

The disciples at Easter indicated the acceptance of faith. Thomas witnessed to the affirmative quality of doubt. On the road to Emmaus the disciples went a step further to show an acceptance of the spiritual reality of Jesus.

But this cosmic drama is not cast in personal terms alone. It involves the characters of the world of affairs. Politics is never sure of the role it should grant to spiritual matters. Pilate stands as a caricature of the effort to pay tribute to the spiritual influence of eternal values at the same time that earthly impulses of the mob are placated.

The social choice between the reckless adventurer and the prophet of righteousness, between the exponent of social consciousness on the ethical level and social aggressiveness on the level of organized self-interest is found in the choice between Barabbas and Jesus. The gamut of human emotions and social relations is run in this drama of history in which the will of God seeks its realization in the affairs of men. True to the conflict, there is the unresolved nature of the tension between the desires of the self that is dedicated to its own satisfaction and the self that is seeking to reveal a will larger than its own.

4. Religious Rites and Emotional Responses

The significance of this symbolic drama for suffering and grieving humanity is difficult to overestimate, for within its framework is the fulfillment of the manifold needs of mind and emotion that makes it an effective healing instrument. It can be lived through again and again by those who need to feel the problems of their lives related to a cosmic drama that includes them in a struggle for life and value.

In relation to sorrow and identification the need is met through a ritualized reliving of the events of the parting of Jesus and his disciples in a symbolic meal at which they were prepared for his death. Through this memorial relived, persons are prepared again for death through incorporating the elements of life and death as an act of identifying with the life of one who was not bound by death because he was completely responsive to the will of God.

The relation of sorrow to substitution is shown in the agreement which was entered into, whereby one who could reveal most fully the will of God was willing to substitute himself in death so that others might find the way to full self-realization before their opportunity was spent. The rite of Communion, with this act of emotional participation in the re-enacted drama, gives each person a chance to engage his feelings in a service of memorial in which his devotion is more abstract and less personal. When such a person has been recently bereaved, he can release his pent-up feelings in an act that gives legitimate expression to his grief, when it is not only justified but desirable. When he has not been bereaved he can develop the mood of participation in preparation that makes it possible for him to anticipate his loss through substitution and so engage his emotions in advance in the abstract grief that will some day become concrete for him.

The drama of Lent, Holy Week, and Easter, as it can be relived individually, can be especially efficacious when the problem of guilt is involved. Guilt, either real or neurotic, is a major problem for the emotions of the bereaved. A clearly established pattern

127

for expressing remorse, doing acts of penance, and impelling one toward acts of retribution is useful. The guilt that is invariably a part of grief may easily be resolved through the act of confession, and the burdensome effects of the grief are relieved by the promise of forgiveness. When this activity is directed toward a creative newness of life, the tendency is to move away from morbid preoccupation with the past toward a healthy participation in the future. "Ye that do truly and earnestly repent . . . and intend to live a new life . . . and are heartily sorry for these [your] misdoings . . . draw near with faith . . . have mercy . . . forgive."

When the person who could forgive is no longer present the effectiveness of an oversoul capable of forgiving is a source of release and comfort. The self-imposed symbolic penalties clear the feelings of any burden of unresolved guilt that the ego feels toward the superego, and in acting out the drama we wisely petition, "Father, forgive." With a wisdom that is more wise than logical, the healing rituals invite a participation that fulfills the needs of body, mind, and spirit. At the same time the rituals are fulfilling basic needs of the human, they are pointing a way toward a philosophy of life that is larger than mere intellectual constructs that have been the basis for much religious expression. Philosophy and theology are important; but neither makes a claim to meet the personality needs which are manifest by that psychological trinity that is so important a factor in life: the unconscious, the preconscious, as well as the conscious.

Such ritualization becomes more than a re-enactment of a historical event. It involves the living person in a drama of relationships that sustain the soul. In a town like Oberammergau it can have a significant social effect, where the acting out of the passion drama so involved the actors that they became more than actors. So in each parish the re-enacting of that part of the passion drama that we call Holy Communion engages the person and his emotions in a way that lets him work through his fears and his feelings of guilt, and develop in their stead a healing relationship of faith and forgiveness.

From primitive rites up to the most exalted rituals, the basic struggles for meaning cannot be denied. They may be ignored for a while but they have a way of re-exerting themselves in new forms. For these ritualized communications become the avenues through which restricted emotions can find an acceptable expression.

The Christian religion has a significance because it becomes the avenue for the highest self-realization at the same time that it asserts the importance of the fabric of social interrelationship. Christianity does not deny but fulfills the long struggle of man to know his nature and to realize his possibilities. Christianity does not limit the mode of man's existence but rather lifts the limits by making the ultimates of life realizable within the soul of the individual, for truly the kingdom of God is within. But it demonstrates that the inner kingdom is not realized without a creative interrelationship through love, for God is love. The incidents of life that involve grief, sorrow, and deprivation are not the ultimates of life, but are truly incidental to the larger meaning and purpose of existence. Rather than being a structure of rituals that insulate man against stern reality, his religious faith should be a pattern of thought and personal involvement that leads him toward the largest reality. The religion that crystallizes long-standing individual and group needs gives creative expression to the totality of life.

The Christian religion opens doors to understanding at the same time that it gives the equipment for involving the mind, emotions, and social impulses. In an inarticulate but effective way, in a total rather than a partial expression, the true interpretation of the Christian faith can lead even the sorely bereaved to understanding and emotional health.

Let us turn now to the more practical aspects of the problem of grief and mourning, and consider what may be done to relieve the acute suffering of the bereaved.

NINE

Types of Grief Manifestation

As we move from the theoretical consideration of grief to its practical aspect, we must first make clear what grief looks like as it is experienced by actual people.

This chapter is largely a detailed description of the grief reactions of three persons. The cases are chosen because they illustrate the three major areas of emotional reaction. The first shows how a normal, healthy person reacts, engages in the work of mourning, and works through it to healthy adjustment. The second deals with a person who uses a variety of techniques to avoid and escape coming to grips with the central problem of loss. The third illustrates the way a grief reaction can precipitate a deep disturbance that makes it impossible for the personality to continue to function normally. Because the terms are not always defined accurately, we hesitate to use the labels "normal," "neurotic," and "psychotic," though some persons might find that classification more explicit.

1. Normal Grief Reaction

Mrs. Arthur Easton, aged fifty-three, was the wife of an executive of a paper manufacturing concern. Her husband had developed lesions in the aorta which made life painful and life expectancy poor. Surgery was advised as the only possible hope for survival, but the surgeons made it clear that the nature of the operation was such that at best there was but a fifty-fifty chance of recovery.

Mr. Easton, a matter-of-fact person, called in his pastor. He explained the nature of his case and said that he was ready for whatever might happen. He had a few questions about matters of faith that he wanted clarified for him and this was done to his satisfaction. When he went to the operating room he was in good spirits, calm and relaxed. He said, "I have the best surgeon possible and a good hospital. Whichever way it goes, I am ready. I certainly can't go on as I have been the last month. I've had a good life anyway, and more than I was entitled to. You have to be sensible about things like this."

The pastor waited with Mrs. Easton after the operation while her husband was in the recovery room. They talked casually and calmly about many things. They talked freely about life and death. After several hours the surgeon came in to report on the operation. He said that the surgery itself was satisfactory but that the structure of the arteries did not look good and anything might happen.

Four hours later the surgeon returned to say that complications had developed and that conditions were deteriorating. Several hours later he came in to say that the heart had given out, and that Mr. Easton had expired without regaining consciousness.

Then began a process of the work of mourning wherein the adjustments of a bereaved person are made to a distressing loss. Note is made of the actions, attitudes, and statements which show the movement of the emotions. For the sake of brevity much of the irrelevant and repetitious material in the case is omitted.

The immediate reaction of Mrs. Easton was to put her arms around the surgeon, bury her head on his shoulder, and quietly weep. The surgeon said nothing for a while but permitted this expression of emotion to continue. Then after two or three minutes she straightened herself up and said, "Doctor J., I know you did everything that was possible. It just wasn't to be."

Then still accepting her expression of emotion, the surgeon gave a detailed explanation of the surgical and medical situation as it had developed in recent hours. He assured her that death came quietly and without pain. He further indicated that the physical condition was such that without the operation her husband would have lived but a few weeks at best. He concluded, "We all did the best we knew how to do under the circumstances, but there was just too much against us."

Mrs. Easton continued, "It all seems so unreal. I knew this might happen, but I never really thought it would." Then she

131

sat down and quietly wept for a few minutes. Looking up at the surgeon again she asked, almost rhetorically, "What shall I do now?"

As if he missed the rhetorical nature of the question, the surgeon continued: "In a case like this you could help us. We have not performed very many of these operations. We are interested in knowing just what went wrong. If you would permit us to perform an autopsy we would appreciate it."

Looking at her pastor, Mrs. Easton said, "What do you think I should do?"

The pastor said: "Knowing your husband as I do, I think he would have approved. He was interested in the medical problem and would have wanted to add to medical knowledge in any way he could. But your feelings are involved, and you must make the final decision."

Mrs. Easton looked at the surgeon: "Yes, that's right. He would want it that way. He wanted to will his eyes to an eye bank. But it seems so unreal and callous to be talking like this." Then she started to weep again.

When she had calmed down the surgeon asked her to sign a release paper for the autopsy. Again he gave some reassurance and concluded by saying: "There are many things about life that we don't know. Medicine is concerned with physical functions. Now you need spiritual help. That can come from your religious faith. Don't fail to use it."

After the surgeon left, Mrs. Easton looked at the pastor and said: "It doesn't seem real. I don't know what to do. What shall I do now?"

The pastor suggested that there were things to be packed and arrangements to be made for the removal of the remains. Together they quickly packed a suitcase, gathered up personal belongings, and left the hospital. Again and again Mrs. Easton said: "It just doesn't seem possible. Poor Arthur. He wanted to come home with me, but now he can't. I knew this might happen but I didn't think it would. Doesn't it seem heartless to just walk out like this? Everything looks the same but it isn't. I suppose I expect too much, but these people all seem to be happy and doing the same as they always do. How can that be when Arthur has just died? Maybe they don't know. It's a big city and a big hospital. Maybe they get used to such things, or maybe they don't know."

On the way home from the hospital, Mrs. Easton talked and wept and talked. She expressed feelings, reminisced, recalled incidents, recounted conversations. She said: "Arthur knew this might happen. That is why he told me just what to do. I have all the instructions at home. I will do just as he said. Arthur was practical and realistic." The pastor said little. He encouraged her to say what she wanted to say and to express her feelings. As they neared home he indicated that there were some things that probably should be done at once and other things that could be delayed until the next morning. He would make arrangements for the funeral and she could call the relatives.

During the next few days Mrs. Easton showed most of the symptoms of acute grief. This was indicated by things she said and did. While she was encouraged to express her feelings, there was no effort made to interfere with the expression of her grief. The pastor remained close at hand, making three or four brief calls a day until after the funeral. He helped with the details of practical decisions but tried to keep from becoming involved in any of the specific feelings she expressed. He did not tell her she was brave. He did not advise her as to what she should do about matters involving her feelings. He indicated to her that her feelings were an important part of herself and that they had been greatly involved in the happenings of the past few days. No one can prescribe another's feelings. We can only respect them.

Mrs. Easton became quite angry at a neighbor who tried to "barge in" and take over certain arrangements. She felt guilty about being angry and asked the pastor if it was wrong to feel so angry. He led her to believe that it was quite natural and normal to act as she had. Her sister came to live with her for a few days, and Mrs. Easton found that she was easily irritated by things her sister said and did. She felt guilty about this but it seemed that she couldn't help it. She just wasn't herself. Her pastor said that was true, that she was under considerable stress and her behavior would quite naturally show the effects.

Also she complained that her food did not taste like food. As she put it, "I suppose I have to eat, but everything I put in my mouth tastes like sawdust." She complained about going around in circles and not being able to get anything done. She complained of a variety of uncomfortable feelings such as tightness in the chest, tightness in the throat, and a fuzzy sort of headache. She said she felt as if she were walking on legs that didn't belong to her. She said, "I feel as if I am going through motions. I don't feel like myself."

At the funeral she was outwardly composed. When the service was over she wanted to remain until the last, so that she would be "the last one to see Arthur." After returning home following the funeral, she spent nearly an hour talking about Arthur, trips they had made, things he had done, and generally painting a rather idealized picture of her husband.

Two days later when the pastor called at the home she became quite confidential and explained in detail about a disagreement they had had years ago as to the best way to provide for his aged mother. She said it was the only real disagreement they had ever had. As she told about it she wept and asked if the pastor thought her husband might have lived longer if they had not had that disagreement.

At the end of a week Mrs. Easton was able to talk quite freely about her husband without involvement of her emotions. She went about the matter of settling his affairs with good sense. She spent time with friends and actively planned for the future.

At the end of a month Mrs. Easton was active in church affairs, more so than in the past. She was making a normal and healthy adjustment to her loss.

At the end of six months she was sharing her home with a schoolteacher whom she had chosen with care for companionship. She was participating in constructive church and community activities. She was doing quite a bit of reading, with variety and interest.

When a woman with no children and few close relatives becomes a widow, it is a severe deprivation experience. Mrs. Easton had faced the full implications of the experience. She had suffered the pains of it and had come through it successfully. Her life had been injured, but she had readjusted. Helpful pastoral care during the difficult period eased the pain, but it did not seek to remove it. She did not build for herself an illusory world of false promises. She did not drown herself in self-pity. She grew through the experience toward greater adequacy as a person.

The case of Mrs. Easton illustrates the movement of the grief situation when it is met well within the range of normal behavior. To be sure, during the early period of the grief work there was the evidence of what might be called "the normal neurosis." Like adolescence, involution, and senescence, there are times in life when neurotic behavior is the more normal and healthy response to circumstance. Her behavior with feelings of guilt, irritation, and uncertainty was the normal behavior for a person subject to great stress. Rather than to repress and deny her feelings, she was encouraged to express them and she did so. She felt bad—mentally, emotionally, and physically—but she did not try to deny her feelings. No one tried to distort reality for her. The surgeon was frank and direct. He immediately precipitated the consideration of stark reality by the discussion of the autopsy. The pastor did not try meaningless reassurance. No one tried to make her feel she was being heroic or brave to ignore her true feelings. She paid off any emotional debt she had toward her husband through confession of past conflict and through present idealization of him. She did not refuse to talk about him. She continued to place him in a framework of realities. She did not want him to die, but she did not try to deny the fact of his death. No one tried to encourage her to build an illusory world of false promises or unreal values. Because she met a difficult situation directly and without limitation, she was able to do the work of mourning quickly and well. She adjusted to a grievous deprivation with complete integrity of her personality. She continued on in complete possession of valued memories. But she was not chained to morbid recollections. She was able to live her own life in the present, free from any enslavement to a love object from which she had not been able to free herself. Any hostile feelings that developed she worked through quickly and economically for the over-all state of her emotional health. While her general behavior pattern was disorganized for a while, she quickly reorganized it about her new set of needs and interests. Still in her early fifties, she has before her many years of happy, healthful, and normal living.

2. Abnormal Grief Reaction

How different is the case of Mr. K., who refused to face his grief. I first became acquainted with Mr. K. when I was asked to visit him in a hospital. He had been admitted for examination of a supposed heart condition. Careful examination had failed to reveal any present or past heart injury that adequately accounted for the symptoms of which he had complained.

During my first visit with Mr. K., I was unable to engage him in any conversation that related to himself. He had been reading Ulysses S. Grant's *Personal Memoirs* along with *A Stillness at Appomattox*. For the best part of an hour he regaled me with detailed descriptions of the planning and execution of military maneuvers. Whenever I tried to change the subject back to him, it merely reminded him of something about the War Between the States, and there we were all over again.

From members of the family I pieced together a picture of what had happened to Mr. K. during the ten years which led up to his hospitalization.

During the summer of 1945, Mr. K.'s only son, the pilot of a Navy Corsair, took off on a mission involved in the operations at Okinawa. He never returned to his carrier and no subsequent report has indicated anything about his action. The Navy assumed he was lost at sea and so notified the family. When the telegram came from the Navy Department, Mr. K. read it with stolidity. At no time did he break down, or show in any visible form an emotional reaction to his loss. Many persons commented on his bravery in bearing up so well under his bereavement.

Although Mr. K. idolized his son, he had been rather strict and critical. When he would remonstrate with him about his attitude and behavior, the boy would say, "Someday you'll be proud of me." When people would comment about his loss, Mr. K. usually said, "My boy told me that I would be proud of him some day. Now I want him to be proud of me."

Mr. K. had been more than ordinarily successful in business. His two older daughters were married, and he had no particular feeling of obligation or concern for them. But he had wanted to provide his son with all he would need for a good start in business. Financial success was important for Mr. K., and he had pressed every business advantage so that he could make more money and more and wiser investments for his son's sake.

With the loss of his son, Mr. K. also gradually lost interest in business, and though his associates tried to keep things going, it was obvious that without his drive there was little chance for continued success. He was finally urged to sell his business, which he did. Had he kept the proceeds of the sale he would have had enough for a comfortable living, but he made further unsuccessful ventures and within a few years had lost most of what he had by unwise and careless operations.

During his busy life in business he had not had much time for reading. Now, more and more, he buried himself in reading about wars, past and present. After a time his reading began to center on the events and personalities of the Civil War. Here he accumulated a great amount of relatively meaningless information. When he could find anyone who was interested, he could talk by the hour. When there was no one to talk with about the Civil War, he sat quietly with his pipe and read more and more.

Increasingly he took a dependent attitude toward his family. He expected them to be near him for emotional support though he never actively shared his feelings with them. Toward his older daughter he assumed an attitude similar to that which he had had toward his own mother. Both were capable and strong characters with a tendency to dominate others. Quite willingly, he moved toward this older daughter as if he welcomed the protection that such domination brought to him. He seemed to resent her preoccupation with her own life and family, and kept urging her to come and spend time with him, though during such time he made little effort for meaningful communication with her.

While Mr. K. had always been an active churchman, his attitude toward the church subtly changed. He complained about the minister and his preaching. He objected to expenditures. He became bitter in a restrained way that made it difficult to challenge his attitude. Although he had always gone out of his way to express patriotic attitudes, he now expressed resentment against payment of income taxes, saying, "All the government wants to do is take, take, take." Yet even there he expressed his attitude in such a way that his grief never became explicit.

Many of the actions of Mr. K. indicate a desire for sympathy which he is unwilling to accept. Such a desire is characteristic of a general attitude by which he refuses to accept his feelings. His loss created so great a problem for his life that he reacted against the demands for adjustment. But while he was able to control some of the more obvious and external aspects of his grief, he was not able to bring under control the internal forces that were slowly and surely conditioning his behavior to the point where his personality was changing. What some people took for a stoic attitude gave evidence of being a regression to a level of emotional action that had satisfied his needs in childhood. Instead of showing bravery, as some people thought, he was building a retreat from life in a world of dependencies and escapes that interfered seriously with the forward motion of his living. As Franz Alexander has put it, "Every neurosis replaces an insoluble actual conflict with a past conflict he has already solved." [1] On the physical level Mr. K. was reverting to a dependence that had protected him from severe choices, while at the same time he was projecting his mental activity into a civil conflict that had already been resolved historically but in which he found a large measure of satisfaction by reworking the incidents in terms of his own inner needs. Here was a war he could fight without having to suffer. Here was a world to which he could retreat in safety.

Many of these aspects of Mr. K.'s behavior show a refusal to do the work of mourning directly, so that his person has become involved in the more disorganizing and disrupting indirect working out of the deep grief. His inability to express his emotions was

138

an indication of difficulty to come. The stimulation of his mental activity was a danger signal when it was connected with no active sense of loss. The fact that there was no casket, and none of the usual supporting ritual of society such as a funeral, made it more difficult to engage in grief work. In his case he tended to acquire the symptoms of the cause of death of his son by a preoccupation with military history. The appearance of a medical problem, psychogenic in nature, was but a further evidence of the depth to which the disturbance had worked in his being. The gradual change in his relationships to his family, his church, his friends, and his country were a thinly veiled indication of a growing sense of hostility against life itself. His illness carried this feeling one step further. While no one of these things was making it impossible for him to continue to function in society, when put together they revealed a personality sorely distressed and in need of help. The real problem was whether or not he could be brought to the place where he would be willing and able to take the help he needed to start belatedly to work through the grief situation that was altering his personality.

3. When Grief Brings Breakdown

Evans B., aged thirty-five, was the only son of a dominant, compulsive mother and a rather weak, rigid, and submissive father. He had lived a quite restricted life except for a period of military service that seems to have been rather uneventful. He was honorably discharged but had not been sent overseas. His military records have not been available for examination.

Evans B. was referred to me by his pastor, who felt the man needed special help and who wanted his judgment confirmed. Evans had held a good job in the personnel department of a large corporation. He was thought to be competent, patient, and of likeable nature. About a year after his mother died he began to have a variety of symptoms that bothered him considerably. He was given a leave of absence to rest, but the symptoms persisted. He usually traveled by subway to get to work, but going down into the subway caused him to have strange feelings. Sometimes he would feel faint and dizzy, and at other times he would break out in a cold sweat. It kept getting worse, and the more he worried about it the worse it became.

Finally he tried traveling by a series of buses. This amused his father, who ridiculed him. Evans became angry and threatened to leave home but could not seem to bring himself to actually do it. His physician suggested that he get some other kind of work. He gave up the personnel work for which he was trained and took a position in a bank nearer his home. Here things went fairly well until he had to do some work in the vaults. Then he was overcome with feelings of distress so great that he could not force himself to remain in the vaults. He ached, perspired, became nauseated, and was finally told by his employer that they had made a mistake in employing him.

For weeks he sat at home in a darkened room trying to rest, and increasingly it became difficult for him to go out into the street. His father was impatient and thought his behavior was all foolishness. As he put it: "If anyone wants to work, all they have to do is go out and get a job and stick to it. I had one job for forty-three years. I never had to be babied."

Evans' father brought him to my counseling room. Evans entered the room uneasily. He said, "You don't need to close the door." I didn't. He said: "Probably you know all about me. I need help and I thought maybe you could help me. I can't do anything any more." He was thin and haggard and continued to wring his hands in a distressed fashion.

After a while he relaxed somewhat and told his troubles. It all began when his mother died. She had been the only one who really understood him. She had been a wonderful person, and he had felt lost ever since she had died. His father never understood him. He thought only of his work. His father was not as smart as his mother. Mother could do almost anything she turned her hand to, but father had no interest in anything. He didn't read anything but the newspaper. He wasn't even interested in the ballgames. He puttered around the house all the time, and noise made Evans uneasy.

Evans talked about his mother. She had died when she was away from home on a visit to relatives. She was taken with some kind of attack while she was riding on a train. She was taken off the train at a distant city and placed in a hospital where soon after she died all alone. His mother spent her life taking care of him and she had no one to take care of her when she needed it. He always gave his mother his money and she helped him to build a good bank account. He wasn't interested in girls very much, though there was one in the choir that he liked to look at. When she came down the aisle in the processional he felt weak all over and wanted to get up and run out of the church. But he never went out with her. He just liked to look at her. His mother had never encouraged him to go with girls. She had understood him and shielded him from his father, who never really knew how he felt.

Evans talked about home. He said that the doctor had told him he must get away from home, but that somehow he couldn't leave it. His father always rubbed him the wrong way, but if he went away from home he didn't feel safe until he got back there again. Perhaps if he got married and had a home of his own he would be all right again. Did I think he needed to get married? He often wondered about it but then he was never sure.

His doctor had tried to arrange for him to go to a veterans' rest camp in the mountains where he would get a two months' rest with good recreation, fine food, and good psychiatric care. But he would have to travel four hundred miles on a train and that would make him sick. He couldn't stand the thought of riding on a train. Then he would have to be away from home and with a lot of strange people. Did I think that would be good for him? Perhaps they were people who did things he wouldn't want to do. That would not be good for him. Even to come a few miles to see me he had to have his father with him. But his father didn't understand him. It was just because the doctor told his father to be very kind to him that he was doing it.

The personality picture that Evans revealed was one of severe disturbance due to the reaction of acute grief. His dependence upon his mother had been so great that though he was thirty-five years old chronologically, he was still a little boy at heart. Because she had been so dominant he had never dared to make his own decisions. His army experience was uneventful, for the army became his temporary mother. Now that she was gone he had deep resentments against her for dying and leaving him unprotected against his father's ridicule in his own home. He wanted to get away but he did not dare to try.

Evans had invested so much of his emotional capital in his mother that his life was bankrupt when she was gone. He tried to carry on for a while but it was too much for him. Though he could not remember any expressions of grief at her death, he did remember that he was sort of numb and unable to say or think very much. As the numbness wore off he was aware of a problem so large that he was unequipped to handle it. He was so closely identified with his mother that anything that might have symbolized death brought an acute physical reaction within himself, so that he had to avoid subways and vaults. But at home he was nearest to the place where the sheltering love and protection of his mother could be felt. Here, if it was quiet and the shades were drawn, he could sit down in peace and feel that he was safe again.

But this was an illusion. Evans knew it was an illusion and he wanted help to get beyond it. But the problems involved were not the kind that could be easily or quickly handled. His grief situation had set in motion a variety of deep emotional forces in his being that called for a skilled and specially trained psychotherapist. The abnormal condition that had been implicit for years had now been made explicit. When he came to a pastor for help, the best help he could get was an arrangement for the type of skilled treatment his sorely disturbed personality needed.

4. An Evaluation of Roles in Dealing with the Grief-stricken

These three cases of acute grief show different ways in which the personality can react under stress. Also they indicate something of the pattern of behavior that can be quite obvious to the trained observer. Anyone as closely related as the pastor to the problems of the grief-stricken would want to be trained to observe those attitudes which indicate potential danger to the personality. First, it should be rather clear in the mind of the pastor or other interested person just what he would want to do in assisting the mourning person.

Erich Lindemann has defined that purpose rather simply as an effort "to steer him through the disturbing period of intense emotional upheaval which ensued during the subsequent weeks" after the bereavement experience.[2] When the pastor is involved in the case at the time of bereavement, he can be most useful by persuading the persons involved to yield constructively to the process of mourning. This involves an acceptance of the discomfort caused by looking realistically at the loss. It seeks to get the mourner to participate actively in the work of mourning instead of trying to escape it or deny it. Mrs. Easton was able to engage in the painful adjustment to reality because in the first place she was an essentially healthy personality, but also because she had been prepared by a wise and realistic husband, and was encouraged to actively work through her feelings by a pastor who accepted them for what they were and encouraged a normal expression of what she felt. Mr. K. was not able to bring himself to face his grief. Personality problems that had been kept under control in the past were revealed by the grief reaction, and to this day he is suffering from a disorganization of his whole pattern of living. Evans B. has suffered a serious disintegration of his personality because of psychological processes at work to deny the basic reality of his loss. While he has been able to incorporate his love object with himself in one sense, he has not been able to do it without a great cost to the health of his personality. It is possible that the process of mourning can be carried through even at this late date with the help of a specially trained therapist, but it will be a slow and costly process.

The grieving period can be delayed but it cannot be postponed indefinitely, for it will be carried on directly or indirectly. If it is not done directly at the time of loss it will be done later at a much greater cost to the total personality.

The pastor is probably more involved in dealing with the emotions of bereaved persons than is any other member of society. He has a professional responsibility for observing carefully the reactions of the bereaved. He has a need to be alert to the danger signals that may be flashed by a disturbed personality. He needs to know the processes by which he can be useful in helping to stimulate the normal healthy processes of mourning work. He needs to use the strategic position his professional status affords him to protect his people against the injurious aftereffects of sorrow and loss. He can help his people to readjust to their loss and reinvest their emotional capital where it can produce satisfactory fruit.

While acute grief is a normal neurotic reaction to distressing circumstances, there are deeper aspects of the personality involved. When grief precipitates these deeper reactions the pastor should be the first to sense the problem and quick to make available, directly or indirectly, the help that can restore the person to personal adequacy. This calls for some personal competence on the part of the pastor in evaluating what is normal, abnormal, or serious as far as grief reaction is concerned. The next three chapters will deal with a more detailed examination of the characteristics of the three levels of grief response.

Grief is one of the most deeply disturbing emotional states a human may endure. To relieve the pain, to ease the misery, is a responsibility and privilege not to be taken lightly. To grow in competence in meeting the needs of the sorrowful is certainly one of the major tasks of the parish minister.

Resolving Normal Grief Situations

Most grief situations are normal. The great majority of persons meet the crisis situations of life with enough strength of personality and momentum to go through them with a capacity they did not know they possessed. How often persons say,"I don't know where I got the strength to go through this but each day seemed to take care of itself." Often persons can meet some of the larger crises of life with more adequacy than they can the simpler day-to-day problems.

1. The Minister's Attitude Toward Grief

The minister, as the person designated by society to deal with the needs of the bereaved, should be aware of the importance of his function. It is not something to be treated casually or in a remote and formal manner. He has a chance to engage the personalities of the grief-stricken in the constructive work of mourning, and he is guilty of professional negligence if he fails to do wisely and well what he is called upon to do.

Sometimes matters of personal inadequacy interfere with the minister's work. One minister refused to make hospital calls because he had such severe emotional reactions to the sights and smells of a hospital. He needed treatment for his disturbed emotions. Another found it so difficult to conduct his ministry to the bereaved that he avoided the home of the mourners, made his arrangement by phone, arrived at the appointed place at the last minute, and read a short, formal, ritualistic service, hastening away as quickly as possible. Even then he was trembling with the emotional exertion involved. He, too, was in need of help in meeting his problem.

Fortunately most ministers are not so obsessed. They are able to participate in the healing relationship their profession places upon them. However, often from lack of knowledge of what is taking place in the emotions of the bereaved, they say and do things that make the work of mourning more difficult and delay the normal processes of withdrawing the ego investment, and placing the emotional capital elsewhere. Using the mood of a familiar poem, they are likely to say in a variety of ways, "He is not dead; he is just away." At other times they may call the most gruesome tragedies the "expression of God's will," and in so doing destroy the basis of any sustaining faith that the individual may carry with him into the tragic circumstance.

If the minister is to be aware of his function as a skilled assistant in helping his people to do effectively the work of mourning, he will want to know what to do and what not to do in dealing with normal grief.

2. Symptoms of Normal Grief

Here the studies of recent years can be specifically helpful, and perhaps none more so than those conducted by Erich Lindemann, of Harvard Medical School. Speaking on the basis of his studies that revealed primarily the reactions of persons bereaved not by slow illness but by tragic accident, he points out that the following symptoms are present in normal grief. There are somatic disturbances, lasting from twenty minutes to an hour. This includes tightness of the throat, choking and shortness of breath, need for sighing, an empty feeling in the abdomen, lack of power in the muscles, chills, tremors, and intense subjective distress described as tension, loneliness, or mental pain. These feelings are usually precipitated by mention of the deceased or by receiving sympathy from visitors. This leads persons to avoid the stimulating factors of their distress, to avoid visitors, to keep the deceased out of their thoughts by diverting action. Not all of these symptoms will occur in all persons, but if and when they do, they are well within the range of the normal. This leads to the following conclusions by Lindemann:

1. Acute grief is a definite syndrome with psychological and somatic symptomatology.

146

2. It may appear at once, or be delayed, exaggerated, or apparently absent.
3. It may involve distortions that are variations of conclusion 2.
4. It is possible to restore the abnormal to the normal through a therapeutic process.

Other characteristics of the emotion of normal grief are feelings of weakness and tiredness. Things feel too heavy, food tastes like sand, saliva won't flow, events seem unreal, the sense response seems disorganized and undependable, and there is fear of loss of sanity. This may be aggravated by irritability, a feeling of hostility that bothers the grief-stricken, a desire to talk considerably and about the bereaved, as well as a restlessness that seems to keep going through motions with no zest or meaning. The person seems to have lost a capacity to initiate actions, has little ability to organize activity, and takes three times as long to do anything as was normally the case.

3. What Grief Work Accomplishes

These symptoms give a picture of a personality that has gone through severe emotional shock and is slowly readjusting itself to a new reality. Someone has called the work of normal grief "the illness that heals itself." When that is the case it is pain with a purpose. Concerning the process Edoardo Weiss writes:

This slow transformation is accomplished by means of a number of changes . . . by which the mourner is forced gradually to renounce his longing for the lost person and to accept the real world without the loved one. In severe grief, this renunciation requires emotional reorientation to all details of the world of reality. At first, unable to bear even the thought of the every day occupations and activities that he associates with the lost person, the grief-stricken survivor must concentrate on every object and situation carrying the association until he can accept it emotionally without reawakening his longing.[1]

Speaking further of what is taking place in the personality of the mourner, Weiss adds:

✓ Confronted with such a loss, the mourner is torn between an uncontrollable desire for the loved one and a recognition of the fact that the loved person no longer exists: and his grief is an expression of the conflict between the inner world of needs, instincts, and drives and the outer world of reality. Desires and "investment of interests" come from urges and instinctive drives belonging to a broad, obscure area of our human personality which we cannot control at will: it is precisely because these forces cannot be easily mastered that grief follows loss. With time, however, the individual usually succeeds in giving up his longing for the deceased person and respect for reality gains the upper hand.[2]

Speaking of the responsibility of the medical specialist in dealing with the grief syndrome, Lindemann says:

Proper psychiatric management of grief reactions may prevent prolonged and serious alterations in the patient's social adjustment, as well as potential medical disease. The essential task facing the psychiatrist is that of sharing the patient's grief work, namely, his efforts at extricating himself from the bondage to the deceased and at finding new patterns of rewarding interaction.[3]

Speaking of the importance of observing the emotional state of the mourner, he continues:

It is of the greatest importance to notice that not only over-reaction but under-reaction of the bereaved must be given attention, because delayed responses may occur at unpredictable moments and the dangerous distortions of the grief reaction, not conspicuous at first, be quite destructive later and these may be prevented.[4]

4. The Pastor's Role in Normal Grief Situations

Then of special interest to the minister in relation to his role with the bereaved, Lindemann speaks of the part religious counselors have usually played and the larger and more important role that may be filled by those who are alert and qualified:

Religious agencies have led in dealing with the bereaved. They have provided comfort by giving the backing of dogma to the patient's wish for continued interaction with the deceased, have developed rituals which maintain the patient's interaction with others, and have counteracted the morbid guilt feelings of the patient by Divine Grace and by promising an opportunity for "making up" to the deceased at the time of a later reunion. While these measures have helped countless mourners, comfort alone does not provide adequate assistance in the patient's grief work. He has accepted the pain of the bereavement. He has to review his relationships with the deceased, and has to become acquainted with the alterations in his own modes of emotional reaction. His fear of insanity, his fear of accepting the surprising changes in his feelings, especially the overflow of hostility, have to be worked through. . . . He will have to find an acceptable formulation of his future relationship to the deceased. He will have to verbalize his feelings of guilt, and he will have to find persons around him whom he can use as "primers" for the acquisition of new patterns of conduct.[5]

It is clearly evident that the pastor's work does not end with the funeral, but that he must engage himself in the process of a pastoral relationship that will help the bereaved to accomplish the adjustments that are necessary to restore him to a right relationship with himself and with others.

Perhaps it would be helpful, now that we have looked carefully at the symptoms of normal grief, to look at two cases of normal grief as they were met and worked through by normal individuals with pastoral assistance. They follow somewhat the same pattern as that of the case of Mrs. Easton, outlined in the preceding chapter. They share the characteristics of many of the grief conditions that the pastor will meet in his parish work.

5. Illustrations of Normal Grief

W. H. was sixty-two, a deeply religious individual who had been both church-school superintendent and a teacher in the high school for many years. He was well loved, well read, deeply rooted in the classics, and had a good working knowledge of psychology. When his wife of thirty-five years died rather suddenly of an acute kidney infection, he was deeply grieved. I arrived at the home shortly after she expired and found him sobbing inconsolably. Little was said during the hour or so that I stayed with

149

him, but he was appreciative and profusely thankful. The next day he was still quickly brought to tears by mention of his wife, and yet he talked about her in superlative terms for quite some time. He described the conditions that led up to her death, and the activities of the days just preceding it. He told with pleasure of the things they had done together. He talked of her religious faith and of the strength he was finding in his. He talked of the fine things she had done for other people through the years and seemed to find real satisfaction in having an appreciative hearing. He talked freely about the funeral service and about her wishes concerning it. Every once in a while he would stop for a few moments and sob as if his feelings could not be controlled. When he stopped he would almost apologize by saying, "It's not that I don't have faith, or that I am fearful of her welfare. I just can't get used to the idea of her being gone."

He proceeded normally through the mourning work, with most of the symptoms. After about two weeks he came to me and asked: "Do you think it would be wrong for me to take a trip so soon after Ella's death? We had planned to take a trip to England and on up into Scotland to visit relatives and I want to do it just as we had planned." I encouraged him to do what he felt impelled to do and indicated that he should feel no guilt for doing what he felt was important. He went and enjoyed the trip. He said he felt it was important for him to complete this bit of unfinished business they had planned together. He said that many times during the trip he felt so conscious of his wife's presence that he caught himself speaking to her. When he returned home he returned to his work with cheerfulness and a renewed sense of sympathy for others.

This case illustrates how important it is in the work of mourning to carry through some symbolic activity that brings to a clear reality the nature of the completed life. Here the symbolism was unusually clear, for it was a matter of completing together the journey that had been planned. By the time the journey was completed the work of mourning was done, and the business of the rest of life could be faced and accepted. The sustaining fact of religious faith, coupled with an ability to give free expression to the emotions, made it possible to find a completely satisfactory adjustment in a short period of time.

But looking at W. H.'s situation, we find several things to be noted. The pastor felt that W. H. was engaging his emotions in a healthy fashion from the beginning; otherwise, the pastor would have been cautious about his taking a trip so soon after. Often, trying to get away is a danger signal, if the emotional response has not been normal. It may indicate an effort to escape the work of mourning. Long acquaintance with W.H. gave the pastor confidence in his secure and mature ego structure, strong positive ties with reality, and practically no feelings of guilt. He did not need active guidance, and the pastor's role was largely that of being present to listen as the normal feelings were expressed. When there was a question concerning the trip, all indications were that it was a healthy action; and then the pastor's role was acceptance of the idea and what little reassurance was needed to make it entirely satisfying. When there is no distortion of reality, no unusual withdrawal, and a normal expression of feelings, the pastor can feel quite sure that the bereaved will work through the loss satisfactorily.

The second case indicates something of the emotional tone that exists in rural sections where the facts of life and death are more specifically a part of everyday experience. In the large cities elaborate efforts are made to protect persons against even the more normal evidences of death. Most dying is done in hospitals, and few have contact with it. In rural areas this elaborate pattern does not exist.

Our mountain retreat in Vermont is located many miles from a village. In the summertime even the village may be without a pastor. One summer afternoon a neighbor from a farm two miles down the road drove up the winding road to our hilltop haven. We could hear his small truck long before we could see it. When he came into sight I went to greet him. He got out and, with simple directness, said, "My wife has died and I came up to see if you could help me out by saying a service over her." I said, "Dan, you know I will." Realizing that he did not want to see anyone else, I did not ask him into the house but suggested that we go up on the brow of the hill and sit down on some rocks there. We did, and looked down a peaceful valley toward the White Mountains fifty or more miles away. We sat there for fifteen or twenty minutes saying nothing. The clouds moved slowly overhead and on a distant farm we could see men and horses at work in a hayfield. We were close to eternal things and words seemed unnecessary. Finally Dan said: "She had a cancer. We did all we could. We couldn't do much. She was a good woman. She was a good wife. She was a good mother. We did everything together. She drove the tractor when we hayed. She won't do it no more." It took Dan about ten minutes to say those few words. There were long pauses between the sentences. He wiped tears from his eyes. His big brown hands were steady. His clear blue eyes had a distant look in them. We sat again for a long time and he watched the light and shadows on the distant hills as if they meant something to him. Then he stood up slowly, shook my hand for a long time, and as he walked toward his truck he said, "Service is day after tomorrow at 2:00 in the church."

The little church was filled with friends and neighbors. The front pews were reserved for the family. At the appointed hour the organist began the Chopin funeral march and the family, in slow and mournful tread, acted out their grief in the symbolic march by which they took their places. After the service they went to another hilltop for the burial. There were tears, but no fuss. There was a feeling of closeness to elemental things. The grave digger leaned on his shovel close by during the committal service. He was one with the group of mourners. When it was over he spoke to me in friendly fashion: "She was a fine woman. Too bad. I've got lots of friends here now. Guess more here than down in the village. I'll be here myself before long."

When I stopped at the farm a few days later, Dan was out in the field. "Got to get this hay in," he said. We talked about his wife and the children. He was making his plans slowly and with a clear sense of reality. He suffered the pains of grief but he was working through them wisely and well. Now, two years later, he is adjusted to the demands of life. The children are able to assume responsibility. The problems of bereavement were met squarely, with reality, for there was nothing artificial about his approach to life or death.

6. The Importance of Ritualized Expressions

Many of the traditional practices that surround the funeral have a useful purpose as far as the emotions are concerned even though they may seem odd at first examination. There is often a folk wisdom that has been accumulated through the years which is psychologically sound as it speaks to the preconscious and unconscious levels of the being. Often the effect is to encourage the mourners to express their feelings, and the paid mourners of the past were certainly capable of creating a mood for contagious emotional expression. The long vigils and the public displays had their place in exteriorizing the feeling that might otherwise have been repressed.

Military funerals have their own special rituals. The caisson is symbolic of the last lonely ride; the firing of the volley illustrates the energy that is spent and gone; and the playing of taps marks the ending of the day of life. The military does not encourage emotional displays, but each part of the military service urges the facing of stark reality.

An interesting custom has been prevalent in New Orleans. After days of intense and visible emotional displays of mourning, the family returns from the cemetery with the stirring music of a brass band playing lively tunes to which the mourners dance and sing. Symbolically the mourning is left behind at the grave, and the future is faced with a song.

7. Three Recommendations to Pastors

The pastor's role as counselor is clearly defined. He is assigned the role by the community of bringing comfort wisely, both for the immediate situation and the longer period of life. Lindemann suggests that there are three things which can be done by a pastor, chaplain, or counselor. These have been found to be specifically useful through the period of acute grief.

First is the maintenance of contact. When one discerning and competent individual keeps an active contact with the person through the important first days, confusion is cut down, a sustained communication with a trusted individual is made possible, emotional stress is relieved, and a measure of emotional security in a framework of unstable things is guaranteed. This person should be able to communicate full information concerning physical matters to the bereaved, so that the reality relationship will be sustained and at the same time the confidence in the counselor made secure.

Second, this counselor should be able to deliver messages that are important to the bereaved so that they can be interpreted and related to other events that are happening. Then he can help the grieving person to deal with his problems wisely. The counselor should not do for him what he can do for himself, but he should help the person do what he can and then relieve the stress where it appears to be too taxing.

Third, as opportunity affords and if necessary when opportunity is made, the counselor should help the person to face the reality of his situation and to think through the deeper meanings of his new responsibilities, his new relationships, and the new problems of adjustment. He should be the backboard against which the mourner can work out his new thoughts and feelings. He should not hurry the person at a speed faster than he can move, nor should he allow the person so to obstruct the process that he will avoid facing the facts of his new life as they must be faced.

8. The Place for Weeping

The counselor should be quick to accept the feelings of the mourner, and should encourage the expression of feelings. It is at this point that an understanding of the function of tears is important. It serves little purpose to try to prevent the use of nature's own safety valves. Of course, there is such a thing as pathological weeping, but it is not likely to be the case at the time of real loss. "The consoling effect of quiet tears suggests an influence as comforting and soothing as the soft flow of the tears." [6] Tears, warm and wet, are soothing in and of themselves and symbolically can serve to wash away the irritants of life. It is the sorrow that is too great to bear that becomes the source of dry-eyed grief. It would be wise for the counselor who is afraid of the flow of tears in himself or others to read carefully the words of Heilbrunn as they interpret the function of the soothing tear:

Under ordinary circumstances the lacrimal glands produce little secretion. . . . Increased secretion occurs promptly however in response to physical stimulation of the eyeball or its immediate surroundings, this response serving to remove the disturbing stimulus as quickly as possible. Pain anywhere in the body may also cause lacrimation, as if the flood of tears could magically wash away even the most distant irritants. Lacrimal discharge caused by emotional pain serves a similar purpose, riddance of the foreign body, so to speak, and maintenance of psychological homeostasis, as suggested by Petö. . . . Whenever stimuli of grief, disappointment, anger, or "overwhelming" joy exceed the tolerance of the organism, the ensuing state of tension is alleviated by a release of energy from various organs or organ systems which abolishes the tension. The shedding of tears furthers the homeostatic principle so well that it is the favorite mechanism of release during childhood. Probably it would so continue throughout life were it not suppressed by the demand of society for emotional restraint and replaced by other modes of discharge.[7]

9. What Not to Do

Just as there are some things it is important to do, there are other things that it is just as important not to do. For instance, there seems to have developed a practice in many of our communities to call the doctor immediately to prescribe sedatives for the grief-stricken. This practice seems to show a lack of awareness of the importance of the work of mourning and the value of having it begun in earnest as soon as possible. The longer it is delayed, the more difficult it is to do it effectively. Paul Hoch, mental health commissioner for the state of New York, has written that the use of sedatives involves the "strategy of knocking out the anxiety-mediating neural mechanisms. . . . It can be rightly pointed out that these measures are not psychotherapy." [8] This almost certainly constitutes a mistaken effort to spare the personality stress, for the work of normal mourning is helpful to the health of the personality rather than injurious as some seem to think. Any reasonable influence than can be used to prevent the postponement of the work of mourning by the use of sedatives should be exerted.

The same thing should be said for the words that pastors often use which serve the same purpose as sedation and are presented for the same purpose. How often words that are clearly designed to warp the reality sense of the mourner are passed off glibly at the time of bereavement! It would be clearly advantageous to the mourner in many instances for the religious counselor to keep his words at a minimum. The time of acute grief is hardly the occasion for a lesson in abstract theology. This may well come with time, and it is important that a person grow in his philosophy of life to the point where he can tolerate stress; but his important immediate need is to face the reality of his loss rather than escape it in vapid words. This would be true for words spoken at a formal service as well as those given in informal counsel. The attitudes that play fast and loose with our best knowledge of the structure of the universe are poor aids to a strengthened reality sense. Though many would follow the poet's impulse to take the world apart and rebuild it "closer to the heart's desire," the wish does not make the reality, and the wishful thinking of the unrealistic counselor does not make the work of the mourner easier.

For several reasons the counselor's task with the bereaved may be more difficult than the usual counseling situation. The circumstance of the counseling itself is not easily controlled by the counselor. It may take place in a hospital waiting room, in a car traveling to a cemetery, in a home involving interruptions and distractions. If there is evidence of a considerable condition of shock, the surroundings probably make little difference, and the actual engaging of the mind and emotions may be postponed until conditions are more satisfactory. But even in unorthodox conditions, the healing communication may be carried on. If arrangements could be made, it would be best to have the bereaved come to the pastor's counseling room, where circumstances can be controlled more easily and problems related to adjustment can be considered in a more neutral atmosphere.

10. Nine Areas of Concern

Probably no more adequate guide for the counselor has been laid down than that of Lindemann, who suggests the areas that may well be considered in the process of such counseling. Lindemann shows that the concerns of the person involved in a normal grief reaction may fall into nine categories. No one person would show a concern at all nine points, but any normal person might have one or more of these problems. Perhaps a word of caution ought to be added, for such a list is not designed to stimulate questioning at any one of these points, but to give a clue to the counselor as to what is to be expected. The counselor would be cautious about starting the discussion at any of these points. Usually the initiative would come from the counselee. These are areas of concern that could legitimately be considered: (1) There may be the problem of the acceptance of the pain of bereavement. This could be raised in such a simple statement and question as, "I feel so awful inside. How long does this feeling last?" It would suffice here for the counselor to imply that such discomfort is natural and not indefinite. (2) The bereaved may want to review the relationships with the deceased. Just talking about these relationships with someone who listens sympathetically is usually adequate. (3) The grieving person may want to talk about his own feelings and how they have changed. (4) Sometimes persons have feelings that they have not had before and consequently may think they are losing their minds. To say that as long as they can think that way they certainly are not—should carry them through that phase of their concern. (5) The bereaved may want to talk about what he is doing to deal with his changed feelings, and in so doing get a clearer picture of what he can do. (6) He may want to consider the reasons for hostility that is new and different and perhaps baffling. (7) He may want to discuss how he should think and feel about the deceased in the time ahead. (8) He may want to verbalize his feelings of guilt. The fact that he has them is no basis for trying to re-enforce them. The counselor accepts but does not amplify. (9) He may want to do some verbal experimenting about new modes of living and with relations to new persons, and the fact that he has a trusted and sympathetic listener may make it easier for him to move from verbalization to action on the basis of his expressed thoughts. Such things can be done legitimately within the framework of pastoral counseling. In most communities, if it is not done there it may not be done at all. But clearly, such a list should never be used as a rubric to be followed in prodding the bereaved. At best it is a clue to what might be normally encountered in such counseling.

11. The Pastor's Personal Role

The period of mourning is a time when a person may temporarily assume a measure of dependency toward another person. The pastor, because of his involvement in the matter professionally, may well become the right and proper person toward whom the bereaved holds such an attitude. The pastor, however, must be wise to know when it is a useful relationship and when it ceases to have usefulness. Unless there are factors of an abnormal nature involved, the usefulness of a dependent attitude should be satisfied by the end of a month, and the pastor should then gradually withdraw himself and place the counselee more and more on his own. No rule of thumb works in such matters, and the pastor would have to evaluate the circumstances, his own approach, the needs of the counselee, and the quality of relationship that has existed both before the bereavement and after it.

There can be a danger in another direction in establishing a relationship with a bereaved person that is proving to be helpful, only to have it abruptly terminated as the pastor becomes related to others who are in the more active stage of their grief. Persons are likely to be sensitive to slight at such times, and too rapid a withdrawal of interest may be misinterpreted. The bereaved have a tendency toward hostility, and this may express itself toward the pastor if he makes a number of calls in two or three weeks and then suddenly "folds his tent like the Arabs" and, as far as the mourner is concerned, "silently steals away." The withdrawal, in most instances, should be done gradually and with such explanation as is required to have it understood and accepted.

One of the important factors of the pastor's work is that of encouraging effective group relationships. As the problems of grief are essentially social problems, so the solutions to the problems involve social relationships. The normal life of the church includes a variety of group activities which may well serve the needs of the person who is emerging from a period of mourning.

12. The Pastor's Institutional Role

Some effective group relationship is important in the working through of grief. Yet it is also the group that may stand in the way of the defenses which people have built. For instance, the church service reminds persons of values, of guilt, and of the relationships that have been broken. People may withdraw from the church to protect themselves from the memories they cannot cope with. It may be that they are employing unhealthy devices to avoid the implications of their grief, and the church is the only place where their defenses do not work. It is important then that their relation to the church be maintained, in order that this place where they can deal with their guilt and do the work of mourning may continue to be available to them.

The J.'s were quite irregular in church attendance after the death of their daughter, who had been a faithful member of the choir. Mr. J. was a research scientist, and both he and his wife were so reasoned in their actions and attitudes that there seemed little place for emotion in their lives. They did not appear to have any difficulty in adjusting to the loss of their daughter. Outwardly, at least, they went on about their living and faced their responsibilities toward their other children. On one of his visits to the family, the pastor mentioned that he had missed seeing them at church. He was alerted by their response: "It brings back too many memories and upsets us. When the choir sings we get lumps in our throats and tears in our eyes, and we just feel it is better to stay away if we can't control our feelings."

This led to a discussion of the importance of feelings, the significance they play in life, and the dangers that exist when feelings are denied. Like many who are skilled in the mechanical sciences, they showed a lack of insight into the functioning of their emotions. Too often the engineer feels that human beings can be manipulated according to the amount of stress or pressure that can be brought to bear. When some of these matters were discussed freely, it was possible for Mr. and Mrs. J. to take a different view of what went on when they came to church. They were assured that their grief was nothing to be ashamed of, and that everyone else in the church either had had or would have an experience of loss that would affect them similarly. They found a new sense of relationship with the congregation, for they learned to see them, not as a group who suspected their feelings, but rather as friends who shared them. They returned to church, and for a while sat in the rear of the sanctuary, but then they resumed their accustomed place when they had worked through their emotions. They found a release in church that they were not able to find elsewhere, and this ability to find a release undoubtedly made it possible for them to so adjust their emotions to the reality of life and death that they were not obliged to go through the less fortunate experience of illness and undesirable personality modification.

13. An Evaluation of the Pastoral Function

An alert pastor can often help to restore persons to right relations so that their feelings may find a normal and healthy expression in an atmosphere where they can be understood and accepted.

The pastor is not only a counselor with psychological understanding and a concern for the welfare of his parishioners' souls, but he is also the custodian of a philosophy of life and a concept of the universe that can replace despair with hope, fearfulness with faith, and guilt with a feeling of forgiveness. These are important functions not to be overlooked in the specific ministry to the grief-stricken. This is not only attested by the experience of many ministers and their people through the years but is recognized as a legitimate function by psychotherapists in the medical discipline. It may be well to close this chapter, in which we have leaned heavily on the advice and counsel of psychiatrists, with three statements that pay a degree of recognition to that special area of competence that has been and continues to be the field of the pastor.

Edoardo Weiss makes clearer, in these words, the role that may be played by a wise pastor in his symbolization of a sustaining faith as a resource to help control the excessive stimulation of acute grief:

When, deprived of the satisfaction of a strong need, an individual loses control over the frustrated urge or desire, he also reacts with anxiety. A child who is abandoned by his mother cannot master his unsatisfied longing for her and is traumatized. The news of the loss of a love object, the shattering of a faith on which one's integrated existence rests, are traumatic excitations which challenge all of the defenses of the ego. When one is able to control the excessive stimulation resulting from such losses, the "mourning work" solves the problem of integration.[9]

The role of the pastoral counselor is further related to the healing process as the mediator of the means of mastery of his grief.

French has pointed out that the continued hope of the individual that he will find a solution for his problem, a means of escape from his trauma, is an important factor in making it possible for him to bind the excessive excitations until means are found for mastery.[10]

It is the function of the pastor to fulfill the sustaining role at the same time that he is alert to those whose disturbance calls for the treatment of a specialist. Lindemann makes this explicit in these words: "Ministers will have to be on the look-out for the more ominous pictures, referring these to the psychiatrist while assisting the more normal reactions themselves." [11]

Now, in the two chapters that follow, let us turn our attention to the more disturbed grief reactions.

ELEVEN

Resolving Abnormal Grief Situations

Probably no more accurate picture of what takes place in abnormal grief has been phrased than in the lines of Macbeth:

> So from that spring whence comfort seem'd to come
> Discomfort swells.[1]

For as Macbeth later observes, "False face must hide what the false heart doth know." [2]

1. The Nature of Abnormal Grief

Abnormal grief reveals emotional conditions that might otherwise have been unobserved. Such grief releases feelings that might otherwise have been controlled. In fact, feelings that the person never knew he had, for they were so deeply buried in lower levels of consciousness, come boiling to the surface to disrupt and disorganize living. This "peculiarly painful and despairing quality of feeling both in grief and mourning" [3] becomes disruptive of life. Weiss describes the neurotic pattern of grief response as follows:

> Mastery is impossible when a state of grief . . . becomes so overwhelming that one loses contact with reality, becomes unable to care for one's own needs or fails to give proper consideration to the requirements of others. In extreme cases of this kind, the individual may have a sense of "distintegration"; the feeling that he is losing his mind.[4]

This type of disrupting grief is likely to grow in persons who have never had a good object relation. It indicates a person who has limited security in the inner world of his being. Often it involves a reversion to an earlier emotional state wherein there were feelings of unreasonable "badness" as a result of unresolved

162

feelings of guilt produced by infantile aggressiveness. The desire to resolve such feelings may have made the individual over-anxious to placate others. Though rooted in lower levels of consciousness, they may appear under stress, and direct the feelings of the person toward emotional goals not directly related to the grief itself. Then they stand helpless before their grief, and even from the springs whence comfort would normally be expected, discomfort swells.

The more extreme forms of this abnormality will be dealt with in Chapter XII. Here we would take into account the factors that can disorganize life and disrupt effective living without bringing a person to the point where he is incapable of carrying on the major aspects of life. They are usually the results of "manoeuvres adopted by the human organism to deal with the unbearable pain of loss." [5] While the maneuvers may be effective for their specific and limited purpose, they are made at too great a cost to the total personality, and health requires that a balance in the economy of the personality be restored.

2. How Abnormal Grief Is Manifest

Sometimes the abnormality shows up first as a physical ailment. Lindemann's interest in the effect of grief on life was initiated by a study of ulcerative colitis, which revealed that a major portion of the patients had been bereaved a few months prior to the onset of their physical symptom. Wilhelm Stekel, in his book *Conditions of Nervous Anxiety and Their Treatment,*[6] says that anxiety may be manifest through cardiac phenomena, chest pains, upper respiratory disturbances, nausea, vomiting, congestion, fainting, vertigo, trembling, shivering, convulsions, disturbance of the menses, cramps, tics, and pains, as well as sleeplessness. The anxiety-producing aspects of abnormal grief account for the presence of many of the same symptoms in the person whose bereavement has loosed deep emotional factors that he cannot control but which seem to be controlling him.

Clues as to what is going on in the mind of the person suffering from abnormal grief may be found in their dreams. One hesitates to mention the subject of dreams in such a study as this. So many persons are reading books such as *The Forgotten Language* by Erich Fromm, *The Meaning of Dreams* by Calvin S. Hall, and *The Handbook of Dream Analysis* by Emil A. Gutheil, as well as Freud's writings on the subject, that it seems a word of warning should be sounded concerning the use of such material by the pastoral counselor. It takes real strength to listen to the . recounting of a dream and not try to interpret it, especially if the interpretation seems clear and obvious. The insecure counselor feels he needs to interpret in order to reveal his competence. It is the experienced counselor who does not feel that he has to prove himself by entering into fields that are not legitimately his. While the insight that may be revealed may be used, certain safeguards should be employed.

Anderson points out that insight into the roots of the abnormal behavior may be gained from dream material. For instance, he tells of a man whose wife had been killed in an air raid in London. The couple had been married for twenty years and had four children, and to all appearance had a good relationship. However, the man was disorganized by strong guilt feelings subsequent to his wife's death. He became seriously disturbed and his dreams gave a clue to his problem. He had numerous dreams of the nightmare type, filled with aggressive action. These dreams revealed a large amount of suppressed aggression in his marriage relationship. As he progressed in treatment and his aggressive feelings were released, his dream content changed, and when his dreams were quite normal he was considered to be well again.

Anderson points out that dreams are never furious or ferocious when a good and adult relationship exists. Bad dreams are an indication of bad relationships.

The dreams of mourning subjects can be divided arbitrarily into two great categories. In one group, the dead object (dead only in reality) appears injured or injuring, persecuted or persecuting, wearing the garb of death, disease or injury, and is bent upon the destruction of the dreamer; or the dreamer is performing the most horrifying actions against the already injured object. In the other group, however, the dead person is alive once more, whole and well and once again past and happy experiences are being re-enacted.[7]

So the type of dream may be a simple but accurate clue to the deep emotional state of the bereaved person, and the knowledge that it makes available may become useful to the counselor in understanding the source of the abnormal reaction.

In general practice the counselor does not raise the question of dreams. If it is raised he accepts it without interpretation. Though Joseph set a precedent as a dream interpreter, the pastor is wise who does not follow in his footsteps. Dreams are specifically the activity of the preconscious mind, and such material should be left in the hands of a specialist for interpretation. However, the pastor-counselor can listen to the recounting of a dream and use all of his training and insight to see more deeply into the nature of the disturbance. He can even use the dream as a basis for helping the person to gain increased insight into himself with no effort at interpretation. For instance, he can limit himself to this type of question, "And what did the dream mean to you?" If it does suggest anything specific it may be readily available for the process of counseling. If it seems to mean nothing it may be dropped though the counselor's insight may well make note of the subject matter for future reference.

Sometimes the abnormal expression is indicated in a false sense of elation and freedom from responsibility. This hypomanic state is usually operating over a background of depression and guilt that the person refuses to face. The hypomanic elation seems to say paradoxically: "It doesn't matter, it hasn't happened, there is no need to undo what has been done." [8] Usually such a person does not want to talk about himself, may be hostile and suspicious, and will ignore the symptoms of his own abnormal condition. This condition should have the attention of a skilled psychotherapist, for it may easily slip into a depression with more alarming manifestations. While as Fenichel points out, "As to neurotic depression, the mildest cases do not need any special treatment," [9] the average pastor is not in a position to make such fine diagnostic distinctions. It is always better to proceed conservatively when the soul of a suffering parishioner is involved.

Menninger warns, in relation to depressed states, that such

persons cannot be cheered up, jollied, or reasoned with. Here again it is better to say nothing than to say the wrong thing. Worst of all is the advice to take a trip to get away from it all, for the person carries with him into unfamiliar surroundings the very mood that has been darkening his life, and it may make his condition worse rather than better. If no form of skilled therapy is available, the pastor may be able to engage the disturbed person in some form of physical activity such as golf or long walks, for as Menninger points out, "Exercise . . . is of some definite relief to most depressed people. . . . Plain hard work will serve equally well for many." [10]

In some instances the main characteristic of grief is an attitude of hostility. This may be directed against the physician who cared for the person, the funeral director, or the minister who worked with the bereaved. The person toward whom the hostility is shown should not take it as a personal judgment but rather as a symptom of the disturbance. While a certain amount of hostility on a short-term basis is to be expected and may be useful to the personality, excessive and prolonged hostility is a danger signal. Such a person should be brought to the attention of a skilled psychotherapist, for such excessive hostility directed outward may at any time be turned against the self with serious suicidal possibilities.

The various symptoms of abnormal grief reactions are efforts to avoid the distressing emotional demands placed on the individual in the working through of his grief. Sometimes the individual seeks delays from starting the work. Sometimes he hardens himself and becomes unable to relax and let go. Sometimes he shows his feelings by his attitude toward talking about the deceased. He may want to talk about the deceased intemperately or not at all.

3. Illustrations of Abnormal Grief

Lindemann gives some illustrations of abnormal reactions to grief. In one case a man of fifty-two, who had lost his wife to whom he had been happily married, had such a severe reaction

166

that he was unable to cope with the situation. He wanted no visitors. He broke down and was ashamed of it. If his wife's name was mentioned, he was swept by a wave of depressive reactions. He asked to remain in the hospital for aid in working through his problem. He became verbally active, finally faced the painful process of mourning work, and found his health in actively working to help others work through their problems. When he was released he returned to his work and was able to achieve a good recovery.

A seventeen-year-old girl seemed abnormally cheerful and accepted the situation of loss, at least verbally. She left the hospital after ten weeks with the same cheerful attitude. At the Cocoanut Grove fire she had lost both her parents and her boy friend and had shown no appropriate reaction. After her release from the hospital, the long-delayed reaction developed, with deep depression, intestinal emptiness, tightness of the throat, frequent crying, and vivid preoccupation with the deceased parents. It was only then that she started the slow process of working through her delayed grief with the help of skilled psychotherapy.

Another case involved a woman of forty who had lost her husband. She wept steadily for three days, said she didn't want to live, and was depressed. Then she started talking and recalled much of his life and activity. She expressed her love for him and her resentment at his fate. She paid any debt she felt she owed him by an idealization of him. Having gone through this process, she was able to make new relationships and a satisfactory recovery.

Sometimes the reaction may be delayed for years and may be transferred from one grief experience to another. A young man was precipitated into acute grief reactions by the loss of a friend. The grief seemed to be out of proportion to his emotional involvement until it was established that his mother had committed suicide when he was a small child, and that this abnormal reaction in adulthood was the delayed expression of the feelings associated with the loss of his mother.

4. The Clinical Picture of Abnormal Grief

Lindemann lists nine abnormal reactions to grief as follows:

1. Overactivity, with a sense of well-being rather than a feeling of loss.
2. Acquisition of the symptoms of the last illness of the deceased.
3. A medical disease, psychogenic in nature, such as ulcerative colitis.
4. Marked alteration in relationship to friends and relatives.
5. Furious hostility against specific persons.
6. Loss of feelings as if acting out life, not living it.
7. Lasting loss of patterns of social relations, with general listlessness.
8. Behavior detrimental to one's own social and economic existence, such as unreasonable generosity.
9. Agitated moods of depression.

He further indicates that the most frequent psychogenic diseases associated with abnormal grief are asthma, colitis, and rheumatoid arthritis. The more easily observed symptoms of disturbance in the autonomic nervous system are enlarged pupils, sighing respiration, "hot waves" in the head, flushed face, and perspiration.[11]

5. Dynamic Factors in Abnormal Grief

Often the disturbed interpersonal relations of a person are reflected in the circumstances that develop at the time of the death of the person involved in the disturbed relations.

Such was the case with Robert C. a Pfc, who was brought, almost bodily, to the chaplain by some of his friends. He was thin, haggard-looking, grayish in color, trembling as if suffering from a chill, and holding his hands tightly as if to try to check the trembling. He was unable to talk in any coherent manner at first, and his friends explained the situation. After a while the chaplain excused the friends and engaged the afflicted soldier in simple conversation. Starting with such questions as, "When did you begin to feel this way?" and "Have you ever been troubled like this before?" he led him to a discussion of his condition. The day before, Robert C. had received word that his father was dying, and that if he were to see him alive he must seek an

168

emergency leave and come home at once. Almost immediately he began to feel disturbed. He went on sick call and was given a sedative. When it seemed to give no relief, he was urged to see the chaplain. It was ascertained that the soldier did not want to go home. He did not want to see his father alive. During a session in which he became increasingly verbal, the soldier told of a tyrannical and evidently sadistic father who abused and tortured him in subtle and direct ways from the time of his earliest memory. For the slightest infraction of rigid regulation, he was brutally beaten. For years he lived in persistent fear of his father. When he grew older this fear turned to a smoldering hatred which he controlled with difficulty. When he started to earn money his father took it away. When he used some of his wages to buy a suit, his father was enraged and threw the new suit into the furnace before his eyes. As the soldier put it, "Never in my life have I seen my father do a kind thing for me. He seemed all right to my sisters, but to me he was a madman." Finally the soldier could no longer endure life at home and left town to get work in a distant city. He had married but his marriage had not been satisfactory because he said he was always upset and jumpy. After an hour and a half of externalizing a large amount of pent-up emotion, he said he felt relieved, and the tremor subsided. No decisions were made as to his plans, but it was decided that he and the chaplain would meet again the next day to talk about the matter further.

When he returned the next day, Robert C. was still anxious, but the more obvious signs were not present. He recapitulated some of what he had said the day before and remarked that he had been doing a lot of thinking since the last interview. He asked directly, "What do you think was the matter with my father?" Parrying the question, the chaplain said, "Perhaps you would like to try to answer that yourself." The soldier tried at an answer and implied that there must be something abnormal about his father. He didn't know what was the matter but certainly that was no way for a father to treat a son. He said, "He always wanted to make me feel bad." Robert was led to see that it did not seem unreasonable that his present reaction was related to this feeling

169

his father always generated in him. He indicated some insight into his father's mood but continued to express an understandable hostility. He said he felt his father's condition had affected him to such an extent that he was not normal either. Toward the end of the interview there were some tears shed, not in relation to his father's illness but because he felt he had been deprived of something important in his life. Robert's hatred of his father and his feeling of guilt about this hatred were evidently beginning to find some expression which relieved his inner tension. He asked if he could return the next day.

When Robert C. returned the third day he said that he had received a long-distance call from one of his sisters saying that his father had died. He felt that he would like to go home for the funeral and also to see the rest of his family. He told more of the things his father had done to him years before, but ended by saying, "There was surely something wrong with anybody who acted that way." When the chaplain raised the matter of his own feelings at this point, he said significantly that he "was glad his father had been cut off for the sake of the whole family" and that he couldn't really feel sad. He knew that that was wrong but he had to be honest with himself. He returned home for the funeral with mixed feelings but enough insight to help carry him through his ordeal. He agreed to report back when he returned from home.

The chaplain consulted with the psychiatrist when the latter made his weekly visit to the base. The psychiatrist agreed that the soldier probably needed some special help to deal with serious traumatic experiences, and arrangements were made to interview him on the date of the psychiatrist's next visit to the base. Interviews continued for several weeks until the chaplain was transferred and lost contact with the case. The psychiatrist, however, reported that a considerable amount of anxiety existed, so that the soldier would need specialized help before his problem could be worked through. His grief was so subordinated to deep feelings of aggression that it did not appear as grief, but rather as guilt and anxiety with physical reactions. Perhaps no real grief could exist for him.

Often those persons who appear to be too competent in meet-

170

ing life may be susceptible to deep disturbances when they are faced by the death of one close to them. Such was the case with Mrs. LTW.

Mrs. LTW seems to have lived a charmed life. She was the only child of a well-to-do and prominent family in a small upstate New York community. She was possessed of unusual charm, physical beauty, and a high IQ. Her parents were so completely devoted that she had everything she wanted and much that she did not need. As she grew up she was accepted with a good deal of deference in the town. At school her natural ability and her special opportunity combined to give her an unquestioned superiority. She won every honor in her senior year in high school and with an act of ostentatious graciousness turned the prize money over to the runners-up for their further education.

In spite of her unusual position she appeared to remain largely unspoiled. She seemed to accept her superiority as a fact that no one could deny. While she manipulated her parents she did it as a benevolent dictator. While she outstripped her peers she did it with a sympathy and graciousness that enhanced her position. She had a pleasant disposition and never seemed to question her place of omnipotence in her world.

When she went to a small upstate college, competition was a bit more strenuous. but she had the ability and by working harder was able in many respects to duplicate her high-school record. In the senior yearbook she was listed as a campus beauty, an honor student, and a class officer, and in her own mind she accepted this as her right, with proper modesty but with an undisturbed sense of her inner power.

After college she returned home to marry the most eligible young man in the area in the most elaborate wedding the town had had in years. It was a sort of fairy tale, with everyone admitting that she was the most beautiful bride and the one most likely to be happy. She was quite willing to agree with such sentiments, not because she was immodest but because she had unlimited belief in her own adequacy.

Shortly after marriage she assumed a place of social and community leadership. Although she had shown few signs of deep religious feeling, her opinions in the village church were given unusual weight. Her position in community service agencies was secure, and various groups sought her support. With considerable energy she worked for these groups and skillfully avoided the pitfalls of small-town tensions.

When she became a mother it was also in an unusually fortunate way, for everyone was sure her young son was bright and good to look at. The years went by swiftly, and she was a good mother as well as a benevolent force in the community. Then the war came and her son, like the rest, was drafted. For the first time in her life she seemed unable to cope with a situation, but went through the motions of life at least. When word came that her son had been killed in the assault on the Italian peninsula, her world collapsed. With the arrival of the telegram, all of her graciousness and adequacy seemed to depart. She went into seclusion, and the few who saw her said she was "changed and like a different person." She lost interest in her appearance and attire. She lost interest in the community. She became completely disorganized in her grief.

The representative of a religious institution in a neighboring community heard of her condition and began visiting her. In effect, he promised a new sense of omnipotence through an authoritarian church that was the sole representative of God on earth. In her emotional state of regression she was much in need of a feeling of relation to an omnipotence to replace the omnipotent feelings that had been so brutally shattered. Her life, which had been a beautiful but unreal dream, now belatedly had to undergo marked readjustments, and it was easy for her to move in the direction of the emotional forces that were so like the ones she had lost. Her friends and family could not understand how she could adopt a religious system so different from her background. She, however, brought all of her considerable intelligence to bear to give support to her emotional need. She became a devoted patron of her new church, and with a bit of her old spirit became its interpreter to all who came within her sphere of influence.

Every young child goes through a period of omnipotence. He cries and food comes. He cries and every essential need is met.

Most persons reach the point where they are weaned from that idea, but with some persons whose circumstances permit, it becomes the mode of life. Mrs. LTW was such a person. Circumstances conspired to re-enforce her immature emotional feelings of omnipotence. When tragedy finally came it destroyed the house of cards of her emotional life. She was so completely disorganized that she was unable to function, and into the emotional vacuum moved a representative of an authoritarianism she would have found entirely unacceptable before the tragedy, to give her a sustaining relationship to a new and surer omnipotence, one that had the answer even to death.

Such a situation does not often occur because the circumstances to support such an attitude are seldom present. When they are present, in even a modified form, the counselor must realize that the traditional approaches to grief will not work. The person involved is not so much in need of insight or exteriorization as he is in need of a chance to get something solid to cling to during a difficult period of emotional reorientation. In such circumstances the counselor may have to assume an authoritarian role to make explicit the direction in which the person must move in regaining the forward motion of life.

6. Methods of Treatment

The indications and illustrations of the disturbed state that develops with abnormal grief reactions should now be fairly clear. Brewster[12] points out something of the method of treatment that is indicated in such cases. He says that the therapist's effort is directed toward the release of the "emotional tie to the deceased despite the attending discomfort of sorrow and subsequently to replace the type of interaction lost." To him the morbid grief state is a "protracted state of emotional preoccupation and impairment of mental functioning." Two conditions may determine the reason for his difficulty in accomplishing the mourning work: "The grieving person may not be able to accomplish this job because of his inability to tolerate the attending emotional distress or because of his excessive need to maintain interaction with the deceased."

To illustrate his method of treatment, Brewster tells of a Mrs. D., aged twenty-eight, of Italian background, who reported to her doctor a difficulty in breathing and a feeling of persistent suffocation. The condition developed at the time Mrs. D.'s husband left for the army and her brother, whom she was nursing, died of rheumatic heart disease. She had anxiety attacks and was in psychotherapy for one year, with one or two interviews a week. She appeared to have no physical abnormality. She had been closely related to her brother during the three years during which she cared for him. Also she had compulsive concern for her twin children. She was dejected, had insomnia, wanted sleeping pills, yet was afraid to sleep for fear of apparitions of her dead brother. In therapy the psychotherapist used the technique that

directed the patient's attention to the memories of her dead brother, reiterating his desire to share these depressing memories with the patient, and repeatedly reassured her that the distressing feelings attendant upon these memories would be compensated by her relief in the future from the symptoms which brought her to the physician.[13]

To be healed, Mrs. D. had to pay the cost of feeling sad. She had to endure dreams of others dying. She went to the funeral of a friend and at the next interview appeared to "tremble all over, to perspire, turned pale, cried convulsively, complained of feeling very weak" for half an hour. Then she seemed to transfer her confidence from her brother to the physician. The anger that she felt against her brother for dying was expressed toward other men. She recovered when she accepted her brother's death. It came about at a wake when, instead of the person in the casket, she saw her brother. She then read the chapter on grief in *Psychiatry and Religion* and gained an insight. Her emotional dependence was broken, especially as it had been related to an individual for whom she had cared for a long period of time. Those who care for invalid relatives who are completely helpless tend to assume the mother's role and develop many of the attendant feelings.

Unshared grief that is suspended and redirected grows from an unaccepted death. This affects all of the other relations of life— social, psychological, and physical. The condition is not corrected until the image of the deceased is released and the reality of his death is accepted as a fact. In this case the therapist moved a deeply disturbed person, with morbid grief reactions, to health by helping her to face and accept the pain of her loss and to work it through with courage and a sense of reality. The fact that the work of mourning was delayed until the physical symptoms developed made it more difficult to engage in the mental and emotional activities necessary to move beyond it.

Sometimes the same forces are at work within the person and are revealed through a dream. A woman whose husband had been dead nearly three years had refused to adjust to the fact. She kept his personal belongings around just as before his death. Then she was obliged to move into another residence. She called her pastor to report a strange dream about which she wanted to talk. She said that in the dream she was packing to move to her new home, but her husband refused to go. She tried to use physical strength but he resisted. Finally she pulled so hard that she pulled him apart limb from limb. Then she packed him in a suitcase, but when she got to the new dwelling she opened the suitcase and to her surprise found it empty. The pastor asked what it all meant to her. She started to cry and said she had been struggling to decide what to do with her deceased husband's belongings. Now she had decided that she could not keep them longer. She called the next day to say that she had disposed of all of them and was moving into her new home to make a fresh start. The dream crystallized her thinking and helped to make explicit the feelings that she could not otherwise verbalize. The pastor's role was merely that of helping in the crystallizing process.

7. The Pastor's Role in Abnormal Grief

The pastor and others closely related to the bereaved have a responsibility to be aware of any peculiarities in the expression of grief, for such may serve as a clue to the special care and attention that is needed. When any of the nine symptoms of abnormality mentioned earlier in the chapter are discerned, it is important to give special attention to the case. Such symptoms may disappear with time. Then all is well and good. Time invested in helping the person to engage in the work of mourning at the early stages can prevent more acute disturbances a few months later. In speaking of this in relation to his observations under wartime conditions, T. A. Ross observed: "In a large number of instances the acute may be cured very quickly. If the case is allowed to lapse into the chronic stage the task of getting the patient well becomes excessively difficult." [14]

The pastor must be aware of the role alcohol may play in the expression of grief feelings. Rather than face the full impact of the work of mourning, the bereaved person may seek to take the edge off his feelings through the use of alcohol. While he may successfully prevent the facing of the grief on a temporary basis, the danger is that the alternative is a chronic state of alcohol addiction. Such was the case with John N., a writer. When his wife died, he was irreconcilable. For weeks he drank considerably and was seldom free from the influence of alcohol. This went on for more than a year until his resources were used up. During this period he did no writing at all. Under financial necessity he tried to write again but his work was unacceptable. In desperation he began doing the most degrading type of hack work, and although he had been a man of integrity and ability, his efforts became careless and prostituted to his need for ready cash. He seemed completely inaccessible to any therapeutic relationship, and after two miserable years of degraded living he died of acute alcoholism. Undoubtedly his grief was responsible for releasing such strong conflicting feelings within his personality that he could not deal with them. He used alcohol as an escape to avoid the facing of his feelings and so thoroughly disorganized his living that he was never able to recover, for he was never able to begin to deal with his inner problem. As the alcohol-dependent person is usually a deeply disturbed, regressive, and dependent type of personality, the loss of an important dependency relationship may precipitate a condition that cannot be brought under effective treatment. However, under such circumstances there are cases where a strong religious attachment supplies the dependency relationship needed, and not only brings the person out of the dependence on alcohol but leads him to a sober, useful, and contented existence. The pastor's role may be primarily that of establishing a contact with a referral group. Alcoholics Anonymous is often able to give the framework of sustaining social and spiritual values that can be effective with those who turn to alcoholic escape rather than work through their grief.

While it is quite normal for the grief-stricken person to show strong feelings of aggression, these expressions may become abnormally strong and so sharply focused as to cause serious personal and social danger. Such was the case with Alfred W. His young son was sleeping quietly in his baby carriage under the trees of his suburban home. A driver, under the influence of alcohol, lost control of his car, which left the road, crossed thirty feet of lawn, and crashed into the baby carriage. Alfred W., the baby's father, was not at home at the time, but when he was informed of the tragedy he was almost beside himself with anger. He persistently threatened to kill the inebriated driver, whom he referred to as a "drunken murderer." The family of the offending driver, with the court's permission, took him out of town temporarily; and the pastor spent several hours a day with the sorely disturbed father. Much of the anger was verbalized through many hours of conversation. Alfred W.'s father had been an alcoholic, and he and his family had suffered severely for many years because of this. Now in this tragic circumstance Alfred's grief was related to the long period of resentment that had never been adequately expressed in the past and was given a clear focus. After a time it was possible to get enough of the anger expressed so that it began to be diffused. This period was marked by a mood of irritability and touchiness. This, too, was worked through during a period of weeks, and as the slow legal processes took their course for the punishment of the offending driver, the father became reconciled to the orderly process of law, gradually accepting the course of events that could not well be changed by any direct action on his part. Such extreme and sharply focused aggressiveness is not usually observed, nor is it normal. But there are circumstances in which the grief is so mixed with feelings of anger and hatred that the work of mourning is not easily dissociated from the expression of the aggressive feelings. When that is the case the

177

pastor may be a useful instrument in encouraging the verbalization and exteriorization of the feelings. Then they can more easily be handled, and a double tragedy can be avoided. However, an accepting attitude toward the feelings must be maintained even while the behavior stimulated by the feelings is brought into question.

8. The Minister's Abnormal Reactions

Sometimes the minister himself is obliged to face the tragic circumstances of life. His ability to express all his feelings is complicated by the public nature of his witness. It is important for him to be aware of his own emotional needs and the importance of a healthy expression for them.

Merton S., a minister, was thirty-eight when his son was killed in a bicycle accident. He bore up under the tragedy with what appeared to be unusual fortitude. He tried in every way possible to carry on as if nothing had happened, because as he said, "I must prove my faith by my actions." Actually he retreated more and more from his people, and finally was seldom seen in the parish aside from the regular services, which he continued to conduct effectively. Question was raised about his work and he made no effort to answer, but withdrew more and more into himself. Instead of continuing his scholarly pursuits to which he had given himself in the past, he spent more and more time puttering around and watching television. But even here there seemed to be no satisfactory diversion from the unresolved feelings of grief within. He was moved to another and smaller parish to see if the change would improve his attitude, but no significant change was noted. No therapy has been instituted, but his disorganized behavior is undoubtedly related to factors involved in the working through of an abnormal grief condition.

Dr. JTS was a brilliant young Baptist clergyman, whose warmth and eloquence appealed to the southern parish which he served with great success. His daughter was taken ill with a lingering malady and finally died. During the months of her illness her father spent untold hours by her bedside, reading to her and showing his concern. He spent many hours in prayer for his daughter's recovery. After the funeral he seemed to be continuing as usual in his parish work. Though more grave in attitude, he was effective and energetic. After a few weeks it was observed that he was losing weight. He complained of abdominal discomfort. One day while calling in the hospital he collapsed. At first it was thought that he had symptoms of typhoid, but his difficulty was finally diagnosed as acute colitis. After a period of grave illness and lengthy hospitalization he was restored to partial effectiveness. Though no psychotherapy was involved this is clearly the type of psychogenic disturbance that could come from repressed grief feelings. The clergyman, with his status in the community so clearly defined in relation to the comfort of the bereaved, may be in a particularly vulnerable position as far as the expression of his own grief is concerned. It is important for him to learn to deal with his own feelings as he would help others to deal with theirs, so that he may work through such grief as comes to him normally.

9. Diagnosis: Professional and Practical

It has been a tradition that diagnosis of illness be a matter for the medical profession. For detailed diagnosis, this is reasonable and proper. But there are matters of general and practical consideration which demand that the responsibility for diagnosis be shared. Parents make a diagnosis when they decide their child is not sick enough to have a physician. Camp directors make a diagnosis when they decide that a sick child must be sent to the hospital for medical care. While the diagnoses may be inadequate, they are working bases upon which persons proceed in practical details of life.

This sort of distinction is even more difficult when one deals with the diagnosis of emotional illness. When the community delegates a portion of the care of its disturbed persons to a group of citizens, it also assumes a degree of competence in determining the degree of the illness involved. This becomes a serious problem when it is a matter of abnormal grief expressions and the professional competence of the clergy to diagnose. Most clergymen would automatically reject the idea of making a diagnosis themselves. Yet at the very time they are making such denials they may be in the process of making the working diagnoses that determine whether they will accept responsibility for a case or will feel that it must be referred to a specialist. This is just as important in a rural community where little or no specialized help is available, as in the large center where psychotherapy is readily accessible. For even in the rural community it is important for a pastor to have a rather clear idea of what he is doing when he works with a disturbed person. Every pastor should be familiar with a basic book in psychiatry such as *The Human Mind* by Karl Menninger, *Psychotherapy in Medical Practice* by Maurice Levine, or *Personality and Psychotherapy* by John Dollard and Neal E. Miller. Such books help to make clear the problems of diagnosis that every pastor is called upon to handle.

Some simple rules, stated in rather brief terms, may be followed that will help the pastor in his effort to protect the members of his parish who are disturbed. It is about as bad to suggest hospitalization for a person who does not need it as to fail to suggest it for a person who does need it, especially as the treatment for mental and emotional illness still carries with it some degree of personal judgment not as specifically present in physical illness.

For instance, it would be easy to confuse the two different types of depression, for many of the more superficial symptoms are the same; but the severity of the disturbance and the needs for specialized therapy differ. H. S. Sullivan writes:

There is just about as much difference between sadness and depression as there is between any two things that pertain to people, but the initial impression does not clearly differentiate them. Depressed people look and sound sad; and if a person looks and sounds sad, the perceived sign is that of sadness. Whether the apparent sadness is a sign of depression—which is a very much more serious and quite different state—will gradually become evident. Sorrow can always be explained. That is, if the person feels willing and free to tell the interviewer what he feels grieved by, the account will be meaningful; there is an adequate explanation for his feeling pretty low in spirit. But the depressed person's explanation for his sadness—if he is able to come out of his depression long enough to make an explanation—puts him in a class with all the great martyrs of history. . . . Sadness is quite apt to change during an interview; even a person who has suffered a great bereavement is apt to cheer up somewhat in the process of giving statistical data, and so on. But the psychiatrist who attempts to change depression has a very difficult task.[15]

While sadness is to be expected in the grief response, the important concern of the pastor is to be able to recognize the difference between normal sadness and the type of response that indicates depression.

Edoardo Weiss . . . separates clinically as well as theoretically a "simple" or "essential" type of depression from the "melancholic" type. According to him, simple depression is characterized by a decrease in the intensity of self-experience of the individual; "he is *less awake* and the external world conveys to him much less intense meaning than it does to other persons." . . . Weiss states that the reason for the lowered ego feeling is to be found in the fact that "the libido is fixated to an object or goal which is rejected but cannot be relinquished," and that this continuous struggle finally exhausts the libido of the person to a degree which results in depression.[16]

This would be the type of emotional involvement generated by acute grief on a temporary basis.

Quite different is the depressed state:

In melancholic depression the patient's narcissism is "injured in the most obvious way." As a consequence, the main characteristics of melancholic depression are loss of self-esteem and the subsequent "development of self-hatred and self-accusations due to feelings of guilt and inferiority, irrespective of what the particular origin of such feelings might be." The "ego feeling" in melancholic depression is, in contrast to the simpler type, not lowered but increased. In brief, simple depression results from exhaustion of ego libido due to an unsolvable conflict (the "ego" is "empty") whereas melancholic depression is due to self-hatred as a consequence of an extensive loss of self-esteem through rejection.[17]

181

As all acute grief involves a measure of depression, it is important to have in mind a clear distinction between the two types; for the simple type usually resolves itself and the pastor can serve well in that process, whereas the melancholic type requires specialized help in getting at the disturbance deep within the personality.

Similarly the distinction between normal anxiety and the type of anxiety that is completely disorganizing should be clear in the mind of the pastoral counselor. Rollo May states it in this way:

Normal anxiety is, like any anxiety, a reaction to threats to values the individual holds essential to his existence as a personality; but normal anxiety is that reaction which (1) is not disproportionate to the objective threat, (2) does not involve repression or other mechanisms of intrapsychic conflict, and as a corollary to the second point, (3) does not require neurotic defense mechanisms for its management, but can be confronted constructively on the level of conscious awareness or can be relieved if the objective situation is altered. . . .

Neurotic anxiety, on the other hand, is a reaction to threat which is (1) disproportionate to the objective danger, (2) involves repression (dissociation) and other forms of intrapsychic conflict, and, as a corollary, (3) is managed by means of various forms of retrenchment of activity and awareness, such as inhibitions, the development of symptoms, and the varied neurotic defense mechanisms. . . .

Thus neurotic anxiety is that which occurs when the incapacity for coping adequately with threats is not objective but subjective, i.e., is due not to objective weakness but to inner psychological patterns and conflicts which prevent the individual from using his powers. . . . A handy distinction between normal and neurotic anxiety is *ex post facto*, i.e., how the anxiety is used; normal anxiety being that which is used for a constructive solution to the problem which causes the anxiety, and neurotic anxiety being that which results in defense from and avoidance of the problem.[18]

The anxiety created by grief can move in either direction, and the pastor should be able to determine the major characteristics that indicate that movement.

When you can talk reasonably with a person and he can act constructively, the evidences of anxiety are probably normal and a reaction attributable to the stress of circumstance. When it seems impossible to engage the mind in a reasonable handling of the major problem or any smaller facet of it, and when constructive action toward a solution seems impossible, neurotic anxiety is likely to be an explanation. The former usually resolves itself as a person works through the grief period, while the latter indicates deeper problems which the grief has brought to light and these invite the attention of a skilled psychotherapist.

Also, it is is important for the pastor-counselor to keep alert to the amount of reality-relation shown by the bereaved. If the latter maintains a good reality sense in spite of his suffering, he will usually work his way through the situation effectively. If, however, in the place of the pain of loss, there is a loss of reality-relation and a retreat to excessive symbolization and fantasy structures, it is a sign that the grief has precipitated factors beyond the normal that call for specialized treatment.

Similarly, if there is an excess of hostility or suspicion it is a danger signal. A certain amount of hostility is to be expected but it is usually specific and directed with some basis of reason. It may also be that some suspicion is the result of a reasonable wariness; but when the person becomes suspicious of everyone, it is a projection of a subjective loss of confidence in himself. So, also, an excess of hostility shows that the person may begin to turn the hostility against the self. In such instances of excess the abnormality of the grief warrants diagnosis and treatment by a specialist.

When a reasonable degree of uncertainty exists in the mind of the pastor, and there will be many instances when such is the case, he may proceed something after this fashion. Such procedure would not be related to the usual work with the bereaved but would be warranted only when such serious reactions occur as to make such a procedure entirely justified. The pastor would say to the person concerned that he would feel better about proceeding with the counseling relationship if he had some of his judgments confirmed by a specialist. He would be glad to make arrangements for such an examination and would appreciate the co-operation of the bereaved. Then, if the psychotherapist finds there are factors involved which call for the attention of a spe-

183

cialist, the counselee is protected and the concern for effective teamwork is fulfilled. If, on the other hand, the psychotherapist finds that the factors involved do not constitute a danger to the person and that the pastoral counseling will serve a healthful purpose, the pastor will proceed with assurance and increased understanding.

As the counseling with those suffering from abnormal grief reactions is likely to follow the actual loss by a period of time it is usually easier to control the setting for such counseling. It is best to use the pastor's counseling room, where the counselee is less emotionally related and may feel freer to express his thoughts and feelings than in a place where relatives may be near and interruptions are likely. The normal counseling techniques would be followed, with careful observation, creative listening, a tentative diagnosis that becomes a working basis in the relationship, and a plan of action that may involve referral, personal counseling, or group involvement. Here, too, the pastor may be specifically helped by courses in counseling, and by a working familiarity with some good handbooks on counseling, such as: The Art of Counseling, by Rollo May; Pastoral Counseling, by Seward Hiltner; Pastoral Counseling, Its Theory and Practice, by Carroll Wise; The Psychiatric Interview, by H. S. Sullivan; and Readings in Counseling, edited by Karl P. Zerfoss.

TWELVE

When Grief Precipitates Deep Disturbance

We have seen how grief is worked through with persons who have an essentially normal grief pattern. We have also looked at the effect that grief may have on persons whose human relations and personal attitudes are easily moved to the abnormal by the acute disturbance of grief. Now we will look at that group of persons who may become acute problems because their grief brings them to a point where they cannot handle themselves or their affairs adequately.

Often these persons have given other signs of their deep disturbance before the bereavement that has made their condition acute. The individual with sadistic attitudes toward a person is likely to become melancholic when that person dies. The person with hatred of an obsessive-compulsive parent is likely to have disruptive feelings of guilt, remorse, and depression at the death of that parent. The person with strong regressive elements in his personality is one who may have that regressive tendency carried to its extreme form. Sometimes social insecurity becomes a factor in the deep disturbance.

R. D. Gillespie[1] found in his study of soldiers under the stress of combat that there was a real correlation between emotional patterns and instability under stress and the stability of their parents and their home environment. A large percentage of the soldiers who broke under stress had emotionally unstable mothers, and a significant number were also the products of homes broken by death or divorce. Similar findings were ascertained by Grinker and Spiegel under comparable conditions.[2] So not only is the pattern of the life of the individual a factor to be observed, but also the conditions of his home background need to be evaluated in relation to any deep disturbance that seems to be evident.

1. Definition of Deep Disturbance

Weiss writes concerning the dynamic factors involved in the deeply disturbed:

Pathological mourning is but one example of the tendency under changed conditions, toward regression from reality to delusions. . . . The successful adaption to reality, including the establishment of emotional rapport with one's fellow beings—occupies a considerable part of the life of the normal human being. The capacity to renounce or postpone one's desire cannot be attained in a short period of time. It is the experiences of childhood, however, that play the most important role, and certain principles deserve special emphasis in the training of children.

The problem of the personality in its acute form arises when deep emotional factors, perhaps of early origin, complicate and impede the normal process of mourning and make it difficult for the person to move beyond a dependence upon that of which he has been deprived.

While most human beings accomplish this adjustment, the mourning work is not always successful. Suicide is an extreme solution: unable to reconcile himself to his loss, the mourner frees himself from an unbearable reality by taking his own life. Others, regressing to the earlier phase of hallucinatory gratifications retreat from the outer world, lose contact with reality, and for real satisfactions substitute delusions. A mother who has lost her child, for example, may continue to believe that he is alive—keeping his room prepared for him, the bed ready, and his toys at hand as if she anticipated his return to the nursery. She may wake with a start, thinking she heard his cry. She may even wheel the carriage up the street, fancying the baby to be inside, or prepare the formula and fill the nursing bottle—all her behavior of such a nature as to deny the death of the child.[3]

Lindemann points out that the grief reaction of the more extreme form is clearly different from the neurotic reaction, for with the neurotic pattern there is an increase of physical and emotional activity while in the more severely disturbed there is a noticeable lack of activity that may be called apathy. The neurotic needs the extra activity to sustain him while he is trying to regain a working relationship with reality. The more deeply disturbed are not bothered by reality. They have found a detour around it, so to speak. For that reason the deeply disturbed are more likely to be retarded both in speech and in action. They seem aimless, lacking in initiative, looking to others for suggestions to follow, lost without the old patterns of life even if they were not satisfying patterns in many respects. They are lost and unable to relate effectively to the immediate problems of the external world. In some instances a hyperactive or manic manifestation may be seen in a cyclical disturbance. This is in reality but the other side of the coin of depression with its aimless activity.

2. Illustrations of Deep Disturbance

Lindemann illustrates this with several cases treated after the Cocoanut Grove fire. In one case of seemingly normal recovery, after eight days a paranoid state was precipitated, and the patient became suspicious of himself, the nurses, and the doctors. In this case there had been a previous history of such episodes and the patient was released, with a poor prognosis, to the care of his family.

Sometimes the problem is one of organic origin in which the brain is so injured that the person is not able to react normally. This may be the case when the person involved has suffered accidental injury. One patient mentioned by Lindemann gave evidence of cerebral lesions, probably due to carbon monoxide poisoning and too long a period of severe shock. The patient was noisy, out of touch with surroundings, restless and disoriented, incoherent, jaundiced, and sometimes lapsed into a period of speechlessness and semicoma. The memory was impaired and there was no improvement in three weeks. The condition was probably the result of asphyxia of the nerve cells of the brain, and the damage was probably of a permanent nature.

In another case mentioned by Lindemann, a young man suffered from minor burns. He was released from the hospital in seemingly good condition. After a while he became restless, could not work, read, or play. He could not carry on a conversation and would break off in the middle of a sentence. He did not seem able to establish a working rapport with anyone for a period of time. He indicated a tension, inability to breathe, weakness and exhaustion, and morbid guilt feelings. He felt he "should have saved his wife but he didn't." He slept poorly, even with sedation. On his sixth day of treatment after returning to the hospital, he jumped from a window to his death.

A young unmarried woman with severe burns about the face and hands was quiet for a month. Then she became increasingly aggressive, used vulgar language, and furiously refused to co-operate. She slept poorly, refused food, disturbed her ward by her noisy behavior. She had fluctuating moods—tearful, then apathetic, then aggressive. In four weeks she was incoherent and hallucinated, with fantasies of destruction. She had a previous history of withdrawal and psychotic episodes under severe stress.

3. Prevalence of Deep Disturbance

Anderson's study,[4] made in an English hospital, shows that nine per cent of the total admissions among the mentally ill were classified as morbid grief reactions. Of this number the following types are listed. Fifty-nine per cent of the total are classified as anxiety cases. Nineteen per cent of the total are hysterias, with seven per cent listed as obsessional reactions, and fifteen per cent as manic depressive. But Anderson further points out that any classification is a device of convenience, for the clinical picture changes as the patient progresses in the work of mourning.

Similarly, Meerloo, in his study,[5] finds a type of regressive group action that may have something of the nature of the dynamics employed by the individual. As "panic is a barometer of inner cohesion," so deeply disturbed reactions in the individual are a barometer of the falling apart of the inner organization of life. As panic is usually related to some form of emergency escape from catastrophe, so the regression of the individual is a comparable form of escape from personal tragedy. As panic is a primitive form of group action, so the regression to early modes of problem-solving in the individual serves the same purpose; in seeking unreasonably for protection from pain, the person is led to unreasoned and unreasonable behavior. And because it is so clearly unreasonable it may be self-destructive. The pain becomes so unbearable that death is preferable. Montaigne indicates the type of reaction: "The siege was remembered for the fear that so seized, contracted and froze the heart of a nobleman, that he fell without any wound stone dead in the breach." [6] In a similar situation, unreasoned fear took its dreadful toll in a London bomb shelter in 1943, where in darkness, fear, and hysterical screaming, over two hundred persons expired in one night with no form of physical injury having been experienced by any of them. The extremes of irrational behavior are almost too bizarre for description, but they tend to serve a purpose for the injured souls who seek in such behavior to avoid the stresses that are too great for their limited reserves to cope with.

The pain that accompanies acute grief is bad enough under normal circumstances, but when it is coupled with an already seriously disturbed personality structure, the results may be extreme. It is in such situations that the pastor-counselor must be alert to protect such persons against themselves and also to protect their families from the excessive burdens that such irrational behavior places on the persons who continue to operate with a strong reality sense.

4. The Pastor's Role with the Deeply Disturbed

The pastor-counselor should be especially alert if there have been previous evidences of inability on the part of the personality to endure emotional stress. Sometimes there are family situations in which the hereditary weakness is clearly discernible. At other times the social factors in the family framework may be known to the pastor to be so disrupted that there is little to sustain the bereaved person in the family structure. In all such situations the pastor may well be alerted to special problems. Also where there is physical injury, he must be prepared to understand and interpret what is happening. Often when one member of the family is killed in an accident, and other members of the family are seriously injured at the same time, the problems of abnormality with a somatic basis arise. Comparable damage may result from senile dementia, wherein the aged person becomes disoriented and confused and expresses such confusion in irrational behavior. Often this is noted in extreme suspicion, aggressive action, and fancied injury. In one case a daughter who had cared faithfully for her father and mother for several years was upset to find that her mother was going to neighbors and friends a few weeks after the death of her husband and begging for protection from her daughter who, she said, had poisoned her father and was now trying to poison her.

Sometimes the pastor is the only one involved in a case in such a way as to deal with all the factors. The physician treats the body and the insurance takes care of expenses, but the pastor deals with persons as persons. In one instance a pastor was standing by with a family when the husband was dying of cancer of the bone. The patient had become irrational with the intense pain, and no drug seemed to be able to relieve it. The man was physically restrained because his activity only added to his injury. The patient's wife felt impelled to remain by his side during visiting hours even though it was obvious she was inflicting severe punishment upon herself by so doing. The pastor tired to convince the woman that she served no useful purpose by such visits, for her husband recognized no one. She persisted, however, and one night after her visit to the hospital she returned home to turn on the gas and destroy herself. In that instance it was clear that the pastor did not sense the intensity of the dynamics at work in the relation of husband and wife. The physician saw the woman only occasionally. Other persons involved were not trained to be aware of the emotional factors at work. The pastor should have been the person to detect and help resolve the problem. Yet while the pastor should feel a genuine concern about his adequacy in dealing with such matters, he should not unreasonably condemn himself for failure to properly interpret all of the forces at work. His obligation is to do the best he knows. There are many situations where the dynamic processes are so deep and well developed that little can be done to correct them. While the physician feels bad when he loses a case, he does not cease his practice and retreat into self-condemnation. Rather, he performs an autopsy to see how he could improve his understanding and technique. While a pastor is not in a position to employ the same approach physically, he is able to examine his failures and to seek increased competence in dealing with similar cases.

5. Cases of Pastoral Success and Failure

The following cases from the parish ministry point out some of the adequacies and inadequacies of the pastor in dealing with some extremely disturbed persons. Sometimes the problem is one of knowing what to do, and at other times it is a problem of knowing how to do it, but also of knowing what not to do.

A Manic State

Deep disturbance may show up in unreasonable elation or a manic reaction. Mr. W. was a steady, dependable individual who lived a normal, conservative type of family life with his wife and three young children, aged six, eight, and ten. Mrs. W. was taken suddenly ill and died. Mr. W. was at first stunned, then deeply depressed, and overborne with feelings of guilt for not getting medical aid as soon as possible. After a few months, and I do not have the exact time interval recorded, he began to do strange and unaccountable things. He started spending their carefully guarded life savings with abandon. He bought a sporty automobile and began going with a physically attractive but rather dull-witted girl who was not yet twenty. He soon came to the pastor to make arrangements for a marriage. The pastor tried to point out some of the problems that were evident, but only succeeded in angering Mr. W., who said that if he had wanted advice he would have asked for it and he was tired of having other people try to run his life for him. He went to a justice of the peace and was married. The effect on his home was severe. The dull-witted girl could not assume the responsibilities of the home and it was soon a shambles. The neighbors said simply, "The man has lost his wits." About six months after the marriage Mr. W. came to the pastor again, depressed and hopeless, "What is the matter with me? I've made a mess of things. My children are suffering; my neighbors avoid me. I want to avoid myself."

191

The possibility of a circumstance like this had been implied by Freud.[7] He wrote that when the grief situation produces a state of melancholia, it is not unlikely that the personality, in ridding itself of the object of the suffering, does it so successfully that a state of unreasoned elation and triumph is achieved which disturbs the judgment and produces a manic state of unaccustomed activity and freedom of action. It is part and parcel of the same illness. It may level off after a time and permit the restoration of normal behavior, or the results may be so distressing that the person is thrown into another period of depression, which is but another phase of cyclic disturbance. In either case, the symptoms are those of a deeply disturbed personality which needs specialized care, usually in an institution.

Depression

Often a person brings to the grief experience an accumulation of feelings that stimulate a depressed reaction. Such was the case with Mrs. R., who first came to my attention at the time of the death of her husband. She was of Jewish background, aged twenty-six, and had been married for three years. She was six months in pregnancy at the time of her husband's death. She was dry-eyed, greyish in color, sluggish in action, and depressed. When I called to speak with her before the funeral service, she kept repeating, "You can't do anything for me so save your time. I want to die and nothing else."

From friends and relatives a reconstruction of her life was made. She had been adopted at an early age, and had been treated with unspeakable brutality for many years of her life. She was shy and suspicious, with a large amount of unexpressed aggression toward others. She had few friends and few interests. In her late teens she left her home to find employment. Here her desire to please and her intelligence won for her repeated promotions. She came to the attention of one of the young executives of an associated company who courted her. At first shy and suspicious, she was slow to make an emotional commitment. However, he was so patient, understanding, and genuinely good to her that she finally gave herself completely in devotion to him. Perhaps she had overcompensated her previous mood and had overinvested her emotional capital. She told friends that she had at last found the happiness she believed could not exist. She was devoted, contented, and seemed to move out of her shy and retiring mode of life. She welcomed her husband's friends and entertained with pleasure. When she became pregnant she expressed joy and said that a child would make her happiness complete. Shortly thereafter her husband was taken ill, and his trouble was diagnosed as a cancer in advanced stages. He died about two months later after a period of severe suffering. She wanted to care for him at home and the physician agreed, for hospitalization would have served no medical purpose. She suffered severely during the last few weeks but seemed anxious to do everything possible to insure her husband's care. He tried to reassure and console her and charged her with responsibility for the care and guidance of his unborn child. When he died she appeared to be in a state of emotional exhaustion.

While the husband had been a man of religious inclination, he did not press the matter, for his wife claimed there could be no God who permitted such suffering and brutality to exist in life. She wanted no part of the minister's presence or words. She wanted me to do what was necessary and as quickly as possible. She said: "You want to tell me a lot of rot about God and love and happiness. I don't want it. I know life and its cruelty. I see the bad enjoy life, and the only truly good person I ever knew dies a miserable death at thirty-five. Now tell me what there is good about that if you can. Death is the only good thing for me and it can't come too soon." She worked off quite a bit of anger and aggression against the pastor. He felt that this might be an important contact with reality for her, and he called repeatedly and always accepted her feelings. There was no preaching, and reassurance seemed so shallow and meaningless that it was worse than useless. She spoke of preachers as "people who prey on others' suffering and can't do them any good for all they know is lies." She condemned her fate for being pregnant, "It is a crime to bring a helpless child into this cruel world." She refused to eat for days at a time and justified her action by saying it was wrong to sustain so miserable a life.

After a few weeks she began gradually to talk about her husband, not in terms of his tragic death but of his life, his interests, his concern for the home, and his friends. After her husband's death she had at first rejected his friends and acquaintances. Business associates were told they need not bother to come. A next-door neighbor, an elderly Polish woman, was probably the most helpful therapeutic agent in the situation. She came in every day at mealtime with some nourishing food. She took a motherly attitude and did a considerable amount of mild scolding. It usually followed this line: "Come now, girl, that is no way to act. You must eat some food. This will be good for you. Your husband, he be mad if you let his little fellow go hungry. You must stop being foolish. This has gone on too long." Mrs. R. seemed to accept this admonition and responded. After a few weeks she was eating regularly again and talking considerably with her friendly neighbor. At the end of her pregnancy she was delivered of a son who seemed well and healthy. In this new responsibility and interest, she found a new sense of direction for living. To my knowledge she has not shed a tear over the loss of her husband. After a period of depression, with much talk about death and suicide, she was restored gradually to a measure of adequacy through the influence of a strong mother figure in the person of the neighbor. Her son also gave her a legitimate object for the investment of some of her emotional capital. There is little doubt that her bereavement had done deep emotional damage that will not be easily resolved, but it was part of the rest of her damaged emotional life. It is also quite probable that her attitude toward her son will be influenced by her condition, and his life will surely show the marks of an abnormal child-parent relationship.

This is an illustration of the healthful influence exerted by an unsophisticated neighbor, who moved in directly upon the situation and, more effectively than the clergy or the representative of the medical profession, played an acceptable role with good results. While the deep personality injury will not be healed without special care, Mrs. R. was guided through an episode of depression and the last months of a difficult pregnancy by a person who was equipped with the right feelings and was able to communicate them.

The Poorly Oriented and Self-destructive

Most ministers are concerned about the type of disorganization that becomes a suicidal threat. Mrs. M. presented this kind of problem. Mrs. M. and her husband bought property in a new development and worked together evenings and week ends to build their home. They were so wrapped up in each other and their work together that they had little or no interest in neighbors or community. When they were asked to join a local church they said, "Our home is our religion." They had a fine garden and beautiful flowers and it seemed they had built for themselves and ideal setting for life.

Mr. M. died suddenly from acute appendicitis with complications. Mrs. M. suffered acute depression of the nervous system and could neither talk nor see anyone. Sedation was administered by a local physician. There was no psychiatrist for miles around. The clergyman was not able to establish effective communication with Mrs. M. because of her state of emotional shock. She had built all her interests around her home and her husband, and without him there seemed to be nothing left for her. She was not able to attend the funeral, and was taken to the home of her brother and his wife some miles distant. There she was kept under the care of a physician and under the constant supervision of the family. While the state of depression continued, there was evidence of improvement of her relationship to others. She was able to eat and talk, even though she remained largely listless and uncommunicative. She seemed to have no emotional expression. At the end of six weeks her brother thought she was well enough to be left alone, and when he returned and found her missing he surmised what had happened. He called police in her hometown. They broke into the house and found that she had committed suicide with gas in the kitchen of her home.

When there is a good healthy relationship between husband and wife, that healthy relationship seems to sustain them in loss. It even becomes the basis for happy remarriage, for it is an evidence of the ability to be accepting. When there is a quality of the abnormal about the relationship, it may easily project into other relations. Mrs. M. and her husband seemed to have practiced a mutual withdrawal from human relationships in their preoccupation with each other. When death came, the basically unhealthy nature of the relationship revealed itself.

Suicidal risks are likely to develop when there is an extreme and unhealthy dependency relationship which leads to a feeling of loss of selfhood in the loss of the object of the dependency. Also, when there are deep aggressive feelings which may be turned against the self, the threat is present. It becomes a form of punishment of others through punishment of self. The elements of depression are invariably present in suicide.

The role of the pastor when there seems to be a suicidal risk is first to establish some form of emergency protection so that the individual is not left alone. This of course is a temporary type of protection. Second, the pastor should make every effort to see that the person involved has psychotherapy, for the person with strong suicidal inclinations is seriously ill. Third, the person's condition should be so interpreted to the family that they will co-operate in relieving the situation rather than acting to complicate it.

It might be useful for the pastor-counselor to acquaint himself with some of the literature in the field. Maurice Levine, in *Psychotherapy in Medical Practice*, has a helpful chapter entitled "Suicide Risks." [8] Karl Menninger's book *Man Against Himself* gives an understanding of the dynamics at work; and Emile Durkheim, in his sociological study *Suicide*,[9] gives understanding of the group and community factors that may be important.

Aggression

Sometimes the deep disturbance is related to problems of religion and religious interpretation. So it was with Ruth K., the twenty-eight-year-old daughter of a retired minister and his wife, who lived with her parents in a small north-shore Long Island community. She had few social interests and lived a sheltered and confined life, caring for the needs of an invalid mother and an infirm father. Ruth was quiet, retiring, her actions studied and formal, and there seemed to be a great deal of unresolved aggression in her being.

Ruth's mother was a product of a strict, rigid New England family. She had one child early in her marriage and then retired with arthritis to a wheel chair. For many years, with a dictator's hand, she had run the household from her wheel chair. Most people gave her sympathy and respect, and expressed admiration for her courageous and cheerful spirit. She had inherited enough money to guarantee her security, and she used this to further her power in family affairs. She spent her money with a clear awareness of the power advantages it would give her over other people.

Ruth's father was a simple, hard-working individual who took his unfortunate lot in an uncomplaining manner, asked little of others, and willingly played his role in the crippled household. He had never made much of a success in his profession because he was obliged to give so much of his time to the needs of his invalid wife. He was conscientious, friendly, helpful, and uninspired, as well as uninspiring. A few years after retirement he was hospitalized for a terminal malignancy, which forced more of the care of the mother on Ruth.

At the time of her father's death, Ruth showed no emotional reaction. Everything she did was proper and formal. She said the right things in the right sort of way. The family quickly settled back into a situation in which they could absorb more of sympathy and less of responsibility. Ruth was now completely under the control of her mother. For years her mother had taught her that men were evil beings, never to be trusted. As far as Ruth's mother was concerned there were no exceptions to the rule.

About two months after her father's death, Ruth attended a service at the church at which the highly symbolic sacrament of communion was administered. Toward the end of the next week the pastor received an eleven-page letter, painstakingly written, with every letter carefully formed. Every inch of every page was covered with criticism of the pastor for his method of conducting the service. The hostility was clear and the purpose was evident. A few sentences from the repetitious content will show the nature of the communication:

Your insincere method of conducting the service was so different from my father's way. He filled it full of sincerity and spiritual meaning. . . . One should not lead a service unless he really means it. My father always meant what he said. He was absolutely honest. He was a good man through and through.

After reading the letter the pastor went to Ruth's home. He was met by Ruth's mother in her wheel chair. When he asked for Ruth her mother was evasive but finally admitted that Ruth had been acting strangely. She hadn't wanted to mention it because she thought it would work out all right in time. Ruth hadn't been seen since Sunday. She was in her room. She could hear her walking around, but she would not answer when called and kept the door locked except when she opened it to get food left at the door by a neighbor who came in to take care of the mother. When the pastor suggested that this was a serious problem which called for a medical specialist, she resisted the idea. She didn't want a psychiatrist entering into their family affairs. The pastor returned every day or two for a week and consulted with the family physician about the matter. They worked out an arrangement for Ruth to be hospitalized and for a practical nurse to care for the mother.

After Ruth had spent two weeks in a sanitorium, the psychiatrist observed that she presented a "veritable chamber of psychiatric horrors." Eight months of hospitalization with intensive therapy followed. Her bereavement had precipitated the psychotic response to the accumulated emotional stress under which she lived, and only the ministrations of a skilled psychotherapist could restore her to even a measure of personal adequacy. The sense of guilt that led her to feel responsible for her father's death explained her irrational reaction to a symbolic service of memorial. By working out some of her aggression in defense of her father, she had sought to satisfy her guilt feelings, but it was too great a problem to be handled by such a device. However, it did open the way for the kind of healing ministry that she needed. The pastor's role in such a case was rather clearly defined. He was an instrument for referral. She now is able to function quite satisfactorily in a limited situation. It would not be unreasonable to expect that the death of her mother may precipitate another such episode.

6. The Pastor and Referrals

In every parish there are probably a few psychotic cases that are never treated because they never present any serious problems as far as maintenance is concerned. Though they are disoriented they are able to function on a limited basis. In many instances they are cases that would not respond to treatment and little can be done for them. However, other situations develop in which treatment is important and therapy can be helpful. In many instances the pastor is the person who can be the instrument for getting these persons to proper treatment. In the soul-healing team of the community the pastor plays an important part in the referral role. He is able to call to the attention of families the nature of the difficulties, and to help in the arrangements that can make proper treatment possible. For that reason the pastor should know the resources of his community and the surrounding area for specialized treatment. He should understand his role as a member of a professional team which can help to make treatment possible. And also he needs to be conscious of the importance of his own training as it makes him a competent member of this team.

The pastor should be able to make some practical judgments in the interests of members of his parish as to resources available. Few persons are able to pay the high fees demanded by the limited number of psychiatrists available. Some psychiatrists are better qualified than others, and though the pastor is not able to pass judgment on matters of professional competence, he can pass a pragmatic judgment on the basis of results observed. It is also well to remember that many persons trained as psychologists and lay analysts are competent and helpful psychotherapists. Increasingly, pastors with special training are able to combine the traditional functions of the ministry with new skills in meeting the needs of those who are disturbed. But in any instance, the major responsibility is to the welfare of those who stand in need.

Physicians take an objective and candid view of their errors and shortcomings. They get together and discuss with brutal frankness mistakes that have been made and the possibility for improving techniques. They take an active interest in the study of the findings of post-mortem examinations. They want to make sure that they learn to improve their understanding and their treatment methods. The pastor, on the other hand, seems to think of failure in personal terms. He is reticent about mentioning his shortcomings. For that reason he may be less likely to overcome them. In some degree this situation is met by the pastors' schools and workshops held increasingly about the country, where men get together in an atmosphere of mutual quest and sharing to compare success and failure. In the area of the pastor's role on the soul-healing team, it would be equally important if some form of professional interrelationship could be established by the clergy and allied professions who deal with those who mourn. This often is done on a superficial basis, with a luncheon meeting once a year. This will continue as an inadequate liaison unless real efforts are made to establish a permanent working relationship with a regular examination of methods and critique of techniques. When that can be done, the role of the pastor in dealing with the severely disturbed will be improved; and when all is said and done, that role is primarily one of referral. Because diagnosis is an important factor in referral, every effort that can be employed to improve the methods of professional interrelationship should be encouraged. Where that is not possible, certain books may be of special help, and it would be wise for every pastor to have on his bookshelf and rather clearly in mind some works on the matters of diagnosis suited to the needs of the layman. Probably *Psychiatry for Social Workers*, by Lawson G. Lowrey, is as good a basic book in the field as one could find. *Psychology for Ministers and Social Workers*, by Henry Guntrip, is also useful. Franz Alexander's

Psychosomatic Medicine gives helpful background understanding, as Edoardo Weiss's *Principles of Psychodynamics* gives a helpful interpretation of dynamic forces at work within the personality.

Jesus won the interest of people in his day because of his work with those who were physically, morally, emotionally, and socially inadequate or disturbed. Those who would seek to follow his leading cannot ignore their responsibility now to use the best personal and group resources for carrying on such a ministry, even to those whose lives seem to be irreparably disrupted by the stress placed upon them.

THIRTEEN

Preparing People for Grief Situations

As we have noticed again and again in our case studies, the emotional conditioning that becomes an important factor in the grief reaction is from an early period in life. This is one of the important insights of modern psychology. The early years of life are important conditioners of the emotions for all of the rest of life. If that is the case, then it is of great importance that the mood and attitude toward death, grief, and deprivation be carefully considered by those who are parents and are training children, and that proper action should be taken to give the child the emotional conditioning which he needs to face the stresses of life.

1. Childhood Conditioning

In studies made of parachutists during World War II, a definite correlation was found between an unresolved fear of falling and an emotional conditioning that developed during that rather strenuous experience encountered in learning to walk.[1] The preparation for death begins before birth, with the attitude of the parents toward life and death. It is difficult to separate the mood of the parent from that of the child through the years of the important learning which immediately becomes a part of the unconscious conditioning of life.

Eissler was called upon to treat a child of four and a half years for obsessional behavior which alarmed the mother. As the psychiatrist had had little experience with children, he prevailed upon the mother to have a few exploratory sessions with him. She repeatedly denied during several sessions any comparable condition in her own childhood. When at the eighth session she recalled the comparable obsessional behavior from her early childhood, she was relieved but also surprised to find that it was immediately remedied in the behavior of her child. The psychiatrist indicated that it seemed to be an evidence of unconscious transference from the mother to the child. If that sort of thing can be observed in anything as specific as obsessive behavior, how much more is it likely to be the case with the more ordinary feelings and attitudes transferred from parent to child in the close associations of the early years.

Under treatment for a disturbed emotional pattern, a youth revealed that after the death of his older brother his mother had taken a vow of silence for a year. She had done the housework, prepared the meals, and shared the physical activities of the home, but she did not utter a word to any member of the family for the term of her vow. The effect on the rest of the children in the family was severe. They could not understand the basis for this breakdown of communication with so important a figure as their mother. The lives of the children were seriously injured by this unwise expression of grief that communicated something that was not intended.

In the book *The Secret Garden* the plot is built around the physical and emotional injury to a child brought on by the unwise attitude of the child's father in mourning for his mother. The child is healed of paralysis and emotional seizures when he is restored to healthy relations with others again and is allowed to face the full facts of what happened to his mother. The book illustrates in dramatic form the powerful forces at work in the mood of grief that can be transferred from a parent to a child.

For these reasons it is important to start any program of preparing people for grief situations as early as possible in the lives of those concerned. Often this involves overcoming serious problems of resistance and false ideas. Some persons feel that it is their duty to surround children with an attitude of falsehood when anything as important as death is involved. When a parent dies, the young child is shielded from the fact by evasive answers and the thought that his "father has gone away." He cannot understand the mood or the feelings so easily transmitted in spite of the words. He may give full rein to his imagination, and the consequences may seem to be much worse than death itself. Children, at even an early age, are able more adequately to withstand the stress brought by their limited understanding of death than they are to withstand the mystery and the implied desertion that would be a part of the fabric of falsehood.

Parents and other adults often ask if it is wise to allow children to visit funeral homes or to attend funerals. Here again a number of emotional factors and previous conditioning have to be taken into consideration, but it would seem as a usual rule that it is wise to do what is honest and what will best sustain the reality sense of the child. The effort should be made to protect the child from wild fantasy and unreasonable flights of imagination which may injure his contact with what it real and honest about life and death. Important learning opportunities are lost when falsehood is employed, and it is inevitable that no fabric of falsehood can be so adequately maintained as to protect the child from ultimately learning the truth. Then the danger is that the truth will be more traumatic, and at the same time the confidence in the integrity of his elders is undermined. A guide such as Gesell's studies of the emotional development of the child may be consulted to determine the needs and capacities of the normal child of a given age.

2. Education in the Church

A program of education in the church might well start with a mothers' group, especially the mothers of young children. Here it would be advisable to discuss the child's tolerance to stress and the effects of the limits of comprehension on that tolerance. The adult usually tends to assume that the emotional content of an experience is much the same for the child as it is for the adult. However, the experience of the child is so different from that of the adult that the content of the experience is surely different both in quality and quantity. The young child has no adequate concept of death. He can sense deprivation and a change in the structure of his security relationships, but to be able to comprehend the meaning of an irretrievable loss is quite beyond the capacity of a young child. The preadolescent begins to share some of the capacity for abstract thought and so is able to comprehend more of death's meaning. But even then he does not understand the change in the structure of social and economic relationships as much as he feels the insecurity, and his changed behavior may become his mode of expression. The ability of parents to understand these factors at work in the lives of their children may make it possible for them to act more wisely in dealing with situations involving death in the home or among close relatives or friends. The naturalness of death as part of a life process may be related to the experience that comes to children in the death of a grandparent.

It is probably reasonable to assume that the earlier a child is introduced to a calm, objective interpretation of death, the sooner he will be able to begin the emotional conditioning that will be his best equipment for effective mourning when the experience of mature years comes upon him. This calm, objective interpretation may often come through unspoken attitude more than through spoken words. The pastor is a special type of teacher in such situations and he must realize that he is also teaching by his attitude as well as his words when he carries on the parish ministry in the presence of death.

A few special sessions might well be planned with the staff of the church school to train them in the matters of dealing with this general area of concern with different age groups. The work of the church-school teacher is continually involved with interpreting matters of life and death. If a teacher has a morbid attitude it can easily be transmitted to his pupils. If he has a healthy feeling, it also may easily be communicated and become a significant factor in the development of a philosophy of life and death. Much of the biblical material is related to the experiences of persons who are being born or are dying, and it is important to know how to handle such material with discernment.

The concern may develop a different context for youth. Our society, with its program of military training and the attending threats of destruction, keeps such thoughts forever in the minds of young people. Some indicate that they never think of death in terms of their own experience but always of the other person's, yet it is not too far-fetched to believe that this is but a device developed to deal with the problem more objectively. Time can profitably be employed within youth groups in the church to think together of the meaning of life and death, so that during the important years when a philosophy of life is being formed, the young persons can give it breadth enough to encompass an adequate thanatology. We can well remember that Bryant was but seventeen when he wrote "Thanatopsis."

3. Preparation Through Pastoral Counseling

The pastor has an unusual opportunity to help prepare persons for grief situations by his ministry to the sick and the aged. It is possible to use the warning signals of terminal illness as an opportunity to face intelligently the feelings that begin to find expression in the situation. Often irritations can be ventilated, and aggressive feelings externalized, so that the death experience does not release all at once the ambivalent feelings that may exist. Also, peace and comfort can be brought in advance of the event through the acts of preparation.

Though much counseling will be of the informal type that is encouraged by the waiting room of a hospital, or the sickroom of a home, it is also important for the pastor to be aware of the chance to counsel with those who are surely faced with the problems of death, grief, and mourning. This is often the case when the potential mourners are rendered inadequate because of serious problems of their own. Mrs. W. called the pastor for an appointment. When she came, she said immediately that she had to have help. She had come to the end of her rope. When asked for clarification she said it was her mother who was driving her slowly insane. It was soon clear that she had strong feelings of ambivalence toward her mother. The reason seemed obvious. She was the only child born rather late in life to parents who idolized her. Her father had died shortly after the daughter's marriage, and her mother had come to live with her. For twenty years the mother had shared the home, supervised the raising of the children, and in every way had imposed her status as mother on a daughter she refused to admit had grown up. Now the mother, in her early eighties, had taken a "queer streak." She stayed in her room and pouted, making life miserable for her daughter when she had friends in. The mother would tell the guests, "My daughter doesn't want me any more. She wishes I would die. But I just can't up and die to satisfy her. Lord knows I would like to end this miserable existence but I can't." This had become so embarrassing that it ended the social life of the daughter and her husband. This in turn had its effect upon his position in business, for as an executive he had responsibilities for entertainment. The daughter said, "I want to take proper care of my mother, but she has dominated my marriage almost from the beginning. Now she is slowly making life miserable with our friends, and I feel as if I were going to lose my mind. Something will have to be done and done soon."

We talked about Mrs. W.'s state of mind. She said she had been able to handle herself fairly well until she became involved in the emotional changes of the menopause. Now she was so jumpy that she was ashamed of herself. Her children loved the grandmother and seemed anxious to bring the great grandchildren back to visit her. They were critical of their mother's impatience with the grandmother. The mother felt threatened both by her children and her mother because she was unable to cope with the problems she faced. She had little capacity to understand anyone else, for she was having difficulty to understand herself and her own unpredictable moods. Here was the type of emotional pattern that could have precipitated deep feelings of guilt and depression at the inevitable death of the aged mother.

How in the counseling relationship could the pastor minister to the needs of this troubled woman so that she would be able to go through the ensuing bereavement without serious damage? A three-point program was approached in the hours that were spent together. First was the effort to encourage every consideration and concern for her own health. With medical care and hormone supplements, she was able to bring her own emotional state into better balance. Then an effort was made to help her understand the nature of the relation that exists between a person suffering from senile dementia and those who surround her. Understanding at this point brought a good measure of relief from feelings of aggression, guilt, and frustration. It also enabled her to see the advisability of care in a home for the aged, where a society of older folk gave a chance for group activity that did not exist in a home in which the aged person was socially excluded because of circumstances beyond anyone's control. Last but not least, she was encouraged to make explicit the feelings of aggression that she had been building up against her mother through twenty years of her involvement in Mrs. W.'s marriage and child training. She had not realized how deeply these feelings were at work in the other problems she faced. The ability to exteriorize her feelings, and to gain some understanding of what they were, how they had developed, and what they meant for her present and future living, gave her a new sense of confidence and freedom in dealing with the practical problems that had brought her near distraction. Two months after the first interview, the aged mother was in a home for persons of her age and condition. She was happier than she had been for years because she now had an independent status at the home for the aged, her mental attitude and physical condition improved. The daughter also felt better and was able to resume her station in the social life of the community and her husband's business. Her mental attitude also was markedly improved with the removal of stress. She went regularly to visit her mother and was able to see her more objectively, and to express toward her the positive feelings of affection that gave satisfaction to both the mother and the daughter. When the mother's health declined and she entered terminal illness, she had every care, and at her death the family was able to go through the bereavement situation without the involvement of the mass of turbulent emotions that had been present when Mrs. W. first sought assistance.

Often, because of his knowledge of the total family picture, the pastor is in a strategic position to be able to detect the trouble spots which can easily develop in eventual bereavement. Within the normal counseling relationship he may be able to assist persons in releasing the feelings that would precipitate abnormal grief reactions or deep disturbance. When he has some knowledge of the dynamic factors at work in human emotions, he can be more sensitive to these situations as they develop and more useful in resolving them. Again it becomes a matter of moral responsibility to prepare as adequately as possible for dealing with these cases which make up so great a part of the normal parish ministry.

4. Pastoral Self-Examination

In preparing himself, it is important for the pastor to re-examine the grief experiences that have been encountered in his own life, the better to understand the movement of his own emotions. Too often a pastor may read into grief conditions the emotional reactions that are rooted in his own experience. While his own experience may be of use in establishing an empathic relationship, it is also possible that unresolved emotional factors may limit his effectiveness and project into other situations feelings that are not legitimately there. So it was with the Rev. John M. No one ever doubted his sincerity or his desire to be helpful to other people. Insofar as most of his ministry was concerned he did creditable work. However, when it came to the matter of ministering to the grief-stricken, he found that he was unable to function effectively. He was bothered by this but did not know there was anything he could do about it until he heard a lecture at a summer conference on psychological motivation. He raised some questions with the lecturer which led to a counseling relationship. It developed that his mother had died at an early age and his father had remarried. The questions he had raised about his own mother and her death were brushed aside and never answered. Although he was treated with kindness, the matter of the death of his own mother was surrounded with a sense of mystery, apprehension, and misgiving. He was never able to come to grips with the feelings and the reactions that developed within himself when he was faced with the death of one of his parishioners. He realized that his attitude was foolish but he could not seem to resolve it. It was not until he had been patiently led back through the maze of emotional developments that had grown up about his early experience that he was able to handle the problem. It had not been a matter of rational control but rather a problem of the release of deep emotional response. When these preconscious feelings were brought to the place where they could be candidly examined they became different. They could then be handled and they were handled. It is unfortunate when one professionally engaged in dealing with the grief-stricken is not able to be reasonably free from the transference of his own disturbed emotions to the experience of his people.

5. Informal Group Support

The life of the church offers opportunities for those who are faced with bereavement to meet together. In one church a group of elderly persons was organized to help them relieve the boredom of life and to find some creative social expression. The middle-aged children of these elderly persons met once a month informally to prepare a luncheon for them. Nothing was ever said about organizing a group discussion, but as the months went on and one after another of the elderly persons died, the members of the group talked the thing over and, in the sharing of their feelings in this informal way, were prepared for the loss that it would soon be their turn to share. Without even making the purpose explicit, the activity served its purpose therapeutically in advance, by preparing their mood and attitude. A further treatment of this important subject is the main emphasis of Chapter XV.

6. Bibliotherapy: Assets and Liabilities

Bibliotherapy has come into prominence in more recent years, with a flood of books that deal with psychology, religion, and related subjects. While there is serious danger present in the steeping of one's soul in illusion-creating, reality-destroying types of reading, that should in no way preclude the use of many carefully written and useful books. Perhaps we have no better rule of thumb in distinguishing the useless from the useful than the standards of measurement Paul used to separate the religious trivialities of his day from the true religious concerns. Looking primarily at the religious situation in Greece, he wrote his followers to beware of three dangerous types of emphasis. One was the esoteric, which claimed that it alone had the way, the truth, and the life. The second was the selfishly immature, which promised its adherents a knowledge of the simple tricks to be used in making God work for them as more of a servant boy than an awe-inspiring creator of the universe. The third was the type that created illusions and false dependencies by the use of miracles and magic in situations in which reality, ethical action, and mature judgment would have been preferable. When a book tends to fall into one or another of these categories, it probably does more harm than good, though as is always the case with such types of books, they tend to shore up a weak and emotionally dependent personality, at least temporarily.

In the use of books or printed materials, the pastor might have three general classifications in mind, and these classifications would determine the use made of the material. There is the literature he himself would use to gain insight and understanding of the problems related to grief and the grief-stricken. Then there is the literature that can be given to the bereaved for their own reading, so that they may gain insight into their feelings and resources for dealing with them. Third is the literature that has a general inspirational and positive quality which can be used to strengthen faith.

In the first group would be studies of personality dynamics, especially as they relate to the problems of death, dying, and bereavement, such as the following:

> *The Psychiatrist and the Dying Patient*, K. R. Eissler
> *Anxiety*, eds. Paul H. Hoch and Joseph Zubin
> *Depression*, eds. Paul H. Hoch and Joseph Zubin
> *Man Against Himself*, Karl A. Menninger
> *Affective Disorders*, ed. Phyllis Greenacre
> *Principles of Psychodynamics*, Edoardo Weiss
> *The Meaning of Anxiety*, Rollo May
> *Beyond Anxiety*, James A. Pike
> *The Funeral and the Mourners*, Paul E. Irion

The type of book that can be profitably read by the average normal reader might include the following list, although it is wise to be aware of the dangers of even such books for the seriously disturbed. As one would not give a medical book to a hypochondriac, so one has to be aware of the limitations of therapeutic reading with persons whose emotional outlook is disordered.

The Common Ventures of Life, Elton Trueblood
Ye Shall Be Comforted, W. F. Rogers
The Courage to Be, Paul Tillich
You Can Be Healed, C. E. Kew and C. J. Kew
On Being a Real Person, Harry E. Fosdick
Peace of Mind, Joshua Loth Liebman
The Mature Mind, Harry A. Overstreet

The books that can be read for inspiration, comfort, confidence, and understanding of personal adequacy would certainly include the Bible, with its varied human experience and spiritual insight. It would include biographies of persons who have met life with courage, honesty, and imagination. Also it would make a place for the inspirational reading that is produced in quantity by the religious presses of the country. Here the matter of taste would be a major factor. Some of the inspirational literature would be considered by one person as unadulterated drivel, while another would feed his soul upon it. The reprints of spiritual classics are useful, as are also the interpretive writings of Margaret Applegarth, Margueritte Harmon Bro, E. Stanley Jones, Russell L. Dicks, and Thomas S. Kepler. While these lists are in no sense complete, they are at least suggestive of types of reading that may be useful when a reading ministry seems desirable.

Reading circles may be guided toward the group-sharing of books that are constructive. When such books are read together, another dimension of human relatedness is added. With the disturbed this is often a valuable therapeutic factor, for as the Kews point out, "All that isolates, damns; all that associates, saves." [2] No one approach to the problems of life is effective for everyone. The fullest variety of healthful methods for engaging the mind and emotions should be encouraged by the church that is seeking truly to minister to its people's needs. This is also true of the pulpit ministry.

7. A Pulpit Ministry to the Bereaved

The type of thought that finds expression in pulpit utterance becomes a conditioner of all of the relations that a pastor has with his people. That would be especially true for those whose emotions are made sensitive by death. If they recall a mood of understanding and confident faith that has been expressed by the pastor again and again in the pulpit, they will turn to him with assurance for guidance through the troubles that assail them. The sermon becomes a conditioner in advance of the fact when it is prepared with an awareness of this function. During the course of the year it is important to make a special effort to preach directly to the needs of the bereaved, not because any large number of the congregation are in mourning, but rather because all the congregation need to know that such a subject is well within the range of competent handling by those who are chosen to minister to their needs. This should not be an excursion into the unreal or the illusory, but rather an honest, down-to-earth meeting of the problems that the bereaved face. Perhaps the best way to do this is through illustration. This I have tried to demonstrate with sermon résumés in the chapter "Preaching to the Sorrow-filled," in my book How to Preach to People's Needs.[3]

Certainly, not all preaching should deal with such matters explicitly, but the attitude of confidence, courageous facing of reality, and the assumption of spiritual resources to help in so doing, should be a part of every sermon. That it is as effective in advance of actual bereavement as it is during the actual time of mourning is indicated by the fact that scores of persons have requested copies of sermons preached months or even years before they were faced with acute loss. They would say something like this, "Do you remember the sermon you preached once about strength to meet sorrow? Well, I would like to read it again now." The act of preparation has served its purpose and the mind of the mourner is now aware of a need and a resource to help meet that need. A message of mature thought, a clear approach to reality, and a constructive use of the resources of the Christian faith now become doubly meaningful. In this way preaching can be an instrument for creating the mood for a wise approach to bereavement and the possibility of effective counseling when it seems necessary. Pulpit utterance should never be insignificant. When it is so, it indicates the failure of the pastor to sense the importance for life of the spoken word rather than a failure of those in need to seek nourishment for their troubled souls.

The church, through its varied ministry, can be alert to the ways of preparing people mentally and emotionally for the loss that may come at any time and will eventually be a part of the experience of all.

FOURTEEN

Special Opportunities in Grief Situations

Often the pastor is called in to minister to the needs of the family that has suffered loss, without his having had a previous acquaintance with the family. He may know nothing of their background, their religious training or beliefs, or the emotional factors that may be released by the loss.

1. Relations with Official Persons in the Community

For that reason there is need for establishing with other official persons in the community who work with the bereaved a clear understanding of how the pastoral function is interpreted. This may be done with physicians, funeral directors, and in some communities, where the police have the only ambulance, with the police.

On one occasion a funeral director called to notify me of a death in a family that had not been connected with the parish. Matters of schedule were checked for the time of the funeral service, and I left shortly thereafter to go to the home of the deceased. Upon entering I noted a tension and embarrassment that I could not explain. Nobody seemed willing to say anything. In my effort to relate to the situation I soon made a misstatement that caused even more agitation of suppressed nature. I said, "I would find it helpful in preparing for the service if you could tell me something about Mr. J. that I could keep in mind as I make selections of scripture and poetry." Finally someone said bluntly: "Perhaps the less said the better. He never found much in life. In fact, he committed suicide this morning." I went directly to the funeral director and asked, "What is the situation with Mr. J.?" His response was, "Oh, he committed suicide this morning." "Why," I asked, "didn't you tell me that when you called earlier? It would have saved an embarrassing situation for the family and would

215

have made it possible for me to minister more effectively in an already difficult situation." Had the pastor interpreted to the funeral director in advance what he considered his function to be, such an unfortunate circumstance would not have developed. There can be a professional relationship that shares background information. When entering a new situation the pastor might ask the funeral director, "Is there anything unusual about this situation that you think I should know?" A funeral director can be a real ally in the work of ministering to the mourning, if he feels that the minister does not treat his responsibility as a perfunctory matter to be handled superficially and as quickly as possible.

A good working relationship with the medical profession will also be helpful in such matters. To be able to go directly to a physician with a question of diagnosis is helpful in determining procedure. A physician who was a minister's son and understood the importance of correlating the ministry of medicine and of religion called me late one evening and said, "Ezra L. needs some help. His wife is in a coma and will probably die during the night. He is a lonely man. They withdrew from the church [and he mentioned a neighboring church in the city] years ago over some disagreement. I think they were sorry afterward, but you know pride. Ezra needs help now. Would you go over?" I went over and spent the night with this lonely man who realized too late that he had made a mistake in separating himself from his church. He was deeply thankful for any friendly gesture that night. We sat by the bedside for hours and talked of many things. He told me all of the details of his withdrawal from his church. He reviewed many experiences of his life with his wife. He talked freely as one may do who has been a lonely person for a long time. Toward morning his wife expired and I assisted in the arrangements that had to be made. Ezra said, "I'd like you to take the service. You know I don't go to church any more but you know why."

During the days that followed I stayed rather close to Ezra, for he seemed to be quite dependent. He continued to talk about many things. We talked about the importance of re-establishing his relationship with his old church. I said there were ties there that could not be replaced at his age, and that he would find real satisfaction in worshiping again with his old friends. About two months after the funeral he called to say that he had rejoined his old church, and he seemed to feel real satisfaction in having done so. This relationship, which helped a lonely man through a bereavement that would have been doubly difficult, was established by a physician who knew the importance of such a relationship and was willing to go just a little out of his way to help establish it. Sometimes the nature of the community is such that a close and friendly relation between the medical profession and the clergy is not easily established. However, there are many ways in which a pastor can express his concern for an effective ministry to people, and many doctors see and respond to such a concern. Often the physician can be especially helpful in indicating any special problems that might be met in the family of the deceased.

2. Procedures in Dealing with Strangers

It is difficult but not impossible for the minister to be genuinely helpful when he is called in at the last minute to assist persons he has not known before. It requires quick and rather superficial estimates of the emotional condition of the bereaved. It means that he has no background for sensing any abnormal factors that may develop in mourning. But it is also fairly sure that persons will respond in rather well-established and almost universal patterns. It is when they do not respond in these ways that special care and concern is warranted. Here the ability to observe and evaluate is important. Also, supplementary sources of information may be available. Relatives, friends, and neighbors may be helpful in acquainting the pastor with the kind of information that begins to build a picture. Of course, it is important to realize that considerable idealization may be involved and the real picture is gained by a careful reading between the lines.

When the pastor is called in to minister on such short notice, he will want, as quickly as possible, to get the best answer he can to three questions in order to determine his own action. He probably can get the answers more by indirection than directly. What is the personal adequacy of the bereaved? What are the religious presuppositions of the bereaved? What is there in the situation that can be used to stimulate the normal work of mourning? The answer to the first question may be rather simple and direct, or it may be so camouflaged that it is difficult to get an accurate answer. A pastor may be met with the assertion, "We are atheists and all we want from you is what is decent for the dead." This is an immediate admission of a breakdown in relationships. But it may be less of an admission than a thin veneer of too obvious piety.

3. The Problem of Religious Opposition

The denial of God is usually subjective and related to strong feelings of rejection in the life of the individual, who feels impelled to project these feelings out upon the universe. Mental note may be made of this fact, but it is usually not the time to begin an apologia for the faith. It is more likely to be a time for a careful evaluation of the relationships that can be observed. Because of the emotional factors that may be released in bereavement, it is better for the pastor to stand by as an accepting friend rather than as an argumentative antagonist. Then in the stress of the next few days, some one or another of the persons may seek out the pastor for personal words which will open the door for a more effective pastoral relationship.

Many of the problems of religion are problems of definition. The facing of ultimate realities has a way of moving people beyond the semantic difficulties to the place where there is a meeting of mind and soul. Often a few hours spent together in a time of crisis can bring persons together more closely than years of normal and casual acquaintance. It is not an unusual experience for the pastor to establish a relation with the bereaved family that becomes a basis for a long and creative friendship. The attitude of the pastor is often the determining factor. A genuine concern to be helpful, a sure measure of professional competence, an indication of the importance of persons whether of long or short acquaintance, a responsiveness to special needs—all may become the basis for establishing and maintaining a healing relationship.

For some, the experience of acute grief comes when they have recently moved into a new community. Here their feelings are compounded of grief, loneliness, and despair. The pastor, as a symbol of a human fellowship that is not bound by any artificial barriers, is able not only to bridge the feelings of loneliness and separation, but also to use the organizations that are at his disposal to relate persons to a community of mutual interests.

4. Using the Universals in Grief

The basic feelings in grief are so universal that the trained pastor can readily develop empathy with even new persons in the expressing of them. While the advantages of long friendship are not to be minimized, and the problems of establishing relationship with total strangers are considerable, the emotions involved in grief are so real that they find an expression without regard to time or place. The pastor who is available becomes more than a person. He becomes a symbol of the mobilized forces of society that express concern and help in meeting acute emotional needs. By using his symbolic status, the pastor may helpfully engage persons in pastoral counseling of the less formal nature. He can encourage persons to express the grief they feel. He does not try to repress the feelings of others, either by word or attitude. He knows it is important for their health to give expression to their sense of fear, anxiety, loneliness, and despair. But when that expression has been made, he is alert to the opportunities that exist for starting the upward climb to renewed faith, confidence, restored relations, and courage for life. He encourages the learning process involved in breaking the bonds that have related to the physical presence of the deceased. He may in a very useful way become the bridge to help the person to replace the bonds of the past with new relationships that can bind him to the future. At all points the pastor seeks to remove the barriers to a useful, wise, and healthy engaging of the emotions.

The pastor is alert to his function as one who can resolve the guilt that may be found in grief. A rural letter carrier moved into the county-seat town after his retirement. Shortly thereafter he died and his wife seemed obsessed with the idea that she must go out to the section of the county he had served and go around his mail route. Her children rejected the idea as foolishness. The pastor, however, sensed the importance of this symbolic action for the bereaved woman, and took most of a day to go with her over the route, meet some of the people, and talk about the life of her husband as it related to these people, their fears, and their pleasures. When they returned home after the day's journey, the letter carrier's widow confessed that her husband had always wanted her to take the trip, but she was always too busy and saw no sense to it anyway. Now she felt she had fulfilled an obligation and could be at peace. A stranger in a large town, she had found an understanding friend in the pastor, and her relation to him and to the church he serves, grew in meaning through his responsiveness to her emotional needs.

5. The Funeral Sermon

The preaching function is also important in dealing with those who are in the process of working through their feelings. While the funeral service is hardly an appropriate time for a lengthy sermon, it is not difficult to bring a brief testimony of faith into the service as the basis upon which later thinking can be built. It is also the custom in some parts of the country for the whole family to attend church in a body the Sunday following the funeral. This gives an opportunity to make a constructive approach to some of the problems that may have been discerned by the pastor in his contact with the bereaved. His approach to such problems from the pulpit, however, should be handled with indirection and discretion; for it has happened that persons were so embarrassed by a service that they did not return again, and the chance to be helpful was destroyed. These are areas of consideration which can legitimately and profitably be made the subject of a sermon: the importance of spiritual values, the problem of suffering, the resources for creative living in spite of difficulty, and the importance and validity of the emotional life.

6. The Funeral and the Bereaved

The funeral service itself is the accepted formal time and place for expressing those thoughts which can be helpful to the bereaved. Though we recognize the limitations of such a service and would supplement it by other pastoral relationships, we must be aware of the fact that it is the only instrument we will have for dealing with some of those persons who come from a distance, arrive just in time for the service, and leave shortly afterward. What can be said or done to give this service meaning? How can it be used constructively to stimulate the work of mourning?

Perhaps it might be well to mention first some things that should not be done. The funeral service is not a time or place to take advantage of bereavement to condemn the behavior of the living. There are probably enough feelings of guilt already operative without stimulating any more. Nor is it a time for a long display of the pastor's skill as a reader. Charles Laughton can give dramatic readings of the Scriptures and they have their place. But the pastor's function is different. I once attended a funeral where a clergyman read endlessly from the Scriptures in a voice that just missed being a chant by a narrow margin. Dripping with sanctimoniousness and steeped in a self-consciousness of form and style, it was an interesting performance, but it did not seem to relate the wisdom of the ages to the needs of the afflicted. The reading of the Scriptures is not an oral exercise nor an example of elocution. It is a form of communion between the accumulated mind and soul of those who have suffered in the past and of those who now represent mankind on the earth, with their continued burden of mortality and their awareness of life's transitoriness. What can be said to man to help him carry his burden with courage?

The funeral, then, should be first of all a testimony of faith. If the people do not have a sustaining faith they should at least be made aware of its presence in the representative of the church, the institution of faith. This can hardly be done in a cold and formal service. It may be well to use a portion of the service to make a simple, direct affirmation of faith that is geared to the most distressing moments of life. This should not be a sermon, or of any great length. But it should be so simple and direct and so clearly a witness to faith that no one will escape the nature of it. It might be introduced by a statement such as this, "Our Christian faith is made for times such as this. It speaks to our most acute personal needs with a wisdom that has been built upon the experience of untold generations who met the tribulations of life and became 'more than conquerors.' " The statement may be related to the deceased if he is a person of faith, but it is not primarily a eulogy. Rather it seeks to undergird the present experience of death with a long-range understanding of the experience.

It would be a time when socially supporting factors are recognized. The church, the community, the home, as social institutions, give significance to the life of the individual. This contribution is clearly felt in times of acute need. The help of sympathetic neighbors adds immeasurably to the strength of the bereaved individual. The funeral service does this without ever having put it in words. The coming together of family and friends to give their supporting presence may be recognized by a phrase in the pastoral prayer, or a sentence in the statement of faith. But whether it is mentioned or not, it is there and it is real.

The funeral also should help rather than impede the normal mourning work. It should avoid any artificial or unreal atmosphere. It should not deny the fact of death even though it is concerned with relating the incident of death to a larger perspective of life. It should encourage the reality sense, help people to accept the pain of loss, and avoid the tendencies toward escape that easily .

While the funeral is not a time for exhortation, it is always important to encourage a realistic look at one's self in relation to others and the rest of life. Persons who are face to face with the ultimates of life are in a position to give careful thought to spiritual values, modification of their behavior, and improvement of their interpersonal relations. To encourage any acts of repentance or works of restitution may be important for resolving feelings of guilt that may be related to the bereavement.

In a day when much of society seems to conspire to keep the reality of death from becoming a part of conscious thought, the church as an institution and the funeral as an instrument serve important functions in keeping the basic realities of life and death in clear perspective. Commenting on the attitude of our society which seeks escape in sensation and the unreal in life experience,

George Buttrick remarks, "The cynic calls religion an 'escape!' In truth, religion alone refuses to be blind to the fact of death." [1]

7. Nine Criteria for Evaluating a Funeral

In gaining insight into his role as one who helps people through the grief experience, the minister can find helpful insight in books that have been especially prepared for this purpose. It is not necessary to do again here the work that has been adequately done in such other books. Paul Irion, in his book *The Funeral and the Mourners*, lists nine criteria for evaluating the personal effectiveness of the funeral:

1. The funeral must deal with death realistically.
2. The funeral must present a vision of God which will be a comfort and help to the mourners in their suffering. This includes the understanding of the love of God, the nearness of God, and his concern for his people.
3. The funeral must see man as an individual of worth, turning man's attention to the importance of his personal integration and the resources which God offers for the strengthening and stabilizing of the self.
4. The funeral must demonstrate that the Christian faith is a resource which enables the individual to mourn, rather than a substitute for mourning.
5. The funeral must recognize and accept deep feelings, rather than cover them up by a superficial aestheticism.
6. The funeral must provide a sense of finality.
7. The funeral must be an aid in recalling memories of the deceased.
8. The funeral is to establish a climate for mourning.
9. The funeral must be sensitive to the individual needs of the bereaved, dynamic, variable in both form and content.[2]

The minister must never forget that his function at the funeral is to face the fullest reality of life in terms of the most daring faith the human mind can generate. W. Earle Biddle, a psychiatrist, speaks of the function of the Christian message which is particularly pertinent at the time of death. He says:

Christianity has not failed. It stands today, as in the time of Christ, a tower of strength, a source of solace, a reason for life. The Christian has failed to recognize or to use the resources it has to offer. . . . The mature, practical Christian needs first of all a strong realistic faith in God as the child has in a loving parent.[8]

In helping people through the crises of their lives, the minister should be the witness to that faith in all he says and does.

FIFTEEN

Resources for Facing New Horizons

We come now in this last chapter to the task of gauging our part in the important work of helping the bereaved to move ahead into life. The crisis has been met. The grief work has been engaged in. The personality is ready to take hold of the tasks and opportunities that lie ahead. But it is not the same personality. Something significant has happened and with every significant experience there is adjustment and growth. The person has had to deal with some ultimate realities and the stress on his personality has been considerable. Though he has weathered the storm, he is well aware of the fact that there was a storm, and he was threatened by it. As he moves into the future he will have a concern for his own adequacy in dealing with life, for he has been reminded of the fact that his days are numbered and that it is important for him to "apply his heart unto wisdom."

Erich Fromm, in *Man for Himself* asserts that we are all forced to face two "existential dichotomies." The personality emerging from a grief experience has faced both. By "existential dichotomies" he means "contradictions which man cannot annul but to which he can react in various ways, relative to his character and his culture." [1] One is death itself. "All knowledge about death does not alter the fact that death is not a meaningful part of life and that there is nothing for us to do but accept the fact of death; hence, as far as our life is concerned, defeat." The second has to do with the feeling that life is too short for a man to find his fullest self-realization. Concerning these basic problems, Fromm finds that there is no solution apart from that of a courageous despair at the ultimate meaninglessness of life. That solution is to

face the truth, to acknowledge his fundamental aloneness and solitude in a universe indifferent to his fate, to recognize that there is no

power transcending him which can solve his problem for him. . . .
There is no meaning to life except the meaning man gives his life by
the unfolding of his powers, by living productively.[2]

1. Courageous Meaning or Courageous Meaninglessness

Against the personal adequacy based on a courageous facing of
meaninglessness there is another concept of personal adequacy
based on the courageous venture of faith that we have outlined
in this book. It is the achieving of a transcendent meaning for life.
It is the fulfilling of a destiny larger than the negative limitations
of philosophy, psychology, or social thought. The values we cherish
refuse to be limited by the formal bounds of mere logic. There are
needs of the total being that are not satisfied by the limited aspects
of man's organized comprehension. The next step is not a counsel
of despair, or a spasm of disorganization, but rather a larger concept
of what makes for human adequacy.

This may come in part through an insight into what makes
for a more mature handling of personal experience. Here the judgment of a medical psychologist like Maurice Levine gives a clue to
this quality of emotional maturity. He lists ten indications of personal adequacy:

1. Ability to be guided by reality rather than by fears.
2. Use of long-term values.
3. Grown-up conscience.
4. Independence.
5. Capacity to "love" someone else, but with an enlightened self-
interest.
6. A reasonable dependence.
7. A reasonable aggressiveness.
8. Healthy defence-mechanisms.
9. Good sexual-adjustment with acceptance of own gender.
10. Good work-adjustment.[3]

But maturity also involves other people, and the person emerging
from a grief experience is bound to face problems of readjustment
at the point of his human relations. Grief is a group experience. It
involves the relationships with another person or persons. Here the

response of the individual must also be measured by the type of standards that make allowance for group performance and the competence with which group relations are maintained. Some criteria that may be useful in gauging a reasonable social response are listed by Foote and Cottrell: (1) health, not as an absence of disease but as a high level functional wholeness, (2) intelligence as the ability to perceive, abstract, relate and communicate meaningfully to others for clearly defined and useful purposes, (3) empathy, the ability to take the role of the other, to feel with others, (4) autonomy, the ability to function with a stabilized set of integrating values and standards, (5) judgment, the ability to bring accumulated experience to bear on present circumstance so that both reason and valid emotion are preserved, and (6) creativity, whereby the imagination can be employed without doing violence to reality, reason or emotion.[4]

As beings with great spiritual potential, we cannot fail to employ it without frustration and impoverishment of life. When spiritual crises develop it is especially important to have the resources to meet them. The loss of a loved one has clear spiritual implications. Important inspiration can come from great personalities of the past and present who have shown their spiritual mastery over life circumstance.

Albert Schweitzer, for instance, has been a source of spiritual strength for many in our age. His philosophy takes into account all of the values of science, culture, and social relations and moves on to establish a daring mental construct that represents spiritual creativity of a high order. His life gives a validity to his thought that proves not only his personal adequacy and interpersonal competence, but his spiritual creativity as well. Not in any trivial sense of self-hypnotic thought, but rather with a solid reason geared to reality, he presents a simple structure of spiritual values rooted in reverence for life, expressed through ethical behavior predicated on that reverence, and fulfilled through a God-consciousness that gives the spiritual basis for both reverence and ethical action. Contemplating such a life adds value and status to the contemplator, and the serious problems of life are more easily faced.

Those who work with the bereaved must be continually alert

to the task of increasing the resources of the personality for dealing with both life and death. The clues found in sources such as these to which we have just referred may well give the starting point from which an individual can grow toward maturity, adequacy, and spiritual competence.

2. The Counselor's Role in Restoring Persons to Useful Living

In his ministry to the bereaved it is important for the spiritual interpreter to possess the daring insights of those who have thought courageously and lived prodigiously. The pastor tries to help healthy people to maintain their wholeness under stress. The true minister seeks to restore those whose wholeness has been compromised by personal disaster. He works not with negatives but with the positives of life. Karl Abraham admitted that psychoanalysis had thrown little light on mourning among normal people.[5] It has been of significant help in dealing with those who have not been able to meet their disturbances with the normal strength of the adequate personality. But the major problems of giving sustaining power to life, even after the significant aid of the medical or psychological specialist has been administered, remains for those who deal with the creative resources of the normal personality.

To that end the pastor does not give satisfaction to the impulse to escape from reality, or encourage the mood of self-pity, or hold up any of the promises of unrealistic solutions to the problems of even the bitterest experience. His aim in counseling and in his pulpit ministry is continually to make real a concept of personal, social, and spiritual adequacy that can be the measure of the abundant life. Those emerging from a period of grief and disorganized living need to have held before them a clear pattern of the person they can become and the life they can find.

The pastor is a teacher of the courage for life. That he has a reasonable task is verified by Joost A. M. Meerloo in his study of the psychology of courage.[6] He believes that persons can be trained in the creative handling of their feelings. He feels that a quality of self-control can be built that is more than a superficial display of bravery to cover up the strenuous fears that lie beneath. He points out that the false philosophy of Nazism produced a mass hysteria that made it easier for people to face death, but this mass hysteria was impotent when it came to building the values to help people live. Nazism in its deeper expression was organized cowardice. There is need for the courage for life that is produced in an inner faith that is able to look ahead and value life for itself. This reverence for life is an obligation of those who would reveal the master of life.

For the bereaved person this revelation is not bound up so much with the mystical as with the practical. His concept of competence is a matter of practical adjustment rather than theoretical speculation. His competence for facing the new circumstances of life can be expressed and developed through the importance of relation, communication, and participation. Here the theoretical becomes practical. Here the readjustment of life actually takes place.

3. The Importance of Being Related

Relation involves the action and reaction between the core of being and the fabric of its interrelatedness to group life. Men have always recognized the importance of relationship as essential to personality growth, but probably never before have they been as well aware of why the health of the individual is bound up with the functional group. Jesus, in his insight into human relations, emphasized the importance of relation. In the parables of relation and separation he points out that life has meaning only as it is effectively related. The security of the individual, the ability to function normally, and the moral integrity of the individual are never separated from group life.

In the parable of the lost coin, the loss of function was inevitable when the coin was removed from circulation; and its function was not restored until the coin was found and made available for its purpose. The coin was lost by accident, but it was restored with intent. Often the loss of life and the incident bereavement tends to take the mourners out of circulation, not so much by design as by accident.

The pastor noted that Mrs. T. had dropped out of things after the death of her husband. On inquiry she stated the case quite simply: "Fred drove the car. Since he's gone I don't get anywhere." She had been put out of circulation quite by accident at the time when she especially needed the sustaining influence of group support. It became a rather simple matter at that point for the pastor to re-establish the group relationships by making this woman's separation a matter of group concern. In fact, there was a joy of satisfaction when she was restored to group life by those who could easily furnish transportation.

Sometimes the breakdown of relation is due to carelessness and neglect. The lost sheep wandered away because of a careless preoccupation with its own interests. The bereaved may be so preoccupied with their problems that they become thoughtless and neglectful of themselves and of their group relationships. Bereavement and loss of self-esteem may go hand in hand. Social adequacy involves a handling of the situation so that self-esteem is restored. Evidences of the loss of esteem may be observed in the carelessness with which a person dresses, keeps house, or ignores the social amenities.

Such seems to have been the case with Mrs. Henry J., a rather self-assured and meticulous schoolteacher, whose attitude toward life changed after the death of her husband. Her appearance changed; she wore clothes badly in need of dry-cleaning; her hair was carelessly arranged; even the house was poorly kept. She was withdrawn from group activity. Circumstances gave her warrant for her feeling of injury, for her husband died in an automobile accident in the company of another woman and in rather questionable circumstances. Self-esteem could well be damaged by such an event and its attendant publicity. The question was, How could a sustaining group relationship help to restore the injured self-esteem and bring this woman back to more normal life?

The "Good Shepherd" in this situation was the pastor's wife, who quietly and patiently began giving special attention to Mrs. Henry J. She stopped in to visit her frequently, took in tasty items of food, and invited her to the parsonage for dinner quite often. This mood of unqualified acceptance had a gradual restorative effect. Mrs. Henry J. was not allowed to withdraw with her injured self-esteem into self-pity and neglect. The pastor's wife served as a persistent social pressure that put the brakes on withdrawal and restored an injured person to a supportive structure of group relationships and activities. At times the path was thorny, but in time the straying sheep was restored to the fold.

At other times the breakdown in relationships is a deliberate expression of aggressive feelings. In effect the bereaved person says, "I want no more of this. Life has done me an injustice and I will deny as much of the rest of life as I can. I will deliberately waste my resources and reject life." The mood of the Prodigal Son is turned against life itself.

Such was the mood of W. D., whose wife died of a malignancy of long and painful duration. He was angry at life and God and people. He showed his aggression against the funeral director, the pastor, and those who tried to speak words of comfort. He rejected with directness every indication of kindness and every effort to restore him to healthful group relationships. His bitterness seemed to be impenetrable. One of the prayer-group leaders in the parish mentioned his case and communicated her concern to the other group leaders. Thereafter, every evening at 9:00 there were thirty or more persons united in intercessory prayer for this bereaved man. In a way that had not seemed possible through direct approach, this man "came to himself," was markedly changed in attitude, and began to function again as a responsive member of the group. Something in the prayer group seemed to establish an identity and a response that was able to modify his attitude and bridge the gap of bitterness.

The spiritual group with its resources may be effective in restoring people to right relationships when nothing else seems to work. Perhaps the first effort should be to keep persons related so that there is no breakdown. This tends to be automatic and the group function is asserted so that bereaved persons proceed in their grief work sustained by the fabric of such supportive relationships. However, when separation does occur, the group can help to restore a healing relationship by meeting the circumstantial factors at work, by using the power of an accepting attitude, either by an individual or a group, or by using those resources of the religious group that may effectively bridge the gap of resistance and thus release the inner inclination toward health and wholeness. The church has a special function at this point as a form of social insurance wherein those who suffer loss can find strength and support from those who have in the past shared the common experience and have felt the benefits of the supportive group.

4. Cultivating a Capacity to Communicate Creatively

We now know much more about the importance of communication as a factor of emotional health than we did a few years a ago. Careful studies of the nature and need for communication have been made by psychologists and sociologists. Something deep within the social being is preserved by the technique of communication, and something surely is lost when communication as an effective human relationship breaks down. This communication is not so much a matter of language as it is a quality of language. People can talk without much communication. People can communicate without much talking.

The Scriptures say, "Let us reason together." The crises of life invite this type of significant communication, but when bereavement comes it often dislocates the process by removing the one with whom communication has been most effective. So the problem of re-establishing communication may be doubly difficult. Just because it may be difficult is reason for giving it special consideration.

Communication in relation to grief work implies a person with sympathy, empathy, and acceptance, with whom one can project through verbalization the deep feelings that exist. Just as a ship takes a shakedown cruise after major alterations, so a person, after acute deprivation, tries out his new feelings and attitudes by attempting to talk through the matter with someone who can share his feelings. The efforts at communication may take a variety of forms. Negatively, one may talk to himself as if he were communicating. Mrs. Y., a widowed schoolteacher, carried on her professional work as usual, but lived withdrawn as far as the rest of life was concerned. In response to efforts to relate her to group life again, she said, "I don't want to be bothered by people for a while until I have been able to think this thing through for myself." While this may indicate flaws in her basic orientation to people, it is her way of inverting the communication process.

When the pastor called on Mrs. L. one afternoon he found her deeply engrossed in a television serial of rather emotional nature. She was weeping gently and did not want to be disturbed until the episode for the day was concluded. Then she explained that she had been getting much comfort from these dramas which had "such nice people who have the same problems I have." In her loneliness Mrs. L. had established a form of communication with television personalities. While she could not talk with them, she could act out her feelings with them, and in so doing find a type of emotional release that seemed important for her.

This ability to communicate through the acting out of feelings is not done through the passive approach alone, as employed by Mrs. L. At the death of his son, Emerson wrote vigorously and with keen penetration. The repeal of the Corn Laws in England was made possible, at least in part, by the enthusiasm with which a young widower went to work to communicate his intense feelings of grief by sharing the lot of those who suffered. The possibilities for communication through the acting out of grief are almost unlimited. Here relationship is carried one step further and strong feelings of success, failure, fear, and guilt are exteriorized. Often the means of exteriorization is verbalization, and such verbalization seems to give a measure of control over the circumstances that are beyond control. It is important in the process of working through the grief to be able to find the most constructive form of communication. This usually is the type of communication that is related to reality rather than fantasy, deals with real people rather than persons who exist only in a remote relationship, and has an accepting and creative orientation rather than a relationship limited by both insight and attitude.

In this creative communication the counselor can play an important role, for he does not stimulate the unreal or direct emotions away from the frames of reference that future living will require. Rather, the counselor approaches the person who is groping in the darkness of grief and helps him gradually to turn on the lights of life again. While the counselor is not critical of

233

the limited forms of communication that may develop, he tries to lead beyond them to the communication that can strengthen life and re-establish the needed relationships of life on a productive and life-sustaining level. This quite naturally leads to the third step in the reorientation of life, the process of participation.

5. The Place of Active Participation in Personality Reorientation

We have always known that there was something health-giving about being able to engage the total personality in constructive action. More than just a matter of relationship, and more than the capacity for communication, there is a value in doing. This may involve no more than the housekeeping activity of life wherein a person participates in preparing meals, making beds, and working in the garden. What we speak of is quite different from the frenzied activity of one who tries to get away from himself and reality by immersing himself in activity merely for the sake of activity. We rather refer to the type of activity that restores one to useful functional relationships with a sustaining group whether it be a family, a religious group, or a business association.

If a family is disrupted by bereavement, there are groups that can effectively serve as substitutes for the family relationship in that they can engage some of the same emotions. Sometimes a person can find a new family relationship in which he cares for others and others care for him in the normal tasks of living. Sometimes the process of counseling takes on some of the characteristics of this relationship. Often persons get an emotional response from worship that satisfies the need for participation at the same time that it protects the privacy of thought and feeling.

In a prayer group made up largely of bereaved persons, it has been observed that there is an identity, a movement of emotion, and a spiritual response that fulfills many of the needs for a family relationship. The participation in the group is voluntary but disciplined. The self is sustained at the very time that thought is directed toward the needs of others in intercession. The total being is engaged in a process of self-giving and self-receiving that reveals deeper levels of the life of the participants. This type of

234

revealed meaning through participation gives a perspective to one's own loss at the same time that it is helping to relieve the burden of another. It also gives a sense of well-being through an understanding faith which gives forward motion to living.

The counselor, the pastor, and the sustaining group are able not only to bring first aid to the bereaved, but to accomplish that more important task of giving impetus for the next stage of living. Through relation, communication, and participation, the person is led to a new feeling of adequacy for the tasks of life. Though the pain of bereavement is real, life is not all pain. Though the burdens are heavy, they are bearable. Though the desires of life are not all fulfilled, there is a revelation of depths of life and being that can be mutually supportive. All can share together in the process of moving from the injuring incident to the feelings and attitudes that are more than incidental. This perhaps is one of the fundamental spiritual revelations that cannot come except through trial and suffering.

This spiritual revelation is not bound by privilege or status. It is the property of those who master the high art of adequacy as human beings. They are the ones who can face the new horizons of life with an assurance that the goodness of the past is somehow related to the goodness of the future. One of the most beautiful testimonies to the achievement of this adequacy came not from the learned, or from the symbolism of the scholar. It came as the expression of the faith of a humble man who had known grief and suffered loss and faced his own death with courage and the confidence of one who had known the goodness of life and was sure in his mind of the goodness of death.

6. A Sustaining Faith to Meet Life or Death

Abraham C. was the senior janitor of a large New York apartment house and a deacon of the Negro Baptist church. He was a person of unusual kindliness and genuineness of spirit. People went to him continually for advice and counsel and he always seemed to be able to lift their spirits and give them a new perspective. He was calm and sure of himself, with no evidence of aggressiveness. He did not engage in the activities of the groups that fought for the rights of Negroes. He thought other people could do that more adequately. He just had so much native dignity and assurance of his place in the world as a child of God that it never occurred to him to fight to change his status. Because his church had a part-time minister, it fell to the lot of Abraham C. as deacon to do much of the supervisory work of the parish. This he did with devotion and a real concern for the needs of other people, as well as a high regard for their possibilities.

When he was taken to the hospital with a terminal illness a neighboring pastor stopped to visit him two or three times a week. When a physician told this pastor that he thought Abraham C. had about a week of life left, it seemed that some pastoral approach to his condition should be made. So the pastor started to talk to Abraham C. about the meaning of the spiritual values and the undying quality of the spiritual life. After an effort in that direction the patient looked up and said, "Pastor, you are being kind to me but you don't need to tell me all these things. The doctor hasn't told me yet but I know I will die in a few days. I am thankful for all of the good things the Lord has done for me all of my life. I have never wanted for anything that I rightfully should have had. I love the Lord and I know he loves me. I am not afraid to meet him face to face. He has been so good to me for so long, I know he will keep on being the same way. My wife and my friends have all gone on before me. Now I can go. So, pastor, don't you worry about me. I'm only going home and no one is ever unhappy about going home."

If in our dealing with those who face the problems of life and death, we can in some measure create a consciousness of the underlying goodness of life, the fear of death will be largely gone. If we can sustain a faith that is not bounded by little assurance but has the courage of great ventures into the world of values and transcendent meanings, the gates of death will be friendly gates. If we can help people clearly to mark the way between what is real and what is false, they will be able to accept life and death with a wisdom that fulfills rather than destroys. Then we can pray and teach the prayer:

O God, give me the serenity
  To accept what cannot be changed.
Give me the courage
  To change what can be changed.
And the wisdom to distinguish
  The one from the other.[7]

NOTES

Chapter I

1. Rollo May, *The Meaning of Anxiety*. Copyright 1950 The Ronald Press Company. Pp. 247-330.
2. Joshua Loth Liebman, *Peace of Mind* (New York: Simon and Schuster, 1946), p. 110.
3. Charles Anderson, "Aspects of Pathological Grief and Mourning," *International Journal of Psycho-Analysis*, XXX (1949), 48-55.
4. Helene Deutsch, "Absence of Grief," *Psychoanalytic Quarterly*, VI (1937), 12.
5. *Collected Papers* (London: Hogarth Press, Ltd., 1950), IV, 152 ff.
6. *Selected Papers* (London: Hogarth Press, Ltd., 1927), pp. 433 ff.
7. *Op. cit.*, p. 191.
8. *Op. cit.*, p. 123.
9. *Men Under Stress* (Philadelphia: The Blakeston Co., 1945), p. 120.
10. *Op. cit.*

Chapter II

1. *Lectures on War Neuroses* (London: Edward Arnold & Co., 1941), p. 3.
2. "Symptomatology and Management of Acute Grief," *American Journal of Psychiatry*, CI (1944), 146. Used by permission of the author and the publisher.
3. Kuno Fischer, *Shakespeare's Hamlet*, p. 206, as quoted from Ernest Jones.
4. Ernest Jones, *Hamlet and Oedipus* (New York: Doubleday & Company, Inc., 1954), p. 77.
5. K. R. Eissler, *The Psychiatrist and the Dying Patient* (New York: International Universities Press, Inc., 1955) pp. 21 ff.
6. For elaboration of this point, see, Freud, *Beyond the Pleasure Principle* (New York: Liveright Publishing Corp., 1950); Ferenczi, "The Problem of Acceptance of Unpleasant Ideas," from *Further Contributions to the Theory and Technique of Psycho-Analysis* (New York: Basic Books, Inc., 1952); and Franz Alexander, "The Need for Punishment and the Death-Instinct," *International Journal of Psycho-Analysis*, X (1929), 260.
7. For elaboration, see Jean Piaget, *The Language and Thought of the Child* (New York: Humanities Press, 1951), *The Child's Conception of Physical Causality* (New York: Humanities Press, 1952), *The Construction of Reality in the Child* (New York: Basic Books, Inc., 1954), *The Origins of Intelligence in Children* (New York: International Universities Press, Inc., 1953); *Emotional Problems of Early Childhood*, ed. Gerald Caplan (New York: Basic Books, Inc., 1955); Donald M. Johnson, *The Psychology of Thought and Judgment* (New York: Harper & Brothers, 1955); Arnold Gesell, et al., *Infant and Child in the Culture of Today* (New York: Harper & Brothers, 1943).
8. Karl Stern, Gwendolyn M. Williams, and Miguel Prados, "Grief Reactions in Later Life," *American Journal of Psychiatry*, CVIII (1951), 289-94.
9. Melanie Klein, "Mourning and Its Relation to Manic-Depressive States," *International Journal of Psycho-Analysis*, XXI (1940), 125-53.

Chapter III

1. Solly Zuckermann, *The Social Life of Monkeys and Apes* (New York: Harcourt, Brace & Co., 1932).
2. Bruno Bettelheim, *Love Is Not Enough* (Glencoe, Ill.: The Free Press, 1950); Fritz Redl and David Wineman, *Controls from Within* (Glencoe, Ill.: The Free Press, 1952); Phyllis Greenacre, *Trauma, Growth, and Personality* (New York: W. W. Norton & Co., Inc., 1952); Bruno Bettelheim, *Truants from Life* (Glencoe, Ill.: The Free Press, 1951); Pollak, *et al., Social Science and Psychotherapy for Children* (New York: Russell Sage Foundation, 1952); David Beres and Samuel J. Obers, "The Effects of Extreme Deprivation in Infancy on Psychic Structure in Adolescence," in *The Psychoanalytic Study of the Child*, eds. Ruth S. Eissler, *et al.* (New York: International Universities Press), V (1950), 212-35.
3. *The Golden Bough* (New York: The Macmillan Co., 1951), ch. lxvi.
4. (New York: W. W. Norton & Company, Inc., 1926), p. 12.
5. *Modern Man in Search of a Soul* (New York: Harcourt, Brace & Co., 1934), pp. 249-50. Used by permission.
6. *Ibid.*, p. 250.
7. Henri L. Bergson, *The Two Sources of Morality and Religion*, trs. R. Ashley Audra and Cloudesley Brereton. Copyright, 1935, by Henry Holt & Co. and used by their permission.
8. Franz Alexander, *Our Age of Unreason* (rev. ed.; Philadelphia: J. B. Lippincott Co., 1951); Erich Fromm, *The Sane Society* (New York: Rinehart & Company, Inc., 1955); Karl A. Menninger, *Man Against Himself* (New York: Harcourt, Brace & Co., 1938).

Chapter IV

1. *The Depths of the Soul* (New York: Moffat, Yard & Co., 1922), p. 123.
2. *Principles of Psychodynamics* (New York: Grune & Stratton, Inc., 1950), p. 72. Used by permission of the publisher and the author.
3. *Ibid.*, p. 73.
4. *Masochism in Modern Man* (New York: Farrar, Straus & Young, Inc., 1949), pp. 233-34.
5. *A Primer of Freudian Psychology* (Cleveland, Ohio: The World Publishing Company, 1954).
6. *Op. cit.*, p. 34.
7. *The Psychoanalytic Theory of Neurosis* (New York: W. W. Norton & Company, Inc., 1945), p. 394.
8. *The Ego and the Id*, tr. Joan Riviere (London: Hogarth Press, Ltd., 1947).
9. *Loc. cit.*

Chapter V

1. *Anxiety*, eds. Paul H. Hoch and Joseph Zubin (New York: Grune & Stratton, Inc., 1950), p. 173.
2. *Man Against Himself*, pp. 265-67. Used by permission of Harcourt, Brace & Co.
3. *Op. cit.*, p. 81.
4. *Children's Humor* (Glencoe, Ill.: The Free Press, 1954).
5. See also "Wit and Its Relation to the Unconscious," *The Basic Writings of Sigmund Freud*, tr. and ed. A. A. Brill (New York: Modern Library, Inc., 1938), pp. 633-805.

Chapter VI

1. *The Concept of Dread*, tr. Walter Lowrie (Princeton University Press, 1944), p. 96.
2. Gordon W. Allport, *The Individual and His Religion* (New York: The Macmillan Co., 1950), p. 86.
3. Roy S. Lee, *Freud and Christianity* (New York: A. A. Wyn, 1949), p. 158.
4. Carroll A. Wise, *Pastoral Counseling* (New York: Harper & Brothers, 1951), p. 91.

Chapter VII

1. Eissler, *The Psychiatrist and the Dying Patient*, pp. 165, 191, 247. Used by permission of International Universities Press, Inc.
2. *The Two Sources of Morality and Religion* (New York: Doubleday & Company, Inc., Anchor Books, 1954, pp. 256, 262, 257.
3. As quoted by Leslie Weatherhead, in *That Immortal Sea*, p. 26.
4. *A Faith That Enquires* (New York: The Macmillan Co., 1922), pp. 264-68.
5. *Phaedo.*
6. *Religion and the Sciences of Life* (Duke University Press, 1935), p. 16.
7. *Moses and Monotheism*, tr. Katherine Jones (New York: Alfred A. Knopf, Inc., 1939), p. 195.
8. *The Self and the Dramas of History* (New York: Charles Scribner's Sons, 1955), pp. 24-25. Used by permission.
9. T. G. Duvall, *Great Thinkers* (New York: Oxford University Press, Inc., 1937), p. 218.
10. Quoted by M. F. Ashley Montagu, in *Immortality* (New York: Grove Press, 1955), p. 17.
11. For a detailed interpretation of this development, see Edgar N. Jackson, *This Is My Faith* (New York and Nashville: Abingdon Press, 1951).
12. *The Courage to Be* (New Haven, Conn.: Yale University Press, 1952), pp. 169-70. Used by permission.
13. Albert Einstein, *Cosmic Religion* (New York: Covici, Friede, Inc., 1931).

Chapter VIII

1. *Patterns of Culture* (New York: New American Library of World Literature, Inc., Menton Books, 1934), pp. 94-212.
2. *Specialized Techniques in Psychotherapy*, eds. Gustav Bychowski and J. L. Despert (New York: Basic Books, Inc., 1952), pp. 41-63.

Chapter IX

1. *Our Age of Unreason*, p. 152.
2. *Annals of Surgery*, CXVII (1943), 814 ff.

Chapter X

1. *Principles of Psychodynamics*, pp. 10-11.
2. *Ibid.*, p. 10.
3. *American Journal of Psychiatry*, CI (1944), 147.

NOTES

4. *Ibid.*

5. *Ibid.*

6. Gert Heilbrunn, "On Weeping," *Psychoanalytic Quarterly*, XXIV (1955), 245. Used by permission of the publisher and the author.

7. *Ibid.* See also Endre Petö, "Weeping and Laughing," *International Journal of Psycho-Analysis*, XXVII (1946), 129-33.

8. *Op. cit.*

9. *Op. cit.*, p. 189.

10. *Ibid.*, p. 189.

11. *American Journal of Psychiatry*, CI (1944), 147.

Chapter XI

1. Act I, Scene 2.

2. Act I, Scene 7.

3. Anderson, *op. cit.*, p. 48. Used by permission of *International Journal of Psycho-Analysis*.

4. *Op. cit.*, p. 10.

3. Anderson, *op. cit.*, p. 48. Used by permission of *International Journal of Psycho-Analysis*.

6. New York: Dodd, Mead & Co., 1923.

7. *Op. cit.*, p. 53.

8. *Ibid.*, p. 54.

9. *Op. cit.*, p. 413.

10. *The Human Mind* (3rd ed. rev. and enl.; New York: Alfred A. Knopf, 1949), p. 128.

11. *American Journal of Psychiatry*, CI (1944), 145-46.

12. Henry H. Brewster, "Grief: A Disrupted Human Relationship," *Human Organization*, IX (1950), 19-22. Used by permission.

13. *Ibid.*, p. 20.

14. *Op. cit.*, p. 30.

15. In *The Psychiatric Interview*, eds. Helen S. Perry and Mary L. Gawel (New York: W. W. Norton & Co., Inc., 1954), pp. 185-86.

16. Phyllis Greenacre, *Affective Disorders* (New York: International Universities Press, Inc., 1953), p. 18. Used by permission.

17. *Ibid.*, pp. 18-19.

18. *The Meaning of Anxiety*, pp. 194, 197, 199.

Chapter XII

1. *Psychological Effects of War on Citizen and Soldier* (New York: W. W. Norton & Co., Inc., 1942).

2. *Men Under Stress* (Philadelphia: The Blakiston Co., 1945); *War Neuroses in North Africa* (Philadelphia: The Blakiston Co., 1945).

3. *Op. cit.*, p. 12.

4. "Aspects of Pathological Grief and Mourning," *International Journal of Psycho-Analysis*, XXX (1949), 48-55.

5. *Patterns of Panic* (New York: International Universities Press, Inc., 1950).

6. Quoted from *Essays*.

7. "Mourning and Melancholia," *Collected Papers*, Vol. IV.

8. (New York: The Macmillan Co., 1945), pp. 160-83.

9. Glencoe, Ill.: The Free Press, 1951.

Chapter XIII

1. Joseph G. Kepecs, "Neurotic Reactions in Parachutists," *Psychoanalytic Quarterly*, XIII (1944), 273-99.
2. C. E. Kew and C. J. Kew, *You Can Be Healed* (New York: Prentice-Hall, Inc., 1953).
3. New York and Nashville: Abingdon Press, 1956.

Chapter XIV

1. *Christ and Man's Dilemma* (New York and Nashville: Abingdon Press, 1946), p. 86.
2. (New York and Nashville: Abingdon Press, 1954), pp. 86-87.
3. *Integration of Religion and Psychiatry* (New York: The Macmillan Co., 1955), pp. 119-20.

Chapter XV

1. P. 41.
2. *Ibid.*, pp. 44-45.
3. *Psychotherapy in Medical Practice* (New York: The Macmillan Co., 1945), p. 286.
4. Nelson N. Foote and L. S. Cottrell, *Identity and Interpersonal Competence* (University of Chicago Press, 1955).
5. *Op. cit.*, pp. 434-35.
6. *Total War and the Human Mind* (London: George Allen & Unwin, Ltd., 1944).
7. Reinhold Niebuhr. Used by permission.

SELECTED BIBLIOGRAPHY

General—The Dynamics of Personality

Ansbacher, Heinz L., and Rowena R. (eds.). *The Individual Psychology of Alfred Adler*. New York: Basic Books, Inc., 1956.

Benedict, Ruth. *Patterns of Culture*. New York: Houghton Mifflin Co., 1934.

Bergler, Edmund. *The Battle of the Conscience*. Westport, Conn.: Associated Booksellers, 1948.

Bettelheim, Bruno. *Love Is Not Enough*. Glencoe, Ill.: The Free Press, 1950.

————. *Truants from Life*. Glencoe, Ill.: The Free Press, 1955.

Bevan-Brown, C. M. *The Sources of Love and Fear*. New York: Vanguard Press, 1950.

Borgatta, Edgar F., and Meyer, Henry J. (eds.). *Sociological Theory*. New York: Alfred A. Knopf, Inc., 1956.

Burton, A., and Harris, R. E. (eds.). *Case Histories in Clinical and Abnormal Psychology*. New York: Harper & Bros., 1947.

————. *Clinical Studies of Personality*. New York: Harper & Bros., 1955.

Bychowski, Gustav, and Despert, J. Louise (eds.). *Specialized Techniques in Psychotherapy*. New York: Basic Books, Inc., 1952.

Calverton, Victor F. *The Making of Man*. New York: Modern Library, Inc., 1931.

Caplan, Gerald (ed.). *Emotional Problems of Early Childhood*. New York: Basic Books, Inc., 1955.

Cartwright, Dorwin, and Zander, A. F. *Group Dynamics*. Evanston, Ill.: Row, Peterson & Co., 1953.

Cassirer, Ernst. *An Essay on Man*. New Haven, Conn.: Yale University Press, 1944.

Clinebell, Howard J., Jr. *Understanding and Counseling the Alcoholic*. New York and Nashville: Abingdon Press, 1956.

Dollard, John, and Miller, Neal E. *Personality and Psychotherapy*. New York: McGraw-Hill Book Co., 1950.

Dunbar, H. F. *Your Child's Mind and Body*. New York: Random House, 1949.

Fenichel, Otto. *The Psychoanalytic Theory of Neurosis*. New York: W. W. Norton & Co., Inc., 1945.

Foote, Nelson N., and Cottrell, Leonard S. *Identity and Personal Competence*. University of Chicago Press, 1955.

Frazer, James G. *The Golden Bough* (3rd ed.). 13 vols. New York: The Macmillan Co., 1952.

243

Freud, Anna. *The Ego and Mechanisms of Defence.* Translated by Cecil Baines. New York: International Universities Press, Inc., 1946.

Freud, Sigmund. *Collected Papers.* 5 vols. London: Hogarth Press, n.d.

_____. *The Ego and the Id.* Translated by Joan Riviere. London: Hogarth Press, 1947.

_____. *Moses and Monotheism.* Translated by Katherine Jones. New York: Vintage Books, Inc., 1955.

Fromm, Erich. *The Forgotten Language.* New York: Rinehart & Co., Inc., 1951.

_____. *Man for Himself.* New York: Rinehart & Co., Inc., 1947.

Green, Harold D. (ed.). *Shock and Circulatory Homeostasis.* New York: Josiah Macy, Jr. Foundation, 1952-55.

Greenacre, Phyllis (ed.). *Affective Disorders.* New York: International Universities Press, Inc., 1953.

_____. *Trauma, Growth and Personality.* New York: W. W. Norton & Co., Inc., 1952.

Grinker, R. R., and Robbins, F. P. *Psychosomatic Case Book.* New York: The Blakiston Co., 1954.

Gutheil, Emil A. *Handbook of Dream Analysis.* New York: Liveright Publishing Corp., 1951.

Hall, Calvin S. *The Meaning of Dreams.* New York: Harper & Bros., 1953.

_____. *A Primer of Freudian Psychology.* Cleveland: World Publishing Co., 1954.

Hare, A. Paul, et al. *Small Groups: Studies in Social Interaction.* New York: Alfred A. Knopf, Inc., 1955.

Hoch, Paul H., and Zubin, Joseph (eds.). *Anxiety.* New York: Grune & Stratton, Inc., 1950.

_____. *Depression.* New York: Grune & Stratton, Inc., 1954.

Horney, Karen. *Our Inner Conflicts.* New York: W. W. Norton & Co., 1945.

Jackson, Lydia. *Aggression and Its Interpretation.* London: Methuen & Co., 1954.

Jones, Ernest. *Life and Work of Sigmund Freud.* 3 vols. New York: Basic Books, Inc., 1953, 1955.

Lee, Roy S. *Freud and Christianity.* New York: A. A. Wyn, 1949.

Lief, Alfred (ed.). *The Commonsense Psychiatry of Dr. Adolf Meyer.* New York: McGraw-Hill Book Co., 1948.

Lindgren, Henry Clay. *The Art of Human Relations.* New York: Thomas Nelson & Sons, 1953.

Lindzey, Gardner (ed.). *Handbook of Social Psychology.* 2 vols. Cambridge, Mass.: Addison-Wesley Publishing Co., Inc., 1954.

Lowrey, L. G. *Psychiatry for Social Workers* (2nd ed.). New York: Columbia University Press, 1950.

Malinowski, Bronislaw. *Magic, Science and Religion.* Boston: Beacon Press, 1948.

May, Rollo. *Man's Search for Himself.* New York: W. W. Norton & Co., Inc., 1953.

_____. *The Meaning of Anxiety.* New York: The Ronald Press Co., 1950.

Meerloo, Joost A. M. *Patterns of Panic*. New York: International Universities Press, Inc., 1950.

Menninger, Karl A. *The Human Mind* (3rd ed. enl. and rev.). New York: Alfred A. Knopf, Inc., 1945.

————. *Man Against Himself*. New York: Harcourt, Brace & Co., 1938.

Menninger, Karl A., and Jeanetta L. *Love Against Hate*. New York: Harcourt, Brace & Co., 1942.

Perry, Helen S., and Gawel, Mary L. (eds.). *The Psychiatric Interview*. New York: W. W. Norton & Co., Inc., 1953.

Redl, Fritz, and Wineman, David. *Controls from Within*. Glencoe, Ill.: The Free Press, 1952.

Reik, Theodor. *Masochism in Modern Man*. Translated by Margaret H. Beigel and Gertrud M. Kurth. New York: Farrar, Straus & Cudahy, Inc., 1949.

————. *The Secret Self*. New York: Farrar, Straus & Cudahy, Inc., 1952.

Thompson, Clara M., and Mullahy, Patrick. *Psychoanalysis: Evolution and Development*. New York: Hermitage House, Inc., 1950.

Tillich, Paul. *The Courage to Be*. New Haven, Conn.: Yale University Press, 1952.

Wolfenstein, Martha. *Children's Humor*. Glencoe, Ill.: The Free Press, 1954.

Grief

Anderson, Charles. "Aspects of Pathological Grief and Mourning," *International Journal of Psycho-Analysis*, XXX (1949), 48-55.

Beres, David, and Obers, Samuel J. "The Effects of Extreme Deprivation in Infancy on Psychic Structure in Adolescence," *The Psychoanalytic Study of the Child*, Vol. V, eds. Ruth S. Eissler *et al*. New York: International Universities Press, Inc., 1950.

Deutsch, Helene, "Absence of Grief," *Psychoanalytic Quarterly*, VI (1937), 12.

Eissler, K. R. *The Psychiatrist and the Dying Patient*. New York: International Universities Press, Inc., 1955.

Ellery, R. S. *Psychiatric Aspects of Modern Warfare*. Melbourne, Australia: Reed & Harris, 1945.

Freud, Sigmund. "Mourning and Melancholia," *Collected Papers*, Vol. IV. London: Hogarth Press, 1950.

Grinker, Roy R., and Spiegel, John P. *Men Under Stress*. Philadelphia: The Blakiston Co., 1945.

————. *War Neuroses*. Philadelphia: The Blakiston Co., 1945.

Heilbrunn, Gert. "On Weeping," *Psychoanalytic Quarterly*, XXIV (1955), 245.

Hiltner, Seward. "*Answer to Job*" by Carl Gustav Jung, *Pastoral Psychology*, January, 1956, pp. 82-83.

Kierkegaard, Soren. *The Concept of Dread*. Translated by Walter Lowrie. Princeton University Press, 1944.

Klein, Melanie. "Mourning and Its Relation to Manic-Depressive States," *International Journal of Psycho-Analysis*, XXI (1940), 125-53.

————. "The Significance of Early Anxiety Situations in the Development of the Ego," *The Psychoanalysis of Children.* London: Hogarth Press, 1951.

Langer, Marion. *Learning to Live as a Widow.* New York: Gilbert Press, Inc., 1957.

Liebman, Joshua Loth. *Peace of Mind.* New York: Simon and Schuster, Inc., 1946.

Lindemann, Erich. *Annals of Surgery,* CXVII (1943), 814 ff.

————. "Symptomatology and Management of Acute Grief," *American Journal of Psychiatry,* CI (1944), 147.

Peto, Endre. "Weeping and Laughing," *International Journal of Psycho-Analysis,* XXVII (1946), 129-33.

Stern, Karl, et al. "Grief Reactions in Later Life," *American Journal of Psychiatry,* CVIII (1951), 289-94.

Pastoral Care

Allport, Gordon W. *Becoming.* New Haven, Conn.: Yale University Press, 1955.

————. *The Individual and His Religion.* New York: The Macmillan Co., 1950.

Bergson, Henri L. *The Two Sources of Morality and Religion.* Translated by R. Ashley Audra and Cloudesley Brereton. New York: Henry Holt & Co., Inc., 1935.

Doniger, Simon (ed.). *The Minister's Consultation Clinic.* Great Neck, N.Y.: Channel Press, 1955.

————. *Religion and Human Behavior.* New York: Association Press, 1954.

Fallaw, Wesner. *Toward Spiritual Security.* Philadelphia: The Westminster Press, 1952.

Fletcher, Joseph. *Morals and Medicine.* Princeton University Press, 1954.

Fromm, Erich. *Psychoanalysis and Religion.* New Haven, Conn.: Yale University Press, 1950.

Gilbert, Jeanne G. *Understanding Old Age.* New York: The Ronald Press Co., 1952.

Guntrip, Henry. *Psychology for Ministers and Social Workers* (2nd. ed.). Chicago: Alec R. Allenson, Inc., 1953.

Hiltner, Seward. *The Counselor in Counseling.* New York and Nashville: Abingdon Press, 1952.

————. *Pastoral Counseling.* New York and Nashville: Abingdon Press, 1949.

Irion, Paul E. *The Funeral and the Mourners.* New York and Nashville: Abingdon Press, 1954.

Jung, C. G. *Modern Man in Search of a Soul.* New York: Harcourt, Brace & Co., 1933.

Kierkegaard, Soren. *Fear and Trembling.* Translated by Walter Lowrie. Princeton University Press, 1941.

Mairet, Philip (ed.). *Christian Essays in Psychiatry*. New York: Philosophical Library, Inc., 1956.

May, Rollo. *The Art of Counseling*. New York and Nashville: Abingdon Press, 1939.

Outler, Albert C. *Psychotherapy and the Christian Message*. New York: Harper & Bros., 1954.

Pike, James A. *Beyond Anxiety*. New York: Charles Scribner's Sons, 1953.

Roberts, David E. *Psychotherapy and a Christian View of Man*. New York: Charles Scribner's Sons, 1950.

Rogers, William F. *Ye Shall Be Comforted*. Philadelphia: The Westminster Press, 1950.

Schnitzer, Jeshaia. *New Horizons for the Synagogue*. New York: Bloch Publishing Co., Inc., 1956.

Schweitzer, Albert. *The Philosophy of Civilization*. Translated by C. T. Campion. New York: The Macmillan Co., 1949.

Spann, J. Richard (ed.). *Pastoral Care*. New York and Nashville: Abingdon Press, 1951.

Standard, Samuel, and Nathan, Helmuth. *Should the Patient Know the Truth?* New York: Springer Publishing Co., Inc., 1955.

Stolz, Karl R. *The Church and Psychotherapy*. New York and Nashville: Abingdon-Cokesbury Press, 1943.

Waterhouse, Eric S. *Psychology and Pastoral Work*. New York and Nashville: Abingdon-Cokesbury Press, 1940.

Weatherhead, Leslie D. *Psychology and Life*. New York and Nashville: Abingdon Press, 1935.

————. *Psychology, Religion, and Healing* (rev. ed.). New York and Nashville: Abingdon Press, 1952.

Wilkinson, Bonaro. *Understanding Fear in Ourselves and Others*. New York: Harper & Bros., 1951.

Wise, Carroll A. *Pastoral Counseling: Its Theory and Practice*. New York: Harper & Bros., 1951.

INDEX

Aborigines, 54
Abraham, Karl, 17, 71, 72, 73, 228
Acropolis, 93
Acts of the Apostles, 51
Adolescence, 42
Adrenalin, 51
Affection, 208
Age of Unreason, 57
Aged persons, 42
Aggression, 89, 90, 177, 207, 208
Aggressive action, 164
Aggressive feelings, 196, 206
Aggressiveness, infantile, 163
Agrarian man, 45
Alcohol, 176
Alexander, Franz, 57, 138, 200
Allport, Gordon, 78
Ambivalence, 20, 32, 42, 50, 52, 79, 88, 89, 90
Ambivalent feelings, 62, 74, 90, 206
American life, 55
Ananias, 51
Anderson, Charles, 164, 188
Anger, 177, 193
Animals, 47
Animism, 48, 50
Amputation, 66
Anthropological studies, 44
Anthropomorphic projections, 50
Anxiety, 16 ff., 85, 161, 170, 188, 219
  abnormal, 182
  among airmen, 18
  attacks of, 174
  neurotic, 182
  normal, 182
Apes, 47-48
Appetite, 68
Aristotle, 110
Army, 92
Artist, creative, 33
Arthritis, 56, 197
Asphyxia, 187
Asthma, 168

Athens, 92
Atropos, 33
Autonomic nervous system, 168
Autonomy, 227
Autopsy, 132, 190

Barabbas, 126
Behavior
  ethical, 227
  obsessive, 202
  regressive, 67
  self-destructive, 189
  unreasoned, 189
Benedict, Ruth, 122
Bergson, Henri, 53, 103
Bettelheim, Bruno, 48
Bible, 114, 117, 212
Biddle, W. Earle, 223-24
Birth, 123
Blood, 78
Books, 210
Breast feeding, 68
Brewster, Henry H., 173
Broken homes, 185
Bryant, William Cullen, 206
Buttrick, George, 223

Caesarean section, 91
Caisson, 153
Cancer and grief, 15
Cannibalism, 90
Cardiac phenomena, 163
Carlson, Evans, 115
Carnot, 107
Casket, 90, 139
Cause-effect relation, 54
Cemeteries, 65, 85, 96
Ceremonial meal, 51
Chest pains, 163
Childhood experience, 23
Children and funerals, 204
Chinese science, 52
Chopin funeral march, 152
Christian faith, 213, 223

249

Christian love, 104
Christian practice, 124
Christian symbolism, 119, 124
Christianity, 129, 224
Church, 117, 138, 139, 159, 160, 214
  as social insurance, 232
  and state, 51
  withdrawal from, 216
Church services, 159
Church-school staff, 205
Civil War, 137
Clergyman, 86.
Clinical observations, 21
Clotho, 33
Cocoanut Grove fire, 167, 187
Colitis, 168
Communication, 45, 46, 50, 113, 124,
  129, 137, 154, 156, 195, 203,
  205, 229, 232 ff.
Communion, 127
Communist, 118
Communist state, 107
Competence, 229
Competition, 38
Confession, 128
Conflict, intrapsychic, 182
Congestion, 163
Convulsions, 163
Corn Laws of England, 233
Cosmic counterpart, 125
Cosmic drama, 126
Cosmic retribution, 96
Cottrell, Leonard S., 227
Counseling, 43
Counseling room, 156
Courage, 118-19, 120, 175, 219
Cramps, 163
Creativity, 227
Creator, 105
Crown and scepter, 51
Crying, 86

Death
  child's concept of, 31
  myths, 50
Defense mechanisms, neurotic, 182
Delusions, 186
Dependency, 86, 158
Dependency, unhealthy, 196
Depressed states, 17
Depression, 17, 19, 20, 165, 180,
  182, 185, 186, 195
  deep, 167
  essential, 181

Depression—cont'd
  melancholic, 181
  simple, 181
Deprivation
  acute, 68
  tolerance to, 36
Depth psychology, 108
Dermatology, 56
Determinist, 54
Diabetes, 15
Diagnosis, 179 ff., 216
Divine grace, 149
Divorce, 185
Dollard, John, 180
Drama, 124
Dream, 52, 85, 163, 164, 175
Drives, instinctive, 148
Durkheim, Emile, 196

Ear weaknesses, 42
Easter, 124, 126, 127
Ecclesiastes, 34
Ecclesiastical control, 51
Ego, 61, 62, 84, 88, 92, 181
Ego concept, 35
Ego investment, 146
Ego structure, mature, 151
Eissler, K. R., 33, 202
Emerson, Ralph Waldo, 233
Emmaus, 126
Emotional capital, 87, 142, 144
Emotional exhaustion, 193
Emotional illness, 180
Emotional maturity, 38, 43, 226
Emotional security, 36, 40
Emotional shock, 147, 195
Empathy, 63, 219, 227, 232
England, 150
Enlarged pupils, 168
Eternal values, 126
European background, 93
Everyman's Search, 15
Exercise, 166
Existential dichotomies, 225
Eye weaknesses, 42

Fainting, 163
Faith, 40, 120, 160, 219, 221
Falsehood, 203
Fantasy, 204, 233
Fantasy structures, 183
Father, sadistic, 169
Fear, 219, 233
Fellowship, 219

Fenichel, Otto, 73, 83, 165
Fetishism, 48, 50, 51, 60, 76, 78, 83
Fetus, 44
Flushed face, 168
Folk wisdom, 153
Food, 68
Foote, Nelson, 227
Forgiveness, 128
Frazer, J. G., 49
Freud, 17, 18, 21, 32, 58, 62, 73, 109, 164, 192
Friday, 37
Froeschels, Emil, 44
Fromm, Erich, 164, 225
Funerals, 58, 68, 81, 85, 97, 99, 139, 149, 153, 170, 195, 220 ff.
  military, 153
  reading at, 221
Funeral director, 166, 215, 216

Germans, 75
Gesell, Arnold, 204
Gestation, 44
Gifford Lectures, 105
Gillespie, R. D., 185
God, 34, 103, 110, 112 ff., 119, 121, 125, 126, 129, 172, 193, 223, 236
  anger at, 231
  denial of, 218
God-consciousness, 114 ff., 227
God's will, 127, 146
Goethe, 111
Grandmother, 207
Grandparent and child, 205
Grant, U. S., 136
Grave, 96
Grave digger, 152
Gravity, 115
Greece, 210
Greek dramatists, 17
Greek mythology, 33
Greek mythologists, 35
Greeks, 104
Grief
  abnormal, 19, 20
  definition of, 18
  delayed expression of, 167
  normal, 19, 20, 130 ff., 145 ff.
Grief reactions, morbid, 15, 175
Grief state, morbid, 173
Grief syndrome, 148
Grinker and Spiegel, 18, 185
Group relationships, effective, 159
Growth, 22

Guilt, 20, 23, 30, 31, 37, 38, 42, 50, 52, 79, 88 ff., 127, 128, 149, 151, 157, 159, 160, 163, 165, 170, 181, 185, 207, 221, 222, 233
  neurotic, 89
  real, 89
Guilt feelings, 164
Guntrip, Henry, 200
Gutheil, Emil A., 164

Hall, Calvin, 69, 164
Hallucinatory gratifications, 186
Hamlet, 31, 32
Harvard Medical School, 146
Hatred, 170, 177, 185
Health, 227
Heart disease, 73
Hebrew literature, 34
Hebrews, 104
Hedonistic satisfactions, 58
Heilbrun, Gert, 155
Hepatitis, infectious, 100
Heredity, 22
Hiltner, Seward, 184
Himalayas, 52
Hindu teachings, 52
Hoch, Paul, 155
Holy Communion, 128
Holy Week, 124, 127
Home environment, 185
Homer, 50
Hope, 160
Hormone supplements, 207
Hostility, 157, 166, 170, 183
Hot waves in the head, 168
How to Preach to People's Needs, 213
Humor, wry, 85
Hypnosis, 70
Hypochondriac, 211
Hypomanic state, 165
Hysterias, 188

Id, 73, 88
Id-cathected longing, 62
Identification, 42, 60 ff.
Illness, physical, 180
Imagination, 119
Immortality, 105, 107, 111, 118, 120
Incorporation, 20, 23, 60
Incorporation, oral, 67
Individualism, 53
Inferiority, 181
Injury, physical, 189
Insomnia, 174

Insurance, 90
Intellect, 119
Intelligence, 227
Interpersonal relations, disturbed, 168
Irion, Paul, 223
Irritations, 206

Jack the Giant Killer, 49
Japan, 97
Jeremiah, 34
Jesus, 111, 114, 116-17, 126, 201, 229
Jew, Orthodox, 99
Jewish custom, 90
Job, 34
Johnson, E. Weaver, 15
Jones, Sir Henry, 105
Joseph, 165
Judas, 125
Judgment, 227
Jung, 52

Kant, 110
Kew, C. E., 212
Kew, C. J., 212
Kierkegaard, 88
Klein, Melanie, 43

Lachesis, 33
Lacrimal glands, 155
Laughter, 86
Laughton, Charles, 221
Learning opportunities, 204
Lent, 124, 127
LeShan, Lawrence, 15
Levine, Maurice, 180, 196, 226
Libidinal investment, 18
Libido, 16
Light, 106
Lincoln, Abraham, 29
Lindemann, Erich, 15, 27, 30, 42, 88, 143, 146, 148, 153, 157, 161, 163, 166, 168, 186, 187
London, 164
London bomb shelter, 189
Loneliness, 219
Loss
  instinctual, 18
  pain of, 163
  trauma of, 19
Lowrey, Lawson G., 200
Lycabettus, 93

Macbeth, 162
McDougall, William, 109

Magic, 48, 51, 54
Magical thinking, 49, 54, 55
Mahatmas, 52
Malinowski Bronislaw, 49, 90
Manic manifestation, 187
Manic state, 191, 192
Marine Raiders, 15
Marriage, 123
Marriage conflict, 89
Mary Magdalene, 126
Masses, 96
Mausoleum, 85
May, Rollo, 15, 18, 182, 184
Mayo Clinic, 56
Mechanical manipulation, 58
Mechanist, 54
Medical profession, 216, 217
Medical profession and grief, 16
Meerloo, Joost A. M., 188, 228
Melancholia, 21, 192
Menninger, Karl, 76, 165, 166, 180, 196
Menopause, 207
Menses, disturbance of, 163
Methuselah, 111
Middle age, 56
Military training, 205
Miller, Neal E., 180
Montaigne, 189
Moral nature, 115
Moralist, 111
Mosaic religion, 109
Mother, compulsive, 139
Mother figure, 194
Mother substitute, 35
Motivation, 209
Mourners, paid, 153
Mourning and Melancholia, 17
Mourning clothes, 65
Mourning, pathological, 186
Mystical intuition, 101
Mythology, 124
Myths, 33, 49, 52, 53, 124

Naples, 41
Napoleon, 64
Narcissism, 181
Nature, laws of, 115
Nausea, 163
Nazi philosophy, 229
Nazi state, 55, 107
Neurotic flight, 56
New England, 64
New Orleans, 153

252

Niebuhr, Reinhold, 110
Nordic race, 55

Oberammergau, 128
Objective reality, 113
Obsessional reactions, 188
Obstetrician, 86
Okinawa, 40, 136
Old Testament, 17, 34, 35
Omnipotence, 54, 171, 172
Oriental religious practice, 52
Orphans, 94
Orthothanasia, 16
Oversoul, 128

Pain, 147
Panic, 188
Parable of the lost coin, 229
Parable of the lost sheep, 230
Parable of the lost son, 231
Parachutists, 202
Paradise Lost, 43
Paradise Regained, 43
Paralysis, 203
Paranoid state, 187
Parapsychologists, 120
Parent
    attitude of, 202
    obsessive-compulsive, 185
Participation, 229, 234 ff.
Pastor, symbolic status of, 219
Pastoral confidence, 22
Pastoral counselor, 101
Paul, 210
Penance, 128
Perception, 108
Personal adequacy, 226
Perspiration, 168
Peter, 125
Petö, Endre, 155
Physical symptoms, 175
Physician, 166, 215
Pilate, 126
Plague, 56-57
Plains Indians, 122
Plato, 108, 110, 119
Poet, 111
Police ambulance, 215
Politics, 126
Polytheism, 50
Portici, Italy, 41
Post-mortem examinations, 200
Potter's field, 34
Prayer group, intercessory, 231

Preconscious mind, 122
Pregnancy, 192
Pride, 66-67
Primitive man, 48, 49, 50, 58, 90
Primitive rites, 90, 128
Psyche, 60, 90
Psychiatric care, 141
Psychiatry and Religion, 174
Psychogenic diseases, 168
Psychogenic disturbance, 179
Psychological homeostasis, 155
Psychoneurosis, 32
Psychophysical activity, 19
Psychosomatic illness, 56
Puberty, 123
Public display, 153
Pueblo Indians, 122
Pulpit utterance, 212-13

Rado, Sandor, 76
Reality, 233
Reality, distortion of, 151
Reality-relation, 183
Reality sense, 39
Redl, Fritz, 48
Regression, 20, 65, 83, 138, 172, 186, 188
Regressive elements, 185
Reik, Theodor, 25, 66
Rejection, 181
Relation, 229
Relationship, 160
Religion, 40, 122
Religious counselors, 148
Religious inclination, 193
Religious process, 119
Remarriage, happy, 196
Remorse, 185
Reorientation, 173
Repression, 182
Restored relationship, 219
Resurrection, 119
Reverence for life, 227
Reversion, 162
Rheumatism, 42
Rheumatoid arthritis, 168
Rites, 124
Rituals, 57, 65, 85, 124, 128
    of death and resurrection, 49
    sacred, 51
Robinson Crusoe, 37
Ross, T. A., 26, 176
Rural community, 180
Rural sections, 151

Russell, Bertrand, 103

Sadism, 55
Sadistic attitudes, 185
Sadness, 180
St. George, 93
Saliva, 78
Santi family, 41
Schmitz, Oskar A. H., 52
Schweitzer, Albert, 227
Scientists, 119
Scotland, 150
Sea, 58
Seclusion, 172
Secret Garden, The, 203
Sedation, 195
Sedatives, 155, 169
Self-accusation, 20
Self-esteem, 20
Self-hatred, 181
Self-injury, 20
Self-pity, 230
Self-realization, 125
Semicoma, 187
Senescence, 42
Senile dementia 190, 207
Sex, 85
Shakespeare, 17, 31, 32, 35
Shivering, 163
Shock, 17, 18, 156, 187
Sighing respiration, 168
Sin and salvation, 126
Situational factor, 23
Skeletons, 85
Sleeplessness, 163
Social insecurity, 185
Socrates, 111, 119
Soldiers under stress, 185
Sorcery, 123
Sorrow, 180
Soul, 50, 58, 107
Speechlessness, 187
Spiritual crises, 227
Stekel, Wilhelm, 60, 163
Stern, Karl, 42
Stillness at Appomattox, A, 136
Stomach ulcers, 56
Stone of Scone, 51
Stress, tolerance to, 204
Students and death, 15
Subjective reality, 113
Substitution, 23
Suffocation, 174
Suicidal risks, 196

Suicidal threats, 195
Suicidally inclined patient, 102
Suicide, 169, 186, 190, 194
Sullivan, H. S., 46, 180, 184
Superego, 70, 88, 92
Survival, 123
Suspicion, 183
Symbolic structure, 122
Symbolism, 58
Symbolization, 46
Sympathy, 63, 232
Symptoms, 139, 163, 166

Taboos, 51
Taps, playing of, 153
Tears, 66
Terminal illness, 102, 206, 236
Thanatology, 16, 17, 40, 206
"Thanatopsis," 206
Theosophy, 52
Thermodynamics, 107
Thomas, 126
Thought patterns, nihilistic, 55
Tibet, 52
Tics, 163
Tillich, Paul, 118
Trafalgar Hospital, 15
Tragic accident, 146
Transcendent factors, 23
Transcendent meaning, 226
Trembling, 163
Tribal hunter, 45

Ulcerative colitis, 15, 163
Unconscious transference, 203
Undertakers, 85
Unreal glorification, 42
Unspoken language, 122
Upper respiratory disturbances, 163
Uzzah, 51

Vaults, 140
Verbalization, 178, 233
Vermont, 151
Versailles, 75
Vertigo, 163
Vigils, long, 153
Vomiting, 90, 163
Vow of silence, 203

WAAC, 64
Weeping, 154-55
Weiss, Edoardo, 60, 62, 84, 147, 161, 162, 181, 186, 201

Western world, 118
White Mountains, 152
Widow, 67
Wilhelm, Richard, 52
Wineman, David, 48
Wise, Carroll, 89, 184
Wishful thinking, 123, 156

Withdrawal, 151, 158
Wolfenstein, Martha, 85
Women, 66
World War II, 17, 41, 202

Yoga, 52

Zerfoss, Karl P., 184